MAR 0 8 2007

AMAZING GRACE

William Wilberforce
and the Heroic
Campaign to End
Slavery

AMAZING GRACE

ERIC METAXAS

HarperSanFrancisco
A Division of HarperCollins*Publishers*

For more information on the image of John Wesley found on page 5 of the insert, see http://gbgm-umc.org/umw/wesley.

HarperCollins books may be purchased for educational, business, or sales promotional use. For information please write: Special Markets Department, HarperCollins Publishers, 10 East 53rd Street, New York, NY 10022.

HarperCollins Web site: http://www.harpercollins.com

HarperCollins®, ♔®, and HarperSanFrancisco™ are trademarks of HarperCollins Publishers

FIRST EDITION

Designed by Sharon VanLoozenoord

Library of Congress Cataloging-in-Publication Data

ISBN: 978–0–06–117300–4
ISBN-10: 0–06–117300–2

07 08 09 10 11 RRD(H) 11 10 9 8 7 6 5 4 3 2 1

To the Claphamites of the twenty-first century,

whose passion for God and their fellow man are inseparable

CONTENTS

FOREWORD

History's landscape is littered with great people whose names have disappeared from the rolls of our collective memory. Such has been the unfortunate fate that befell the heroic William Wilberforce. Wilberforce—humanitarian, parliamentarian, and voice of the voiceless—fatefully receded somewhere into the far-off memory of Americans over the past century. Wilberforce and his name once stood as monuments to freedom, faith, and humanity. Were Abraham Lincoln and Frederick Douglass to cite their sources of inspiration, Wilberforce would be high, if not first, on their lists. Today, that memory is resurrected in this magnificent book.

Eric Metaxas's work will stand as a living landmark not so much for its obviously beautiful prose and detailed narrative of the life of Wilberforce, but because it artfully captures the essence of a spiritual strength, moral clarity, human frailty, and divine purpose that dwelled among men at the end of the eighteenth century and beginning of the nineteenth. Bold men and women, Wilberforce first among equals, challenged the prevailing currents of their time to eradicate the scourge of the slave trade. Ultimately, their strategies, defeats, and victories "mounted up with wings like eagles" to call attention to slavery as more than just a "peculiar institution." In Wilberforce's mind, there was nothing peculiar about slavery. Peculiar to him was the ability of so many refined and seemingly polite members of society to stomach slavery's bile and to turn a deaf ear to the cries of millions. To Wilberforce, slavery and other civil ills were forces that destroyed life and its viability. As a result of his courage and efforts, freedom's bell was rung for millions and the thirst for liberty has continued to echo throughout history.

William Wilberforce's courage, zeal, and actions as recounted in this biography are a modern reminder of work unfinished. That he suffered from poor health likewise reminds that even in the context of human weakness, divine work can still attend. His situation begs the question, What can I do today?

Today, in every corner of the world (the United States and Great Britain are not exempt), there remains great work to do. Slavery in Africa is still a reality. Today, the "filthy ships" of European slave traders are dry-docked in our distant memory, but human beings are still stripped of their essence and exported to far-off and hostile places. In too many corners of Asia, Eastern Europe, the Americas, and the Middle East, trafficking in women to serve the baser desires of men is thriving; work unfinished remains.

Scripture is bursting with admonitions to remember. There is power in remembrance, recalling, and memorial celebration. This biography allows us to place Wilberforce in two contexts and to witness the miracles that still occur.

First, Metaxas's biography allows us to put into crystal-clear focus the life of a man born to comfort but discomforted by the dire conditions of suffering people. Wilberforce saw the chemistry of oppression as changing the oppressor as well as the oppressed. In his own available way, he acted boldly to change the world. This boldness, while temporarily forgotten in human history, is ultimately honored and rewarded by Heaven itself.

In a second way, Metaxas's work on Wilberforce's life allows us to witness that God has not finished His creative work. Like Wilberforce, we have the ability to create a better world, that "beloved" community of which Jesus Christ and the prophets spoke.

Wilberforce's obsession with slavery's end was a blessing to those he would never know. Blind acts of love are often redemptive—sometimes painful, but always redemptive. Wilberforce's early defeats and setbacks early in his legislative life were all vindicated by his delayed victory in the House of Commons years after he introduced his first antislavery measure; love is indeed longsuffering, as we are reminded in Paul's epistle to the nascent church in late ancient Corinth. His real redemption and justification were not accomplished during his lifetime nor in the House of Commons. The greatest benefits of his work and toiling are still being realized when oppression is confronted today, racism is challenged everywhere, and a better, more loving world is ultimately created.

The single greatest institutional memorial to Wilberforce is the university that bears his name. One hundred fifty-one years ago, men and women joined head and heart across the lines of race, class, and confessional statements to create America's first private historically black college and university. Not in London, but in the states of the former British colony, stands an African-American college as a memorial to a white British Member of Parliament. The irony is not lost.

At the time of the university's establishment, there was polite conversation in America's parlors and colleges about the basic humanity of African Americans. Even more unrealistic for many in that conversation was the ability of African Americans to learn, contribute to society, and exist beyond the pale of forced servitude.

Today, Wilberforce University welcomes many of America's poorest and most underserved populations and transforms their educational dreams into realities. The average household income of Wilberforce students hovers just above the nation's poverty line, but its students have not surrendered their hunger for excellence and thirst for achievement in the midst of economic and social challenge.

In one small town named Wilberforce, Ohio, Wilberforce's legacy was never forgotten. At every commencement, the "Wilberforce Bible" is read, and in the margins are the unmistakable musings and notes of none other than William Wilberforce. Thousands of African Americans, Afro-Caribbeans, and Africans have presented their minds, bodies, and spirits at an altar of educational improvement. As a result, countless physicians, educators, lawyers, presidents of liberated African nations, members of Congress, and church leaders have graduated from Wilberforce University and now make the world a better place. It is more than ironic that in one of the few places where his name is remembered that miracles continue to happen every single day.

"Lest we forget" seems a fitting admonition in present times, in the midst of change's whirlwind. As the world recognizes Wilberforce, his work, and his Savior, let us not fall into former pits of forgetfulness.

Floyd Flake

*President, Wilberforce University, former U.S. Congressman (NY),
and author of* Practical Virtues *and* The Way of the Bootstrapper

INTRODUCTION

We often hear about people who "need no introduction," but if ever someone did need one, at least in our day and age, it's William Wilberforce. The strange irony is that we are talking about a man who changed the world, so if ever someone should *not* need an introduction—whose name and accomplishments should be on the lips of all humanity—it's Wilberforce.

What happened is surprisingly simple: William Wilberforce was the happy victim of his own success. He was like someone who against all odds finds the cure for a horrible disease that's ravaging the world, and the cure is so overwhelmingly successful that it vanquishes the disease completely. No one suffers from it again—and within a generation or two no one remembers it ever existed.

The roots of the thing Wilberforce was trying to uproot had been growing since humans first walked on the planet, and if they had been real roots, they would have reached to the molten core of the earth itself. They ran so deep and so wide that most people thought that they held the planet together.

The opposition that he and his small band faced was incomparable to anything we can think of in modern affairs. It was certainly unprecedented that anyone should endeavor, as if by their own strength and a bit of leverage, to tip over something about as large and substantial and deeply rooted as a mountain range. From where we stand today—and because of Wilberforce—the end of slavery seems inevitable, and it's impossible for us not to take it largely for granted. But that's the wild miracle of his achievement, that what to the people of his day seemed impossible and unthinkable seems to us, in our day, inevitable.

There's hardly a soul alive today who isn't horrified and offended by the very idea of human slavery. We seethe with moral indignation at it, and we can't fathom how anyone or any culture ever countenanced it. But in the world into which Wilberforce was born, the opposite was true. Slavery was as accepted as birth and marriage and death, was so woven into the tapestry of human history that you could barely see its threads, much less pull them out. Everywhere on the globe, for five thousand years, the idea of human civilization without slavery was unimaginable.

The idea of ending slavery was so completely out of the question at that time that Wilberforce and the abolitionists couldn't even mention it publicly. They focused on the lesser idea of abolishing the slave trade—on the buying and selling of human beings—but never dared speak of emancipation, of ending slavery itself. Their secret and cherished hope was that once the slave trade had been abolished, it would then become possible to begin to move toward emancipation. But first they must fight for the abolition of the slave trade; and that battle—brutal and heartbreaking—would take twenty years.

Of course, finally winning that battle in 1807 is the single towering accomplishment for which we should remember Wilberforce today, whose bicentennial we celebrate, and whose celebration occasions a movie, documentaries, and the book you now hold. If anything can stand as a single marker of Wilberforce's accomplishments, it is that 1807 victory. It paved the way for all that followed, inspiring the other nations of the world to follow suit and opening the door to emancipation, which, amazingly, was achieved three days before Wilberforce died in 1833. He received the glorious news of his lifelong goal on his deathbed.

Wilberforce was one of the brightest, wittiest, best connected, and generally talented men of his day, someone who might well have become prime minister of Great Britain if he had, in the words of one historian, "preferred party to mankind." But his accomplishments far transcend any mere political victory. Wilberforce can be pictured as standing as a kind of hinge in the middle of history: he pulled the world around a corner, and we can't even look back to see where we've come from.

Wilberforce saw much of what the rest of the world could not, including the grotesque injustice of one man treating another as property. He seems to rise up out of nowhere and with the voice of unborn billions—with your voice and mine—shriek to his contemporaries that they are sleepwalking through hell, that they must wake up and must see what he saw and know what he knew—and what you and I know today—that the widespread and institutionalized and unthinkably cruel mistreatment of millions of human beings is evil and must be stopped as soon as conceivably possible—no matter the cost.

But how is it possible that humanity for so long tolerated what to us is so obviously intolerable? And why did just one small group of people led by Wilberforce suddenly see this injustice for what it was? Why in a morally blind world did Wilberforce and a few others suddenly sprout eyes to see it? Abolitionists in the late eighteenth century were something like the characters in horror films who have seen "the monster" and are trying to tell everyone else about it—and no one believes them.

To fathom the magnitude of what Wilberforce did we have to see that the "disease" he vanquished forever was actually neither the slave trade nor slavery. Slavery still exists around the world today, in such measure as we can hardly fathom. What Wilberforce vanquished was something even worse than slavery, something that was much more fundamental and can hardly be seen from where we stand today: he vanquished the very mind-set that made slavery acceptable and allowed it to survive and thrive for millennia. He destroyed an entire way of seeing the world, one that had held sway from the beginning of history, and he replaced it with another way of seeing the world. Included in the old way of seeing things was the idea that the evil of slavery was good. Wilberforce murdered that old way of seeing things, and so the idea that slavery was good died along with it. Even though slavery continues to exist here and there, the idea that it is good is dead. The idea that it is inextricably intertwined with human civilization, and part of the way things are supposed to be, and economically necessary and morally defensible, is gone. Because the entire mind-set that supported it is gone.

Wilberforce overturned not just European civilization's view of slavery but its view of almost everything in the human sphere; and that is why it's nearly impossible to do justice to the enormity of his accomplishment: it was nothing less than a fundamental and important shift in human consciousness.

In typically humble fashion, Wilberforce would have been the first to insist that he had little to do with any of it. The facts are that in 1785, at age twenty-six and at the height of his political career, something profound and dramatic happened to him. He might say that, almost against his will, God opened his eyes and showed him another world. Somehow Wilberforce saw God's reality—what Jesus called the Kingdom of Heaven. He saw things he had never seen before, things that we quite take for granted today but that were as foreign to his world as slavery is to ours. He saw things that existed in God's reality but that, in human reality, were nowhere in evidence. He saw the idea that all men and women are created equal by God, in his image, and are therefore sacred. He saw the idea that all men are brothers and that we are all our brothers' keepers. He saw the idea that one must love one's neighbor as oneself and that we must do unto others as we would have them do unto us.

These ideas are at the heart of the Christian Gospel, and they had been around for at least eighteen centuries by the time Wilberforce encountered them. Monks and missionaries knew of these ideas and lived them out in their limited spheres. But no entire society had ever taken these ideas to heart as a society in the way that Britain would. That was what Wilberforce changed forever.

As a political figure, he was uniquely positioned to link these ideas to society itself, to the public sphere, and the public sphere, for the first time in history, was able to receive them. And so Wilberforce may perhaps be said to have performed the wedding ceremony between faith and culture. We had suddenly entered a world in which we would never again ask whether it was our responsibility as a society to help the poor and the suffering. We would only quibble about how, about the details—about whether to use public funds or private, for example. But we would never again question whether it was our responsibility as a society to help those less fortunate. That had been settled. Today we call this having a "social conscience," and we can't imagine any modern, civilized society without one.

Once this idea was loosed upon the world, the world changed. Slavery and the slave trade would soon be largely abolished, but many lesser social evils would be abolished too. For the first time in history, groups sprang up for every possible social cause. Wilberforce's first "great object" was the abolition of the slave trade, but his second "great object," one might say, was the abolition of every lesser social ill. The issues of child labor and factory conditions, the problems of orphans and widows, of prisoners and the sick—all suddenly had champions in people who wanted to help those less fortunate than themselves. At the center of most of these social ventures was the Clapham Circle, an informal but influential community of like-minded souls outside London who plotted good deeds together, and Wilberforce himself was at the center of Clapham. At one point he was officially linked with sixty-nine separate groups dedicated to social reform of one kind or another.

Taken all together, it's difficult to escape the verdict that William Wilberforce was simply the greatest social reformer in the history of the world. The world he was born into in 1759 and the world he departed in 1833 were as different as lead and gold. Wilberforce presided over a social earthquake that rearranged the continents and whose magnitude we are only now beginning to fully appreciate.

Unforeseen to him, the fire he ignited in England would leap across the Atlantic and quickly sweep across America—and transform that nation profoundly and forever. Can we imagine an America without its limitless number of organizations dedicated to curing every social ill? Would such an America be America? We might not wish to credit Wilberforce with inventing America, but it can reasonably be said that the America we know wouldn't exist without Wilberforce.

As a result of the efforts of Wilberforce and Clapham, social "improvement" was so fashionable by the Victorian era that do-gooders and do-goodism had become targets of derision, and they have been so ever since. We have simply forgotten that in the eighteenth century, before Wilberforce and Clapham, the poor and suffering were almost entirely without champions in the public or private sphere. We who are sometimes obsessed with social conscience can no longer imagine a world without it, or a society that regards the suffering of the poor and others as the "will of God." Even where this view does exist, as in societies and cultures informed by an Eastern, Karmic view of the world, we refuse to believe it. We arrogantly seem to insist that everyone on the planet think as we do about society's obligation to the unfortunate, but they don't.

No politician has ever used his faith to a greater result for all of humanity, and that is why, in his day, Wilberforce was a moral hero far more than a political one. Alexander Solzhenitsyn and Nelson Mandela in our own time come closest to representing what Wilberforce must have seemed like to the men and women of the nineteenth century, for whom the memory of what he had done was still bright and vivid.

Thomas Jefferson and Abraham Lincoln both hailed him as an inspiration and example. Lincoln said every schoolboy knew Wilberforce's name and what he had done. Frederick Douglass gushed that Wilberforce's "faith, persistent, and enduring enthusiasm" had "thawed the British heart into sympathy for the slave, and moved the strong arm of that government to in mercy put an end to his bondage." Poets and writers such as Harriet Beecher Stowe and George Eliot sang his praises, as did Henry David Thoreau and John Greenleaf Whittier. Byron called him "the moral Washington of Africa."

The American artist and inventor Samuel Morse said that Wilberforce's "whole soul is bent on doing good to his fellow men. Not a moment of his time is lost. He is always planning some benevolent scheme, or other, and not only planning but executing. . . . Oh, that such men as Mr. Wilberforce were more common in this world. So much human blood would not be shed to gratify the malice and revenge of a few wicked, interested men." The American abolitionist William Lloyd Garrison went further yet. "His voice had a silvery cadence," he said of Wilberforce,

> his face a benevolently pleasing smile, and his eye a fine intellectual expression. In his conversation he was fluent, yet modest; remarkably exact and elegant in his diction; cautious in forming conclusions; searching in his interrogations; and skillful in weighing testimony. In his manner he combined dignity with simplicity, and childlike affability with becoming gracefulness. How perfectly do those great elements of character harmonize in the same person, to wit—dovelike gentleness and amazing energy—deep humility and adventurous daring! . . . These were mingled in the soul of Wilberforce.

An Italian nobleman who saw Wilberforce in his later years wrote: "When Mr. Wilberforce passes through the crowd on the day of the opening of Parliament, every one contemplates this little old man, worn with age, and his head sunk upon his shoulders, as a sacred relic: as the Washington of humanity."

We blanch at such encomia today, for indeed, ours is an age deeply suspicious of greatness. Watergate seems to have come down upon us like a portcullis, cutting us off forever from anything approaching such hero worship, especially of political figures. With the certainty of a Captain Queeg, we are forever on the lookout for the worm in the apple, the steroid in the sprinter or slugger. And lurking behind every happy biographical detail we see the skulking figure of Parson Weems and his pious fibs about cherry trees and—of all things—telling the truth.

If ever someone could restore our ability to again see simple goodness, it should be Wilberforce. If we cannot cheer someone who literally brought "freedom to the captives" and bequeathed to the world that infinitely transformative engine we call a social conscience, for whom may we ever cheer? Especially knowing that he has been more forgotten than remembered, and that he himself would have been the first to denigrate his accomplishments—as we can see from his diaries and letters, which show us that he went to the grave sincerely and deeply regretting that he hadn't done much more.

In the thick of the battle for abolition, one of its many dedicated opponents, Lord Melbourne, was outraged that Wilberforce dared inflict his Christian values about slavery and human equality on British society. "Things have come to a pretty pass," he famously thundered, "when one should permit one's religion to invade public life." For this lapidary inanity, the jeers and catcalls and raspberries and howling laughter of history's judgment will echo forever—as they should.

But after all, it is a very pretty pass indeed. And how very glad we are that one man led us to that pretty pass, to that golden doorway, and then guided us through the mountains to a world we hadn't known could exist.

Eric Metaxas

New York City
September 2006

CHAPTER 1

LITTLE WILBERFORCE

" . . . if it be a work of grace, it cannot fail."

On August 24, 1759, William Wilberforce was born into a prosperous merchant family in the city of Hull. The impressive, red-brick Jacobean mansion in which he was born was situated on the city's High Street, overlooking the Hull River. The Hull in turn flowed into the much larger Humber, which flowed eastward into the North Sea.

The Wilberforce family proudly traced its lineage in Yorkshire to the twelfth century and the reign of Henry II. *Burke's Peerage* places them as one of the very few families who can be traced to the far side of the river 1066 and Saxon times. In those days and for centuries afterward, on into Wilberforce's own century, the family name was Wilberfoss. It was changed by Wilberforce's grandfather, who seems to have had something of a "forceful" personality, as evinced in part by his penchant for changing whatever he disliked. It's likely that he wasn't fond of the roots of the suffix *foss*, which means "vassal" or, in Irish, "servant." That wouldn't do for a political figure with grand ambitions to wealth and power. And Wilberforce it became.

As a boy, the young Wilberforce could see the river from his house's windows and watch the great sailing ships unloading American tobacco and Norwegian timber and Prussian iron before they were loaded with local exports and then sailed away, down the Hull, and down the Humber, and out to the oceans of the world. In his own lifetime, Hull would become an important whaling port, complete with the seasonal stench of rendered cetaceans. But most important to our story are not those cargoes that came in and out of Hull's harbor, but the one that didn't. Though Hull was the fourth-largest port in England, it was the only one that did not participate in the slave trade. It was this happy detail that would enable Wilberforce to remain in political office in years hence. Any member of Parliament from Bristol or Liverpool, whose economies depended on the slave trade, would not have been able to get away with leading the abolitionist movement for long.

Though the Wilberforce family had been merchants in this part of England for two centuries, it wasn't until the eighteenth century that their fortunes rose dramatically. The rise was due largely to William's grandfather, also named William. (Though he had changed Wilberfoss to Wilberforce, he did not fuss with the name William, which means "valiant protector.") Born in 1690, Wilberforce's grandfather had found great success in the Baltic trade and had inherited considerable property from his mother, an heiress of the Davye family. It was this William Wilberforce, twice elected mayor of Hull and thenceforth known as "Alderman" Wilberforce, who was the patriarch of the family.

The Alderman's second son, Robert, married William's mother, Elizabeth Bird, and joined the family business in Hull, taking over as managing partner in 1755. The Alderman's first son, William, had opted out of the family business by marrying Hannah Thornton and moving to London, where her father was director of the Bank of England and a member of Parliament. It was this couple who, following a series of unexpected events, would soon end up having more influence in the life of the young William than his own parents.

⚬⚭⚬

By all accounts, William Wilberforce was a glorious little child, a veritable cherub of twinkling luminosity. Upon his death in 1833, his middle sons, Samuel and Robert, began a five-volume biography of their father, which was published in 1838. An "unusual thoughtfulness for others marked his youngest childhood," they tell us, and of course they would have had access throughout their lives to many who had known their father as a child. We have only one first-person recollection of him during this time, from a visiting guest sometime in the early 1760s: "I shall never forget how he would steal into my sickroom, taking off his shoes lest he should disturb me, and with an anxious face looking through my curtains to learn if I was better." Indeed, according to all who remembered his earliest days, he was possessed of a "temper eminently affectionate."

What we know of him in later years seems to corroborate this picture perfectly. Already as a little child he had a weak constitution and poor eyesight, as he would all his life. Wilberforce often said that in less "modern" days he wouldn't have stood a chance at survival. But despite his sickliness and myopia, he seems from the very beginning to have captivated all who knew him. Most of us have met children like that, whose piercing innocence and brightness are a refreshment for the adult soul. Little Wilberforce seems to have been one of these—the sort of boy who could lead even the most jaded misanthropes to think that perhaps the supremely cracked-up race of bipeds of which they were a member was not entirely, not hopelessly, unredeemable.

In 1766, when William was seven, he was enrolled at the Hull Grammar School, which the poet Andrew Marvell had attended as a boy during the previous century. Wilberforce was said to have been tiny all of his life; he never grew taller than five-foot-three, and his boyish frame was so slight that, as an adult, during one of his many illnesses, he weighed seventy-six pounds. One can only imagine how tiny he was at the age of seven.

Now and again he would visit his grandfather, who had removed to the bucolic village of Ferribly, on the Humber, seven miles away. But, truth be told, men like Alderman Wilberforce never really seem to retire. Indeed, it was this grandfather who roughly pulled some strings to install one Joseph Milner as the Hull Grammar School's new and very young headmaster, at the age of twenty-three, just in time for little Wilberforce to start there. This power play was

executed over the objections of the other members of the corpora-
tion and town of Hull. But the crafty old Alderman was not about to
let a mere seven miles' distance mitigate his considerable and hard-
won powers over the town he'd run since two King Georges before.
We cannot divine his reasons for wanting to install Milner in that
post, but the Alderman's meddling in this affair would soon end up
having some unintended and ironic results, as we shall see.

The new headmaster was the son of a humble weaver from
Leeds. But Milner had left behind the simple homeliness of the
family's wool looms to go up to Cambridge, where he distinguished
himself in no uncertain terms by winning the Chancellor's Medal.
After Cambridge, Milner became curate and assistant schoolmaster
at Thorparch in Yorkshire, where he caught the shrewd eye of the
old Alderman.

Accompanying Joseph was his seventeen-year-old brother, Isaac,
an unrefined and positively gargantuan figure who would serve as
a temporary assistant, or "usher," but whose accomplishments at
Cambridge in a few years' time would far outshine even his brother's. Indeed, this clumsy giant would eventually reveal himself to
be the owner of one of the brightest minds on the surface of the
planet. Three decades after his lowly stint as temporary usher at the
Hull Grammar School, he would occupy the most famous academic
chair in the world, the Lucasian Chair of Mathematics at Cambridge,
among whose previous occupants had been Isaac Newton and whose
future occupants would include Paul Dirac and Stephen Hawking,
who occupies it at the time of this writing. At Cambridge, Isaac
Milner would later become president of Queens' College and vice
chancellor of the university, and he would also be elected to the
Royal Society—as an undergraduate.

Before he had been rescued to help his brother teach at Hull,
Isaac had sat glumly at his father's looms, a hulking and sulking figure
reading Tacitus on the sly. But things were suddenly looking up. For
one thing the Hull schoolroom didn't reek of wool, nor was reading
Tacitus rewarded with imprecations and buffets about the head.

It now fell to this younger Milner to assist in the schooling of
tiny children, one of the tiniest of whom was a remarkable little
imp named William Wilberforce. Decades later, when Wilberforce

had become famous throughout London society for his extraordinary voice, both as a singer and a speaker, Milner proudly recalled that even as a diminutive schoolboy, "his elocution was so remarkable that we used to set him upon a table and make him read aloud as an example to the other boys."

❧

William Wilberforce was the third of four children born to his parents, and their only son. When he was eight, his eldest sister, Elizabeth, died. She was fourteen and had been at a prestigious boarding school in London. Soon after her death, Wilberforce's mother gave birth to another daughter, her fourth child. But a few months later her husband died suddenly, at the age of forty. A few months after that, Wilberforce's mother fell ill with a serious fever, and so it was decided that Wilberforce—"Billy" as he was then called—should go to live with his Uncle William and Aunt Hannah in Wimbledon.

We can only imagine what it was like for this brilliant and sensitive little boy to see his parents suffer the loss of their darling daughter—and then to lose his own father. For his mother to then become so sick must have been devastating. It would certainly have been difficult to be sent away from her and all that he had ever known, and to live with an unknown aunt and uncle at their country villa in faraway Wimbledon.

But off to Wimbledon Wilberforce now went. His new guardians were extraordinarily wealthy. His Uncle William's brother-in-law was John Thornton, one of the wealthiest men in all of England. In addition to their Wimbledon home, called Lauriston House, they had a magnificent home in London, in St. James's. Wilberforce was now ten, and they enrolled him at the Putney School, which, as Wilberforce remembered, was not terribly distinguished. "Mr. Chalmers, the master," he recalled, "himself a Scotsman, had an usher of the same nation, whose red beard—for he scarcely shaved once a month—I shall never forget." Even many years later the usually gracious-to-a-fault Wilberforce shuddered to describe Mr. Chalmers's assistant as "a dirty disagreeable man." "I can remember even now," he wrote, "the nauseous food with which we were supplied, and which I could not eat without sickness." One wonders whether his lifelong stomach difficulties weren't exacerbated or even instigated during these years. As for the quality of the education, he was no longer basking in the terra-watt brilliance of the Milner brothers. Wilberforce said that at Putney he was "taught everything and nothing."

If Wilberforce disliked his new school, however, he quickly came to love his aunt and uncle, whom he visited on holidays. And they fell in love with the extraordinary boy who had been dropped into their lives. "They had no children," Wilberforce wrote, "and I was to be their heir. . . . I loved [them] as if they had been my parents." Without question the greatest influence they had on him was spiritual.

The society to which they exposed him was a far cry from what he had known in Hull. Hull was a gay, prattling world of card parties and theater—second only to London for its worldly amusements—but in terms of anything deeper, in terms of real "soul" food, the larder was, as it were, bare. Wilberforce's mother and father, like the rest of their wealthy and fashionable friends, did not encourage introspection or deep thinking on the meaning of life. That was not the sort of thing one trilled about at card parties. One's "spirituality" was confined to one's rented wooden pew. One attended one's church, and one stood and one kneeled and one sat at the proper times and did what was required of one, but to scratch beneath this highly lacquered surface was to venture well beyond the pale in that society and invite stares and whispers and certain banishment. Wilberforce was from the beginning as serious as he was charming and fun-loving, and his sensitive and intellectual nature was now, at Wimbledon, for the first time fed something far more satisfying than the niceties—the thin gruel and weak tea—of High Church Anglicanism.

That's because Wilberforce's aunt and uncle, quite unbeknownst to his mother and grandfather, were at the epicenter of a spiritual renaissance in England at that time. They were close friends with one of the greatest figures of the eighteenth century, George Whitefield—the principal human force behind the social earthquake known as the Great Awakening, which transformed not only England but the thirteen colonies across the Atlantic. They were also very close with John Newton, another larger-than-life figure whom most of the world knows today as the former slave-ship captain who wrote the hymn "Amazing Grace." It was he who would have given little Wilberforce his first knowledge of slavery. These two connections and many more can be traced to Wilberforce's aunt's half-brother, John Thornton, who, besides being extremely rich, was at that time, according to the secretary of the Treasury, "in great credit and esteem, and of as much weight in the City as any one man I know." Thornton had been converted to a serious faith through the itinerant preaching of Whitefield around 1754. Since then, he had become known less for his wealth than for his generosity, funding many efforts to help the poor and suffering.

It is worth dilating for a moment on George Whitefield and the state of the Christian faith in England in the middle of the eighteenth century. Since the time of the Puritans and the religious wars of the previous century, England had decidedly turned its back on any expressions of what we might call serious Christian belief. Having led to so much division and violence, religion was now in full-scale retreat. The churches of mid-eighteenth-century England all but abandoned orthodox, historical Christianity and now preached a tepid kind of moralism that seemed to present civility and the preservation of the status quo as the *summum bonnum*. And so, understandably, people looked less and less to the churches for the ultimate answers to their questions, and a fog of hopeless and brutal superstitious spiritualism crept over the land. The poor, as is ever the case, would suffer the most from these changes in Britain's religious atmosphere.

But three young men arrived at Oxford University in the 1730s who soon changed things rather dramatically. John Wesley and his brother Charles were two of the three. They formed a small group called the Holy Club whose members prayed fervently and conspicuously. They were soon mocked as "Methodists" because other students thought they were too "methodical" about how they spent their time. George Whitefield, the third of the trio, soon came to Oxford and joined them.

After a few years, something surprising occurred. All of the trio's fussy doctrines and white-knuckled efforts to be "holy" and "moral" melted away when Whitefield came to a realization that would have far-reaching effects. He saw that the Bible didn't teach that we must work harder at becoming perfect and holy, but that we must instead throw ourselves on God's mercy. Moral perfection wasn't the answer: Jesus was the answer. Jesus had been morally perfect and we weren't supposed to save ourselves—we were supposed to ask him to save us.

No less than discovering electricity or splitting the atom, this theological about-face was the beginning of a revolution. When Whitefield began to preach this new revelation, people came running to hear it. No one had heard anything like it, and soon thousands were coming from near and far to hear him. He was just twenty-two at the time. Shocking the starched theological establishment of his day, Whitefield even began preaching in open fields so that more people could hear him, and crowds approaching thirty thousand people would gather.

The phenomenon that was George Whitefield is scarcely conceivable to modern minds. Lives by the thousands were changed all across England. Bitter miners wept and sang, and nasty fishwives leapt for joy. No one had ever told these poor people what this man with the voice like a trumpet was telling them, but it was as if they were hearing something they had always known was true but had forgotten. Their previous experience with religion was nothing like this. They had exchanged cod liver oil for sunshine and would never be the same. Whitefield touched down across England like a tornado, and what was left in his wake was unrecognizable from what had been there before. After he had thoroughly scrambled the English countryside and given hope and joy and meaning to the miserable poor who came to hear him, he hopped on board a ship like a fugitive and took his egregious troublemaking to the American colonies. And then returned to England. In his lifetime Whitefield would cross the Atlantic thirteen times.

As one might imagine, Whitefield was despised by the Church of England. But the press and those opposed to religion hated him too. He didn't mince words on the subjects of sin and hell, and he was increasingly impossible to avoid as his fame grew and grew. Whitefield was forever on the march, like some one-man salvation army. He carried a collapsible pulpit with him and sent handbills and posters ahead to the towns where he would preach; in his lifetime, he preached eighteen thousand sermons, none dull. As one would expect, Whitefield was viciously mocked for every aspect of his ministry and person, including the grave sin of being noticeably cross-eyed. For this pronounced ocular abnormality, he was tagged with the unflattering moniker "Dr. Squintum." But some admirers, seeking to put a positive spin on things, said that "even his eyes make the sign of the cross upon which Jesus died." *Touché*.

In the American colonies, Whitefield preached in fields from Maine to Georgia and routinely addressed crowds of thirty thousand there too. That he accomplished this without microphones almost seems to throw natural selection into doubt, arguing for the decline in vocal projection and/or hearing in the last two and a half centuries. Either that or the crowd numbers were exaggerated, as Benjamin Franklin, good Yankee skeptic that he was, initially suspected might be the case. When Whitefield came to Philadelphia in 1739, Franklin—ever the empiricist—resolved to walk around the circumference of the crowd and measure its size for himself. After completing the vast circuit, Franklin estimated that there were indeed at least twenty thousand there, and he said that he had never been out of the range of Whitefield's voice. Franklin eventually became a fan and friend of Whitefield's, and later became his publisher, though never quite a convert.

There was a great fear among those in power, especially ecclesiastical power, that men like Whitefield—and John and Charles Wesley—were threatening the social order. The lower classes were being encouraged to think for themselves, to resist the more orderly religion found in most of the Church of England congregations. Blacks and women were finding a place in this new, vibrant form of Christianity, and it was all very troubling. Social ferment and movements like the Great Awakening inevitably seem to echo Euripides' *The Bacchae:* wild Dionysian forces threaten to tear society apart, and are fought by the repressive forces of Apollinian order.

George Whitefield departed England for his final trip to America in 1769, about the time Wilberforce went to live with his Aunt Hannah and Uncle William, and so even though they were close friends with

Whitefield, it's unlikely that he and Wilberforce met. Wilberforce would have certainly mentioned such a meeting to his sons, who give us no record of it.

But Wilberforce did come to know another giant figure in English evangelicalism at the time. John Newton, "the old African blasphemer," as he called himself, and the man who surely introduced the young Wilberforce to the evils of the slave trade, was at that time the parson of a church in Olney. He came to London regularly and often visited the Wilberforces for what was called "parlor preaching." The Wilberforces also visited Newton and his wife in Olney many times while their nephew was with them. Newton became very close to the Wilberforces, and during the time William lived with them the little boy and the former sea captain formed a strong bond. Wilberforce said that he revered Newton "as a parent when I was a child." The weak-eyed, sickly, extremely nimble-minded boy must have been utterly captivated by the former slaver who at age eleven—William's age when they met—had gone off to sea for a picaresque adventure unimaginable to the wealthy and pampered merchant's son. The huge, fat, rough figure must have been quite a contrast to the little boy, whom the childless Newton was said to think of as a kind of son.

The great poet William Cowper also lived in Olney during that time. Newton spent much time caring for Cowper, who acted as an unofficial curate at Olney, helping Newton in much of his pastoral work, but Cowper also suffered terribly from depression. Newton suggested that as a way of dealing with it Cowper might write hymns each week for the Sunday service. Cowper took Newton's advice, and many of the hymns he wrote are the most beautiful in our language. Between them, Newton and Cowper wrote some 370 hymns that were eventually collected into the *Olney Hymnbook;* many continue to be frequently sung today.

⸎

When Wilberforce's mother and grandfather sent him to live with his aunt and uncle, they hadn't the slightest idea that they were sending the boy into a glowing hotbed of Methodism. And the idea that he would be parleying with a rough former sea captain on the horrors of slavery! It would have been no less horrifying to discover that the boy had ended up in the South Seas living with tattooed Maoris and dining upon human flesh. Evangelicals, as the movement came to be called, were hated by the cultural and social elites of mid-eighteenth-century England. The term of derision then was "Methodists," or "enthusiasts," and to give them any quarter, much less sympathize with them, was shocking.

In Hull and in London's most fashionable circles, the Methodists were criticized for their unctuous piety; for their moon-faced over-earnestness in all matters, as though appreciating irony were a grave sin; for their grotesque displays of ecstatic emotionalism (some at Whitefield's gatherings were said to bark and howl); for their lack of sophistication; and for their general disdain for the regnant social order and the myriad proprieties that attended its upkeep. So the idea that Alderman Wilberforce had delivered his namesake into the hands of these savages—that they were disguised as his own eldest son and the daughter of a member of Parliament and director of the Bank of England was of no matter—would have made him wonder whether the blue sky had cracked and was falling in pieces to earth.

It's hardly a wonder that surrounded as he was by such love, and by such inspiring figures, this bright, sensitive boy soon fell into their way of thinking. "I often accompanied [them] to church and to chapel," he wrote. "Under these influences my mind was . . . much interested and impressed by the subject of religion."

We don't know how long it took before Wilberforce's mother and grandfather caught wind of the situation. But at some point they were forced to the unpleasant realization that their best-laid plans for little William had gone agley—and rather badly agley at that. His letters and his behavior when he came home to visit surely had raised his mother's suspicions that he might have imbibed some of the fatal waters of Methodism—as, of course, he had. Alderman Wilberforce's opinion of the situation was to the point. "If Billy turns methodist," he barked, "he shall not have a sixpence of mine."

Years later Wilberforce would tell his son Robert: "It is impossible for you to have any idea of the hatred in which the methodists were then held. I cannot better explain it to you than by saying that it is more like the account given in Ivanhoe of the persecutions against the Jews, than anything else I know."

Her suspicions raised, Elizabeth Wilberforce's course was clear. She traveled from Hull to London to rescue her son. For Wilberforce, it was a deeply painful turn of events. He was utterly heartbroken at having to leave his beloved aunt and uncle, not to mention the entire world of fascinating and loving figures. He had been with them for two years.

Hannah Wilberforce and her husband were crushed. When Elizabeth arrived to rescue her son, Hannah remonstrated and tried to convince her sister-in-law of the opportunities available to him by remaining in their circle, describing the advantages of a "religious" life. But Elizabeth had seen all the "religious" life she wanted. And of course Hannah was concerned for her nephew's soul. "You should not fear," Elizabeth replied cynically. "If it be a work of grace, you know it cannot fail."

"Being removed from my uncle and aunt affected me most seriously," Wilberforce later wrote. "It almost broke my heart, I was so much attached to them." In a letter to them shortly after his departure, he wrote: "I can never forget you as long as I live."

Upon returning to Hull, the twelve-year-old was not sent back to his old grammar school. In the two years since Wilberforce had been away, Joseph Milner, the beloved headmaster whom Alderman Wilberforce had installed over the objections of much of the rest of the town, had turned Methodist too! As if Milner's conversion wasn't enough, he had also become a real force for Methodism in Hull, eventually preaching Methodist sermons in the Hull church and finding a following there too. Milner would publish many essays and sermons and eventually became famous for the multivolume *History of the Church of Christ*. He lived to complete the first three volumes; two more were added by his brother Isaac, the jumbo savant, who also reedited the previous volumes in 1810.

And so Wilberforce was sent off to Pocklington, his grandfather's school, thirteen miles away. He would remain there five years.

Although Wilberforce's return home was a brutal blow, he was determined to cling to his faith. But so was his mother determined to swamp it by any means necessary, and she and Alderman Wilberforce had much at their disposal to undertake the siege, not least time. So terrified was his mother of stoking whatever embers of Methodism remained in Wilberforce that she forbade him even to go to the anti-Methodist and boring church that she attended. In a letter to his Aunt Hannah, Wilberforce wrote that one of his "greatest misfortunes" during that time "was not being able to hear the blessed word of God, as my mama would not let me go to high church on a Sunday afternoon, but the Lord was everyday granting me some petition, and I trust I can say that I increased in the knowledge of God and Christ Jesus whom he sent, whom to know is life eternal."

For something like three years he put up an impressive fight, desperately trying to maintain his faith amidst the din of social distraction. Wilberforce later recalled that Hull was

> as gay a place as could be found out of London. The theatre, balls, great suppers, and card-parties were the delight of the principal families in the town. . . . The usual dinner hour was two o'clock, and at six they met for sumptuous suppers. This mode of life was at first distressing to me, but by degrees I acquired a relish for it. . . . As grandson of one of the principal inhabitants, I was everywhere invited and caressed: my voice and love of music made me still more acceptable. The religious impressions which I gained at Wimbledon continued for a considerable time, but my friends spared no pains to stifle them. I might almost say that no pious parent ever laboured more to impress a beloved child with sentiments of piety than they did to give me a taste of the world and its diversions.

These were deeply unhappy years for him, but he bravely fought on, writing secret letters to his aunt and uncle and others. The rift between Alderman Wilberforce and his Methodist eldest son must have been bitter. In September 1772, having just turned thirteen, William takes "the opportunity of writing by a maid who goes away tomorrow: thinking it the better way than sending to my uncle, since grandpa might perhaps see the letter."

Wilberforce says that when he was first taken to a play, "it was almost by force." It seems severe and ridiculous to us that what he had imbibed of religion would make him think the theater sinful, but we have to appreciate the circumstances and shibboleths of that era. Sir John Hawkins, who was the literary executor to Samuel Johnson, once said: "No sooner is a playhouse opened in any part of the Kingdom than it at once becomes surrounded by a halo of brothels." Prostitutes would sell their wares immediately outside theaters, and sometimes— responding to the Roaming and Invisible Hand of the Market—inside too. The modern concept of the theater as a place of deep seriousness and importance where giants like Ibsen and Strindberg fleshed out their progressive intellectual ideas was far in the future. The theater in Wilberforce's day was a place of decidedly impious diversion, not to say vulgarity.

Wilberforce now spent a great deal of time with the family of Joseph and Marianne Sykes. He grew to be like a brother to them, spent many vacations with them, and was under Mr. Sykes's guardianship for a time during these years. The Sykeses were held in great esteem by the wealthiest families of Hull. From Elizabeth Wilberforce's point of view, they were as far from world-hating Methodists as she could have hoped. William became quite close to Marianne, one of their daughters who would later marry his cousin and closest friend, Henry Thornton. The Sykes children wanted their old, fun-loving friend back, and they played a large part in returning him, slowly and against his will, to the world he had previously inhabited.

Years later Wilberforce's son Robert wrote that, when his father was an adolescent in Hull, his "talents for general society with his rare skill in singing rendered him everywhere an acceptable guest, and his time was wasted in a round of visits to the neighbouring gentry. Already, however, he gave proofs of an active mind, and one remarkable anticipation of his future course is yet remembered." Robert Wilberforce was referring to an account by the Reverend T. T. Walmsley—who had been at Pocklington with Wilberforce in those days—in which he claimed that when not more than fourteen, Wilberforce held the slave trade in abomination and wrote an essay against it. That is the first evidence we have of his taking any interest in the subject.

At Pocklington, under the elegantly bland direction of the Reverend Baskett, Wilberforce grew slowly out of his Methodist straitjacket and blossomed into the full half-measure of worldly maturity. His genius allowed him to distinguish himself as a scholar superior to all of the other boys there, though his work habits were not disciplined. Wilberforce recalls: "I was naturally a high spirited boy and fiery. This pushed me forward and made me talk a great deal and made me very vain. This idle way of living at home, of course, did not dispose me for exertion when I returned to school."

By 1775 he seems to have become much the kind of sixteen-year-old his mother and grandfather had always hoped he would be. Vain and full of fun, he had lost the seriousness that so rattled them a few years earlier. What's more, his manners and social graces had been buffed to a high sheen, and his premature *gravitas* had been nicely leavened with *levitas,* if not entirely expunged. And thus very properly outfitted to gambol and cut capers—if not quite play the fool—William Wilberforce went up to Cambridge in October 1776.

CHAPTER 2

INTO THE WIDE WORLD

"There was no one at all like him
for powers of entertainment."

Wilberforce was barely seventeen when he entered St. John's College at Cambridge in 1776, but it was not unusual in that era to begin college at that age or younger. William Pitt, who would in a few years become Wilberforce's closest friend, was the same age as Wilberforce but had already been at Cambridge three years when Wilberforce arrived, having entered at the age of fourteen. Andrew Marvell, who had preceded Wilberforce at Hull Grammar School a century before, began his Cambridge studies at twelve. Still, Cambridge represented rather a great leap for Wilberforce. It was one thing to be familiar with the worldly society of Hull and Pocklington, and another to arrive at an environment of such aggressive debauchery as to make Hull seem puritanical in comparison.

"I was introduced, on the very first night of my arrival," Wilberforce says with almost comic timing, "to as licentious a set of men as can well be conceived. They drank hard, and their conversation was even worse than their lives. I lived amongst them for some time, though I never relished their society,—often I was horror-struck at their conduct,—and after the first year I shook off in great measure my connection with them." In another place he describes them as "two of the most gambling, vicious characters in all of England." For the pleasure of being introduced to these scoundrels he had his own tutor to thank, one William Arnault, the person who was supposed to guide Wilberforce's studies. It was a case of the blind leading the blind, only worse, for Arnault seems to have been practically headless. He actively discouraged Wilberforce from studying. To someone with Wilberforce's penchant for distraction and entertainment, this was as close to a fatal injury as anyone might have done to him at that extremely formative time. For the rest of his life he struggled terribly with self-discipline and always attributed this weakness to his wasted and feckless years at Pocklington and Cambridge, where slacking off was encouraged and his superior mind always enabled him to do just what needed to be done, and done brilliantly, at the eleventh hour. But whatever faults can be laid at the feet of poor Arnault, he surely had his own difficulties: he would go insane some six years later.

Wilberforce's time at Cambridge over two hundred years ago sounds extraordinarily like the experience of many college students today. He seems to have studied only when he had to, which, owing to his extraordinary mind, was very little. He spent most of his time entertaining himself and others and picking up a smattering of learning—getting what was really a "cultural education" that would put him in good stead in the society to which he would soon graduate.

Thomas Gisborne's rooms were right next to Wilberforce's during these years, and as much as Wilberforce didn't study, Gisborne did. "There was always a great Yorkshire pie in his rooms," Gisborne remembers, "and all were welcome to partake of it. My rooms and his were back to back, and often when I was raking out my fire at ten o'clock, I heard his melodious voice calling aloud to me to come and sit with him before I went to bed. It was a dangerous thing to do, for his amusing conversation was sure to keep me up so late, that I was behind-hand the next morning."

Gisborne became a minister in the Church of England and in later years was renowned as one of the very best preachers in the country. Though just acquaintances at Cambridge, he and Wilberforce eventually became great friends. He had a country home in Staffordshire called Yoxall Lodge, where Wilberforce would spend vast amounts of time during the coming decades.

"There was no one at all like him," Gisborne said, "for powers of entertainment. Always fond of repartee and discussion." Gisborne recalls seeing Wilberforce holding court here and there on the streets of Cambridge, "encircled by a set of young men of talent, among whom he was *facile princeps*."

By every account, Wilberforce seems to have been extraordinarily charming; from earliest childhood to the end of his life, he captivated others with his mind and with his singular voice. He was brilliantly witty, indefatigably effervescent, and brightly cheerful, not to mention generous. He had a supreme gift for hospitality that would go a long way toward helping him in his political career in years hence, but at Cambridge it manifested itself less grandly and to no particular purpose. He threw dinners in his rooms for all and sundry. The deaths of his grandfather and, in 1777, of his dear Uncle William had made Wilberforce a very wealthy young man indeed.

Gisborne continues: "By his talents, his wit, his kindness, his social powers, his universal acceptability, and his love of society, he speedily became the centre of attraction to all the clever and idle of his own college and of other colleges. . . . His rooms swarmed with them from the time when he rose, generally very late, till he went to bed. . . . He spent much of his time visiting."

But Wilberforce wasn't the determinedly debauched sort of wastrel that he might have been. Though hardly a prig, he was no drunkard, and he seems not to have joined in the venereal adventures of some of his friends. In his second year at Cambridge, he managed to shake off the worst of the ne'er-do-wells and gamblers in his circle and settled in with a superior group. Still, Wilberforce was hardly studious, and many years later he took some of the men with whom he'd associated at Cambridge to task for their influence on him. Wilberforce felt that they had almost worked at keeping him idle. If they found him studying, they would chide him severely, saying that studying, or "fagging," as it was then called, was for "saps" like Gisborne. They browbeat him into being a very model of insouciance—for this was the studied pose of the upper classes of that day.

So Wilberforce drifted, reading what he liked and spending the lion's share of his waking hours throwing parties and singing and playing cards and going to concerts and dances, and to the horse races and to the pleasure gardens and Vauxhall and to the theater. He traveled to the great country houses of other wealthy friends, and there they would sing and dance and play cards, and Wilberforce's endless resources of wit and charm would find opportunities to exhibit themselves, in all their glory and to no particular purpose. He was headed nowhere in particular, and at a particularly rapid rate.

Wilberforce had an extraordinary knack for collecting friends and acquaintances, often of distinction and note. He seems to have known everybody there was to be known. At Cambridge two of the friends Wilberforce acquired were William Cookson and Edward Christian. Both came from the famously picturesque Lake District; he visited them there during term vacations and would later spend many summers and autumns in the area. The Lake District, of course, would be made famous in part by the poet William Wordsworth, who was Cookson's nephew. Edward Christian's relationship to fame—or notoriety—was by way of his younger brother, a future mutineer by the name of Fletcher.

Two others who were at Cambridge would figure prominently in Wilberforce's eventual decision to take up abolition as a cause. Gerard Edwards, also at St. John's, was close to Wilberforce during this time and would be his lifelong friend. Edwards would marry the daughter of Lord and Lady Middleton—both evangelicals—and it was during his visits with Edwards and his wife that Wilberforce met the Middletons and others who would launch him into his life's work and become his dearest friends. Also at Cambridge now was William Pitt, though he and Wilberforce were not yet friends. Pitt was the brilliant son of the great prime minister William Pitt (the Elder) and as such ran in a higher set than Wilberforce did.

But by the winter of 1779–80, Wilberforce had begun to spend a great deal of time in London and often met Pitt in the gallery of the House of Commons, where they would sit and watch the debates. Pitt was born to be there; under his father's careful and deliberate tutelage, he had lived and breathed politics all his life. Wilberforce acquired his taste for politics during this time, but what precisely drew him to it we can only guess. We know that his grandfather had twice been mayor of the great port city of Hull, the first time at age thirty-two. Surely that had some influence upon his grandson. Sitting there in the gallery, perhaps Wilberforce simply got caught up in the proceedings below and a desire bloomed in him to join the debate and say for the historical record what he was already thinking; perhaps he thought he might do as well as those extemporizing down on the floor and wished to try.

By now his cousin, Abel Smith, had taken over the family business, and Wilberforce could continue to expect revenues from it, inasmuch as it was in such, dare we say, able hands. Wilberforce manifestly lacked the personality to sit over an account ledger and do whatever was necessary to be a successful businessman in the merchant trade back in Hull. Indeed, it would have been like asking a dervish to set the tea table. But if ever Wilberforce had entertained a desire to return to Hull and preside over the family business, surely now he was unlikely to do so, not after having traded quips in the gallery of the House of Commons with his new bosom friend William Pitt.

Pitt's influence on Wilberforce during these crucial early days was considerable. Wilberforce was Pitt's equal or superior in intelligence, charm, and wit, but Pitt was leagues ahead in the political game. Not only was he the son of the famous prime minister, but since earliest childhood he had been groomed by that self same prime minister to be a statesman, to be one of those men on the floor below them whose words shaped the history of their great nation. When Wilberforce had been joking, playing cards, and dancing reels, Pitt had been memorizing long passages from Virgil and studying the speeches of Demosthenes. And while Wilberforce was in 1779 a newcomer to parliamentary debate, Pitt had been watching it for years, not merely as an observer but as the son of one of the principal players in the drama. Pitt had been in the gallery of the House of Lords in 1775 when his father, by then already a mere shadow of his previous self, strongly warned against the North government's hard line with the American colonies. And Pitt had been there the next time his father spoke, warning that if Britain didn't make peace with the colonies, it would be drawn into a wider war with France and Spain and would live to regret it.

At the time, Pitt wrote to his mother: "I cannot help expressing to you how happy beyond description I feel in reflecting that my
father was able to exert, in their full vigour, the sentiments and eloquence which have always distinguished him. His first speech took
up half an hour, and was full of all his usual force and vivacity. . . . He
spoke a second time. . . . This he did in a flow of eloquence, and with
a beauty of expression, animated and striking beyond conception."

As we know, Britain continued to prosecute the ill-fated war
against the colonists. And we know that in October 1777, when the
British lost the battle at Saratoga, the tide of the war turned decidedly
in favor of the Americans and would never turn back. This embold-
ened France to join the fray, just as Pitt had predicted. Lord North,
whose blundering leadership during the war tagged him forever as the
man who "lost" the American colonies, became very dispirited during
this time and asked King George to accept his resignation, wanting to
give the reins of leadership to Pitt. But the king despised Pitt, calling
him "that perfidious man," and refused North, who was condemned to
the horror of continuing to live with his errors, now compounding.

The Elder Pitt's last appearance in Parliament was on April 17,
1778. In dramatic fashion, he entered the chamber supported by his
son William, then eighteen, and his son-in-law, Lord Mahon. The
entire assembly rose to greet him, and though he could hardly speak
or stand, he spoke and stood one last time, powerfully exhorting
England in "God's name" not to cower before France, its "ancient
inveterate enemy." "Shall this great kingdom," he asked, "fall prostrate before the House of Bourbon? Shall a people that fifteen years
ago was the terror of the world now stoop so low as to tell its ancient
inveterate enemy, 'Take all we have, only give us peace'? In God's
name . . . let us at least make one effort; and if we must fall, let us fall
like men!"

He then fell himself, collapsing to the floor. William and his
brother John rushed to their father's aid. Four weeks later he was
dead. The scene must have been fresh in the mind of Pitt as he sat
with Wilberforce, while the very drama in which his late father had
participated in continued below.

On the floor of the House of Commons was a living pageant of
historical personages, with a brace of speakers whose marble busts

today cover the country. Lord North, Charles Fox, and Edmund Burke led the pack. Burke was a staunch conservative, famous as one of the greatest orators of the century. North was a close friend of the king's, and Fox, North's political enemy, was internationally famous for being a dissolute rogue. The king hated Fox ferociously: not only was he a political enemy, but he had led the king's eldest son astray, though to lead the Prince of Wales astray was like leading a hungry lion to a lame gazelle. Lord North's famously deep voice had earned him the nickname Boreas, meaning "North wind," and both he and Fox were quite overweight, though North had the lead in this department by a wide mile. The spectacle of these living caricatures savaging each other day after day in the wittiest of exchanges must have been terribly entertaining.

It was sometime during the spring of 1780, while he was visiting Hull, that the idea formally lodged in the mind of William Wilberforce to run for election to the House of Commons that fall. He was all of twenty at the time, but he would be just twenty-one by the time of the September 11 election. Hull was an important district, one of the top twenty in all of England, so it was a bold and ambitious idea, and it would certainly cost a small fortune. Elections in England were almost literally bought at that time, and in later life, when he had become a serious Christian, Wilberforce said that if he had had to enter politics again under those openly corrupt circumstances, he would have remained in private life. It was an odious process whereby one wined and dined one's constituents and gave speeches. It was all many degrees more shameless than anything we complain of today, not least because one was quite literally expected to pay each elector two guineas as a bribe. If one paid four guineas, the elector would not exercise his second vote, increasing the value of the first. The electors, who were hereditary freemen, saw this payment as a birthright, and if they lived in London, as three hundred of the Hull electors did, they expected—and received—ten pounds for traveling expenses.

Wilberforce gamely spent the entire summer "canvassing" for votes, throwing lavish dinners to which the electors were invited and giving speeches. But nothing could ever compare to what he did on August 24, his twenty-first birthday. He had decided to celebrate his coming of age—quite nicely timed just two weeks before the election itself—by throwing a good old-fashioned ox roast, with a monstrous bonfire blazing and food and drink and music for everyone in the town.

An entire ox roasted whole over a bonfire was a grand spectacle. A rare and extremely festive event—the *ne plus ultra,* as it were, of outdoor meat cookery—an ox roast always signaled an occasion of particular importance. One was held at Windsor in 1809 to celebrate the Golden Jubilee of King George III, and another was held in 1887 to celebrate the Golden Jubilee of Victoria. And here now, in Hull in 1780, an ox roast was held to celebrate the twenty-first birthday of the grandson of the late Alderman, the scion of the great Wilberforce family, a tiny, brilliant, and exceedingly ambitious young man who happened to be standing for Parliament in the general election just two weeks hence.

The famished Hullish masses descended on Wilberforce's land and "a good time was had by all." The eight-hundred-pound ox had twirled round and round over the coals for twenty-nine hours on a specially constructed, eighteen-foot-long spit. Ten tons of wood were consumed to roast the ox, and the entire ox was consumed to elect Wilberforce, who, after paying for the ox roast and all those other dinners, had consumed nearly £9,000 of his own money in just a few months. But two weeks later, on September 11, in what was by all accounts a sharply contested election, Wilberforce took 1,126 votes against Lord Manners's 673 and David Hartley's 453. It was duly noted that the newly minted twenty-one-year-old had won exactly as many votes as his two opponents combined, which gave him a nice little push as he entered Parliament—the ox had not twirled in vain.

CHAPTER 3

WILBERFORCE ENTERS PARLIAMENT

"I was then very ambitious."

On October 31, 1780, at age twenty-one, Wilberforce sat for the first time in the House of Commons as a member of Parliament. His friend Pitt, surprisingly, had lost his bid for the Cambridge University seat during the September election, but he was somehow able to get another seat for the borough of Appleby a few months later. Pitt very quickly distinguished himself as someone "to the House born." He immediately became the unofficial leader of a group of new, young parliamentarians, many of whom had been at Cambridge together.

Wilberforce's entry into Parliament was quiet, and it's unclear when he made his first speech. But Pitt, once in, leapt to the forefront almost immediately. His maiden speech made quite the splash. Lord North deemed it the finest he'd ever heard, and Edmund Burke, one of the greatest orators of all time, said that Pitt was "not just a chip of the old block; he is the old block itself!" Not long afterward, Pitt gave another powerful speech, and Wilberforce himself wrote that "he comes out as his father did, a ready-made orator, and I doubt not but that I shall one day or other see him the first man in the country."

Wilberforce had no idea just how quickly his prescient remark would come true.

Wilberforce deferred to Pitt's superior political knowledge and experience and looked to Pitt for clues on how to navigate what were, for him, uncharted waters. But he remained independent of Pitt politically, even though they were basically united. They were both Tories, and therefore members of the opposition party. At that time the opposition party was led by Shelburne and the Duke of Rockingham, who opposed Prime Minister Lord North's policies, especially regarding the disastrous war with the colonies, which by now was in its pathetic endgame.

And so the same battles that raged when he and Pitt had watched from the gallery a few months before raged still, the war being foremost, and the two leviathans, Fox and North, were still going at it. The only thing that had really changed was that now Wilberforce had a front-row seat at the proceedings. In a letter from that time, he recounted having voted with North on a particular issue, saying: "I staid in with the old fat fellow; by the way, he grows every day fatter, so where he will end I know not." Dr. Johnson, who was a terrifically bulky fellow himself, once said of North that "he fills a chair." When North received word of Cornwallis's loss at Yorktown in 1781, he is supposed to have cried, "Oh! It is all over! It is all over!" With his genius for mimicry—just one of his many social gifts—Wilberforce was able to "set a table at a roar" with his dead-on imitation of the elephantine statesman.

Wilberforce's social gifts were soon being displayed in far higher circles than he had been used to. His overwhelming success in the election had launched him very nicely into London society, giving him an increased measure of social respectability. He was put up for membership at five clubs and accepted at all of them. Wilberforce was obviously socially ambitious. He'd always known he was capable of great things, but he also knew that as the son of a merchant from Hull, he would always be looked down upon by some. Now, somehow, he knew that he had arrived.

"When I went up to Cambridge," he recalled years later, "I was scarcely acquainted with a single person above the rank of a country gentleman; and now I was at once immersed in politics and fashion. . . .

The very first time I went to Boodle's I won twenty-five guineas off the Duke of Norfolk. I belonged at this time to five clubs—Miles and Evans's, Brookes's, Boodle's, White's, Goostree's." What a heady thing it would have been for the recently graduated Wilberforce to suddenly find himself mixing on something like equal terms with the men who were the celebrities of his day. These men were giants of their era and would remain legendary figures in England for generations to come.

George Selwyn was one. Renowned as a wit and celebrated as a macabre connoisseur of corpses, criminals, and executions, he was something like a combination of Truman Capote and Vincent Price. When Selwyn called upon his old rival Henry Fox (the father of Charles James Fox) when he was dying, Selwyn was told he couldn't see Fox, and so he simply left his card. When Fox was later told of Selwyn's visit, he said: "If Mr. Selwyn calls again, show him up. If I am alive, I shall be glad to see him, and if I am dead, I am sure he will be delighted to see me!"

Wilberforce writes: "The first time I was at Brookes's, scarcely knowing anyone, I joined from mere shyness in play at the faro table, where George Selwyn kept bank. A friend who knew my inexperience, and regarded me as a victim decked out for sacrifice, called to me 'What, Wilberforce, is that you?' Selwyn quite resented the interference, and turning to him said, in his most expressive tone, 'Oh, sir, don't interrupt Mr. Wilberforce; he could not be better employed.' Nothing could be more luxurious than the style of these clubs. Fox, Sheridan, Fitzpatrick, and all your leading men, frequented them and associated upon the easiest terms; you chatted, played at cards, or gambled as you pleased."

For the merchant's son from Hull, it was heaven. Wilberforce's acceptance into these five clubs drew him into the very center of the London society of which he had longed to be a part. What a cast of characters it was! Selwyn was a man-about-town and a close friend of Hugh Walpole's, whose cynicism and wit were legendary. Richard Brinsley Sheridan, the famous playwright and member of Parliament, was also a member there. Sheridan was friends with Fox and had just entered Parliament himself.

But the club Wilberforce frequented most regularly was a smaller one, called Goostree's, where Pitt and other Cambridge contemporaries could be found nearly every night, dining and playing cards. Wilberforce gambled along with everyone else because it was simply what was done among members of that class. But one night after he won £600 he decided to quit altogether. He didn't quit because he thought gambling wrong, but because it bothered him, sensitive as he always was, to see that the man who'd lost would have difficulty in paying him.

At Goostree's, Wilberforce's friendships with some of the Cambridge set grew and deepened. Gerard Edwards, William Grenville, Pepper Arden, Henry Bankes, and Edward Eliot were all part of what Wilberforce called "the Gang" or "the Goostree's Gang." And of course, at the center of so much of it was Pitt, who was a startlingly different person when at ease among his friends. With this group and with Wilberforce especially, Pitt could forget for a moment the great pressures and expectations that attended the rising son of his famous father.

Wilberforce reckoned Pitt the wittiest person he had ever known, rather a powerful compliment coming from the man whom everyone else reckoned the wittiest person *they* had ever known. No less a connoisseur of wit than the famous Madame de Staël would one day call Wilberforce "the wittiest man in all of England."

Wit and its employment as a weapon not only in political combat but in playing with one's friends was at the core of the Goostree's Gang. Their favorite pastime was trading quips and being witty— what they called "foyning," or "foining." The term "to foin"—originally French—means to thrust, as with a rapier sword. "Foining" swordplay with lighter swords and rapiers had replaced the earlier kind of swordplay with broadswords, which involved cutting and slashing. So "to foin" meant to parry deftly and thrust with one's wits; the term "rapier wit" is a cousin of "foining." It was an era in which wit was greatly valued, and Wilberforce and his friends, all inveterate wits, were dubbed by Edward Eliot "the Foinsters."

During these first years in London, Wilberforce led a life that was essentially a continuation of the life he had led at Cambridge. There was endless foining and drinking and dancing and singing. Singing what were called "glees" and "catches" was very popular in men's clubs of the eighteenth century. Catches were three- or four-part songs, usually with humorous and sometimes bawdy lyrics, while glees were less about the lyrics than the music; of course, the word survives in what we today call glee clubs.

Wilberforce was greatly renowned for his singing voice and came to be known as the "Nightingale of Commons"—probably not only for the remarkable quality of his voice but for the hours at which he sang. In 1782 Wilberforce sang at the Duchess of Devonshire's ball, prompting the Prince of Wales to remark that he would go anywhere to hear him. And George Selwyn wrote that, leaving one of these fabulous parties, "I left in one room a party of young men who made me, for their life and spirits, wish for one night to be twenty. There was a table full of them drinking—young Pitt, Lord Euston, Berkeley, etc., singing and laughing *a gorge employee,* some of them sang very good snatches; one Wilberforce, a MP, sang the best."

Wilberforce had inherited his Uncle William's villa in Wimbledon, with its eight bedrooms, and the Goostree's Gang would repair there whenever possible, to escape London and their official duties. A few years later, after Pitt had become prime minister and the cares of life lay far heavier upon him, Wilberforce wrote a letter to him: "You may reckon yourself most fortunate in that cheerfulness of mind which enables you every now and then to throw off your load for a few hours. I fancy it must be this which, when I am with you, prevents me considering you an object of compassion, tho' Prime Minister of England; for now, when I am out of hearing of your foyning . . . I cannot help representing you to myself as oppressed with cares and troubles."

The two of them became so close during this time that Pitt used Wilberforce's Wimbledon house as his own whenever he pleased. Wilberforce writes that for "weeks and months together I spent hours with him every morning and while he transacted business . . . Hundreds of times, probably, I have called him out of bed and conversed with him while he was dressing. I was the depository of his most confidential thoughts."

These were wealthy sons of privilege all, and they enjoyed their wealth and privilege to the fullest extent. No more self-centered than others, and certainly not more wicked, they were nevertheless in no way aware of nor troubled by the unfathomable suffering in the world beyond their immediate ken. The term "noblesse oblige"—the idea that those who have been blessed with much are to use it to help those who have not been so blessed—would not be coined for another half-century, and Wilberforce had yet to discover the relevance of any such idea to his own life. Nonetheless, he possessed a moral quality that others noticed, even though he had traveled miles away from the moral seriousness of his early teen years and seemed wholly dedicated to entertaining himself and others. In 1782 Gerard Edwards wrote: "I thank God that I live in the age of Wilberforce and that I know one man at least who is both moral and entertaining."

During his first sixteen months in Parliament, Wilberforce said little, and what little he said touched only on issues concerning his district, Hull. But on February 22, 1782, Wilberforce waded for the first time into deeper waters. The date was appropriate for his debut, for it was—certainly unbeknownst to Wilberforce—the fiftieth birthday of George Washington, the man who had driven Lord North and King George to the brink of madness and frustration. And it was on that date that Wilberforce stepped out beyond his previous parochial interests and, revealing his frightening gifts of sarcasm and oratory, launched an utterly devastating attack on Lord North and his administration. It was as if the unassuming little fellow had all these months been concealing a blunderbuss beneath his coat, and now he rose and suddenly revealed it to the rotund North, who sat there aghast and goggle-eyed, fingering his slingshot.

It was in the next two years that Wilberforce came into his own as a parliamentary debater, often laying waste to his opponents through his sarcastic wit and extremely agile repartee. When, in April 1783, Lord North joined forces with his traditional enemy, Charles James Fox, to form the short-lived Fox-North coalition, Wilberforce attacked their unprincipled union with especial vigor and brilliance. There was a giddy abandon and fury to his oratorical sorties that no one would ever forget, especially Fox, who would resent Wilberforce for years to come for these devastating attacks.

To be sure, the Fox-North coalition was a grotesque sideshow horror, as if someone had crudely sewn together a mongoose and a cobra and presented it as a single fabulous beast. Formerly they had been the bitterest foes, but behold, they were now united against their common enemies—common decency and common sense! The king was unhinged at the treachery of the union. Fox had been his bitterest enemy and North his friend and ally against Fox. The two of them, in this monstrously cynical political union, had come together solely to defeat Lord Shelbourne, whose policies they opposed. But for the king the whole thing was worse than politically hideous and cynical; it was bitterly personal because of Fox's pernicious influence on the king's eldest son, the Prince of Wales.

Fox was internationally known for his immoral and rakish behavior; his appetites were less Falstaffian than merely swinish. As we have said earlier, he had encouraged the Prince of Wales in his already outrageously dissolute lifestyle. We may say what we like about his politics, but the king was a faithful husband who sincerely felt that those in power ought to comport themselves with decorum and restraint for the sake of the country. And he felt that his son, as the heir apparent, ought especially to behave himself to set an example for the nation. But the way his son behaved seemed to express a wish for England's ruin, and father and son became bitterly estranged. The king blamed Fox for a great part of the situation. And now North had joined Fox. It was too much to bear.

The king tried desperately for several weeks to avoid appointing what he called "the most unprincipled coalition the annals of this or any other nation can equal." But in the end he had no choice, and the double-headed freak took office on April 2, 1783. While in office the king did all he could to oppose them, and Fox further infuriated the king by attempting to give the Prince of Wales an income of £100,000 from the Royal Treasury. The prince's gambling debts were breathtaking and would continue to be for decades to come, but surely it was wrong for him to be bailed out by the government. The king tried to persuade Pitt, though he was only twenty-four, to form a government and become prime minister, but the time for this was not yet favorable, and so, for the time being at least, the political jackalope that was the Fox-North coalition survived.

⚮

In September of that year, Wilberforce, Pitt, and Eliot decided to travel together to France. Before they crossed the Channel, though, they would spend a few days together at the Dorset country home of Henry Bankes, their Cambridge and Goostree's pal. They felt that before leaving England for the Continent, a bit of partridge hunting was in order; they'd fill their lungs with English air and their bellies with English birds. How many British birds they bagged is lost to history, but what we do know of this outing is that Wilberforce, notoriously shortsighted and not much of a shot, nearly blasted England's future prime minister clean out of the history books—not to say out of the future itself. Pitt didn't look much like a bird, but Wilberforce didn't shoot many birds either. His myopic error gave new meaning to the phrase "a shot at greatness," and the others teased him about it for years. Of course, history might have been quite changed had the mistake been more serious. Perhaps most scandalous of all, they waited many years before informing the press.

When Wilberforce, Pitt, and Eliot finally arrived in France, the comedy, appropriately, turned farcical. They discovered that each of them had relied on the others for proper letters of introduction. In a day when society observed infinitely stricter rules than today, a lack of proper letters of introduction could be disastrous, as theirs now was. The one letter of introduction they could obtain at the last minute turned out to be to a grocer in Rheims. The grocer was affable and did his best to make them comfortable, but someone who wore an apron and dispensed figs and raisins was probably not the right person for introductions to the local nobility. At first, believing him to be a nobleman, they were sure that his deadpan impression of a grocer was *trés charmant* but took things a bit too far. But alas, the humble grocer was not playacting—the poor fellow wore his actual apron without irony—and once the trio came to understand this, they realized that they were quite stuck. The three young men spent ten unfortunate days at an inn doing nothing.

But in a sleepy town in Rheims in the summer, three young men doing nothing began to look suspicious, and eventually they came to the attention of the local police *intendant,* who, figuring he had stumbled upon some sort of plot—and right under his nose too—brought the scamps to the attention of the secretary to the Council of State, the Abbé de Lageard, who was officially in charge when the archbishop was traveling. The *intendant* described them as three

Englishmen "of very suspicious character." He told the *abbé* that their "courier" claimed that these characters were important gentlemen—*grand seigneurs*—and that one of them was the son of the famous Earl of Chatham! As far as the *intendant* was concerned, it was all a ruse; they were undoubtedly *des intrigants,* low schemers of some sort, or possibly English spies, and he asked for permission to launch *un investigation officieul.*

Fortunately for our three vagabonds, the *abbé*'s instincts told him things weren't necessarily what the *intendant* feared. And so the *abbé* decided to visit the three *grand seigneurs* himself. It didn't take the *abbé* long to get to the bottom of things, and once their identities were cleared up, Lageard put himself at their disposal, asking how he might improve their situation. Pitt was the first to pipe up. "Here we are in the middle of Champagne," he said, "and we cannot get any tolerable wine!" It's unlikely that this was the first time Pitt had made this ironic observation during their ten-day sojourn with the un-ironic little grocer, but now there was someone besides Eliot and Wilberforce with whom he could lodge his plaintive *cri du coeur.* The *abbé* remedied the situation immediately and invited them to dinner the next day, promising them some of the best wine in the region, and soon thereafter gave proper introductions to the local nobility, none of whom sold raisins or figs.

Lageard also allowed them to hunt on the archbishop's land—and no one got hurt. Eventually they met the archbishop himself, who was the uncle of the famous French diplomat Talleyrand, who would figure in all of their lives a few decades hence. But the horrors of war were far in the future, and the three former schemers were enjoying themselves tremendously. It would have been unthinkable to imagine the dark forces that were about to be unleashed in their world. They played billiards with the archbishop and dined with him and the *abbé* on many occasions during this stay. At one meal where some of the local vintages were doubtless flowing with particularly unimpeded eloquence, the *abbé* felt comfortable enough to express himself on the political situation in England. He asked how "a country so moral as England can submit to be governed by a man so wanting in private character as Fox?"

At last the trio headed for Paris, and on October 16 the archbishop introduced them to the French court. On the morning of the seventeenth, Wilberforce and Eliot went via chaise to see the king, whom Wilberforce describes in his diary as a "clumsy, strange figure in immense boots." In a letter to Bankes, he describes Louis XVI as "so strange a being of the hog kind, that it is worth going a hundred miles for a sight of him." Given similar descriptions of the French king by others, as well as the look of unmitigatedly dim hauteur in some of the paintings and engravings of him, it is an effort to dismiss Wilberforce's sketch of him as an aloof, porcine oaf. The pretty Marie Antoinette, however, Wilberforce found entirely charming: "At Fontainebleu we dined and supped with ministers," he writes, "and every night we spent with the Queen, who is a monarch of most engaging manners and appearance" and was always "mixing in conversation with the greatest affability."

At the royal court they learned that the news of their initial difficulties at Rheims had traveled faster than they had. Marie Antoinette herself teased Pitt about it, on several occasions asking whether he had that day seen his friend, the earnestly aproned grocer.

On October 20 the three dined at the home of the Marquis de Lafayette, where they had the great surprise and honor of meeting Benjamin Franklin, who was at this point an international celebrity. There was no figure who loomed larger on the world stage. Franklin was the Enlightenment incarnate, only wigless—a living icon of homespun American can-do-ism, and the man who, in the words of the French financier Turgot, "snatched lightning from the sky and the scepter from tyrants," and the man whom Immanuel Kant had called "the new Prometheus." And here he was now, in the flesh, all of these things and many more—inventor and printer, Founding Father and Francophilic flirt, "Silence Dogood" and "Poor Richard"—jawing away in his Philadelphian French with Lafayette's charming young wife.

It was an extraordinary moment: the brilliantly witty twenty-four-year-old Wilberforce meeting the brilliantly witty seventy-seven-year-old Franklin. Franklin probably knew of Wilberforce's opposition to the American war and to Lord North's government, and doubtless Lafayette knew it too. Perhaps even more significant is that here at the same table were two champions of abolition meeting at a time before either had entered the lists on its behalf, as it were. Wilberforce would begin his five-decade battle against slavery three years hence, in 1787, and Franklin, who had spoken against slavery many times, would in 1790, the eighty-fourth and final year of his life, sign a petition from the Pennsylvania Abolition Society to Congress pressing them to "take such measures in their wisdom, as the powers with which they are invested will authorize, for promoting the abolition of slavery, and discouraging every species of traffic in slaves"—which would only come to pass seventy-some years later.

But the trip was now cut short. On October 24, Pitt was summoned to return home. There he found the king trying desperately to bring an end to the conjoined abomination that was the Fox-North coalition. When Fox proposed his famous East India Bill, the king saw his chance. Fox would have given himself vast powers of patronage had it succeeded. Even for the unprincipled Fox, the bill represented particularly naked political opportunism, and everyone in the opposition especially was disgusted. The king now cashed in all his political chips, soberly informing the House of Lords that anyone who voted for Fox's bill would be his sworn enemy. And so the East India Bill was defeated. On December 18, 1783, the king, with the greatest glee, showed the door to the Janus-faced indecency that was the Fox-North coalition—and now appointed William Pitt, then just twenty-four, the youngest prime minister in English history.

❧

The notion of a twenty-four-year-old leading a country was nearly as shocking to the world of that day as it would be to ours. Pitt's youth was immediately blasted from all quarters. Someone in the opposition composed a mocking jingle with the title "Billy's Too Young to Drive Us." A group of versifying wits published mocking squibs in the *Morning Herald:*

> A sight to make surrounding nations stare,
> A Kingdom trusted to a school boy's care.

Pitt may have been prime minister, but his situation was politically still very precarious. Every one of the ministers in his new government was from the House of Lords, so Pitt found himself virtually alone in the House of Commons. Wilberforce, only twenty-four himself, was Pitt's greatest ally there, and he stood staunchly by his friend's side during this time, both of them using their powerful oratorical skills to the fullest.

Still, it was only a matter of time before Pitt would have to call for a general election in which he would, in effect, sink or swim. The arcana and complications of British politics are far too confusing to untangle here, but suffice it to say that something like a town meeting, only on a county level, was called for the county of Yorkshire for March 25. It would be held in the vast grassy yard of York Castle. Wilberforce would speak, defending Pitt and Pitt's government. He well knew the importance of this speech for his friend, and its role in deciding his own political future. But what Wilberforce had in mind now was something that went well beyond defending Pitt.

Though we can hardly understand it, and Wilberforce himself never quite made sense of it during his lifetime, he now entertained the outrageous idea of using this opportunity to become one of Yorkshire County's two representatives in Parliament, something that was effectively impossible. York was the most powerful constituency in all of England, and it was always represented by landed gentry who had particular contempt for the sons of merchants, like Wilberforce. Nor was there any vacancy: both seats for Yorkshire were filled. Taking all of these things together, anyone could see that the magnitude of this ambition was outrageous. Somehow, however, Wilberforce had this idea in his mind, although he wasn't entirely clear how it had gotten there and why he had allowed it to stay there—and part of him always wondered whether it had originated elsewhere.

Wilberforce confided to a friend some time afterward: "I had then formed in my own breast the project of standing for the County of York, though to anyone else it would have appeared a mad scheme. It was very contrary to the aristocratic notions of the great families of the County to place the son of a Hull merchant in so high a situation." He explained, "It was a very bold idea, but I was then very ambitious."

The day itself was as miserable and raw as one can imagine in Yorkshire County in March: bitterly cold, with powerful winds and rain. For good measure, there was also hail. And yet what was taking place was so important to the future of the nation that four thousand freeholders showed up and stayed. The speeches started midmorning—

there were twelve of them—and they continued for six hours. Today the idea of standing in the cold and wind and rain—and hail—for hours to hear long political speeches is inconceivable. Finally, at about four that afternoon, Wilberforce's turn to speak came.

There was a kind of wooden canopy, and underneath it a table served as the improvised speaking platform. Just as he once had been lifted by Isaac Milner onto a table to charm the classroom with his elocution, now Wilberforce mounted a table in the midst of a vast castle yard to charm the four thousand, to support Pitt, and to change the political landscape of the nation.

By this time, however, the bad weather had grown worse. It was now so windy that one observer expressed concern for Wilberforce, saying that it looked "as if his slight frame would be unable to make head against its violence." But Wilberforce's exquisite voice was a force of nature itself, and as rude and harsh as the wind and rain were, Wilberforce's voice was glorious and beautiful. Indeed, it seemed to outwit the weather, nimbly threading its way through the clumsy wind to the ears of its audience, like a child running between the legs of a thick-witted giant to safety. Despite the raging weather, everyone there, all the way to the edges of the vast crowd, could hear him, could hear that voice, and they were transfixed.

A newspaper account from that day read: "Mr. Wilberforce made a most argumentative and eloquent speech, which was listened to with the most eager attention, and received with the loudest acclamations of applause. It was indeed a reply to every thing that had been said against the Address; but there was such an exquisite choice of expression, and pronounced with such rapidity, that we are unable to do it justice in any account we can give of it."

Amazingly, James Boswell was there that day, en route from Edinburgh to London to visit the old Samuel Johnson, to whom he had affixed himself like a lamprey for life. Boswell's recollection of hearing Wilberforce that day is memorable: "I saw what seemed a mere shrimp mount upon the table; but as I listened he grew and grew, until the shrimp became a whale."

"Wilber the Whale" spoke brilliantly for an hour; it was one of the greatest speeches he would ever deliver, and he held the weather-beaten crowd with his every word as only he was able to do. The high sheriff, Danby, who was the official who had called the county meeting, said that Wilberforce "talked like an angel." It's difficult to appreciate the powers over a crowd that a speaker like Wilberforce could have in those days. Whitefield had had the same powers, the same ability to hold many thousands rapt, convinced that if they turned away for a moment they would miss something.

What made Wilberforce one of the best speakers of his day is complex. Many felt that his eloquence derived principally from the mere sound of his voice, from its variable tones as he spoke. One parliamentary reporter some years later described Wilberforce's vocal tones as "so distinct and melodious that the most hostile ear hangs on them delighted." The same reporter said that "his address is so insinuating that if he talked nonsense you would feel obliged to hear him." Everyone who ever heard him seems to have agreed that the exceeding excellence of Wilberforce's speaking ability was less in what he said than in how he said it.

Sir James Stephen probably explained the phenomenon best. "The students of history of those times," he said,

> who shall read some of the discourses which won for him so high a reputation, will scarcely avoid the belief that it was very ill-merited. But if he had *heard them fall from the lips of the speaker*—if he had *seen* him rising with a spirit of self-reliance which Mercutio might have envied, and had listened to those tones so full, liquid, and penetrating, and had watched the eye sparkling as each playful fancy crossed his field of vision, or glowing when he spoke of the oppressions done upon earth—the fragile form elevating and expanding itself into heroic dignity—and the transposition of his gestures, so rapid and so complete, each successive attitude adapting itself so easily to each new variation of his style—he would not more have wondered at the efficacy even of ordinary topics and of commonplace remarks from such a speaker, than at the magic of the tamest speech from the lips of Garrick or Talma.

On this particular day at York Castle, the topic upon which Wilberforce spoke was of vital interest to every man within earshot.

The slight figure standing on the table was delivering a soliloquy for the ages, but it was a soliloquy in a play in which they themselves played a vital role. What he was saying would affect them for years to come. And so they listened to each and every syllable that had cleverly dodged the dumb raindrops to find their happy ears.

Then suddenly, if it were possible, the drama rose even higher: about an hour into Wilberforce's stem-winder, a king's messenger on horseback galloped into the castle yard, as if on cue. He had raced all the way from London through that weather, two days' riding, having begun early in the afternoon of the day before. But his arrival at this moment could not have been timed to greater effect. All eyes followed him as he dismounted and hurriedly approached the speaker. He handed Wilberforce the letter he'd carried northward all those miles, traversing half the country through rain and wind and hail.

Wilberforce had stopped his speech and now paused to read the letter. It was from Pitt. Wilberforce, with the flair he had for such things, now announced to the crowd, with Pitt's authority, that Parliament had that day been dissolved. At the end of this letter was a personal note to him in Pitt's hand: "Tear the enemy to pieces."

Wilberforce now looked at the crowd. Improvising brilliantly, and capitalizing on the suddenly changed situation, he implored his listeners directly, as if his whole speech had been logically building up to the arrival of this letter, which he had no idea was arriving until he and everyone else had seen the horse carrying the rider carrying the letter and handing it to him. "We are now to decide upon a solemn crisis," he said. "You are now upon your trial." He shaped the situation before them and now asked them to do what their honors dictated.

It was a performance for the ages, one of the finest speeches of Wilberforce's life, and there can be no question that it propelled him into the seat as much as any speech could have done. It was one of those moments in a man's life upon which all else seems to hinge; there is a curious inevitability about it, as though it couldn't have happened any other way, and at the same time there is a sense that what happened couldn't have happened, that it was a miracle. The timing of the letter's arrival alone was magnificent. Before he was through, there were cries of, "We'll have this man for our county member!"

Another speaker followed Wilberforce, as unenviable a position as can be imagined, no matter what the hour and weather, and afterward the culmination of it all arrived: the vote. A show of hands decided the matter, as simple as pie, in favor of Pitt and the king. It was a monumental and historic triumph for Pitt. And the little shrimp upon the table who'd grown into a whale would get the sea lion's share of the credit! It was simply too much, as if the rain and hail had turned into a shower of falling pearls.

Immediately afterward, there was a big public dinner at the York Tavern. The giddy celebration was soon riven by division and drunken quarreling, but Wilberforce, with his newfound celebrity as the hero of the day, was able to step in and repair the breach, which further endeared him to those present. "This confirmed the disposition to propose me for the county," he wrote, "an idea which had begun to be buzzed about at dinner, amongst all ranks."

Just as they were breaking up at midnight, someone cried: "Bravo, little Wilberforce!. . . I will give five hundred pounds towards bringing you in for the county!" With that, the others exploded into a chorus of approval: "Wilberforce forever! Wilberforce and liberty!" There were still several twists and turns to accomplish—and some of them almost impossible—if Wilberforce was actually to become the new Yorkshire County representative. But with a genuinely strange inevitability, it happened. Wilberforce had become "Knight of the Shire for the County of York." It was an unprecedented and truly shocking leap, like someone pole-vaulting into the balcony at the opera. *Is this seat taken?*

And of course, his astounding ascension had a powerful and decisive influence on the rest of the general election, which went on for days, as they did then. When it was all over, Pitt had overwhelmingly won the House of Commons, and as politically weak as he was before the election, he was now strong. It was an historic and glorious reversal, and little Wilberforce was at the very center of it all. On April 8, Pitt wrote to him from Downing Street: "My dear Wilberforce, I can never enough congratulate you upon such glorious success."

The change that had occurred in the political landscape was profound and dramatic and historic, and would affect the nation for years and years to come. But there was another change coming too.

CHAPTER 4

THE GREAT CHANGE

Amazing Grace! How sweet the sound
That saved a wretch like me.
I once was lost, but now am found,
Was blind but now I see.

When Wilberforce returned to London, he did so as a national hero, riding higher than even he—an exceedingly ambitious twenty-four-year-old—could have imagined. As his son Samuel put it, "He possessed already enough to intoxicate his mind, whilst prospects of gratified ambition seemed to open without limit before him. He attended constantly through the first sessions of the new Parliament, and swelled the triumphant majorities, which secured the supremacy of his friend."

On May 14, 1784, he took his seat for the county of York. Having an ally like Wilberforce in the House of Commons was an incalculable boon to Pitt, who said that Wilberforce possessed "the greatest natural eloquence of all the men I ever knew." Many thought that Wilberforce's ploy all along in winning the seat for York—and in helping his friend Pitt so dramatically—was to secure a ministerial post in Pitt's government. There is little doubt that he could have had one, had he asked for it. But Wilberforce had a special relationship with Pitt and simply wouldn't do such a thing. He respected their relationship too much to use Pitt, even though he certainly deserved whatever post he might have asked for.

William Wilberforce had, at twenty-four, the most coveted seat in all of Parliament. He seemed unstoppable. With his extraordinary eloquence, brilliance, and charm—and with the prime minister as his dearest friend—there seemed no end in sight to where he might rise. But where might he rise? That Wilberforce could hardly know.

When the autumn came, Wilberforce made plans to spend the winter on the French and Italian Rivieras, principally for his sister Sally's health. The plan was to take two carriages. His mother and Sally and his cousin, Bessie Smith, would ride in a coach, along with a maid; Wilberforce and a male friend would ride ahead of them in a smaller post chaise. Wilberforce had no particular plans for the trip, but he knew that he wanted a companion with whom he would enjoy conversing, for they would share an infinity of hours together on the bumpy roads of the Continent.

He invited an Irishman, Dr. William Burgh, a dear friend of his from York. Burgh was bright and had a pleasant disposition, but was unavailable. Later that summer, Wilberforce and his family went to Scarborough, which was where many of the wealthier set of Yorkshire spent their summers. There he fell in with Isaac Milner, the weaver's son from Leeds who had been his tutor at Hull Grammar School nearly two decades before. Milner was now a tutor at Queens' College, Cambridge, and had already become famous in academic circles. By anyone's judgment, Milner was simply his own category, a fantastically outsized figure—a veritable giant—literally and otherwise. We don't know what he weighed or how tall he was, but according to Henry Thornton's daughter Marianne, he was "the most enormous man it was ever my fate to see in a drawing-room." He was a behemoth.

As for his mind, it was entirely beyond reckoning: indeed, while at Cambridge, he'd been given the unprecedented distinction of being pronounced *incomparabilis*. He was what we would today call a "super genius," but the closer one looks, the more one gets the impression that even that superlative doesn't quite capture him, which is both ridiculous and true. The facts are these: he was elected to the Royal Society while still an undergraduate; his performance on his Cambridge Tripos exams was so spectacular that the examiners left a blank line in the record books to separate him from the other candidates; and he both distinguished himself and published in the subjects of physics, chemistry, algebra, and religion. He was ordained in 1775. As we have earlier said, he later occupied the Lucasian Chair in both mathematics and chemistry. Milner even captured the popular imagination of all London by famously solving the puzzle of the "contrivance of the invisible girl," a magician's feat that had maddened the goggling populace when it was performed in Leicester Fields. As if these feats of genius weren't enough, Milner was widely renowned as a conversationalist and wit worthy to succeed the legendary Dr. Johnson. He was famously and irrepressibly jocular and told comic stories in the Yorkshire accent of his youth. Wilberforce himself said that Milner was "lively and dashing in his conversation." On the downside, Milner was also described as an "arch hypochondriac" with an inexplicable but violent antipathy toward thunder and "the east wind."

If not for the anachronism, one would be tempted to simply dub Milner Chestertonian and be done with it, but even Chesterton, for all his huge size and vast accomplishments, seems at least plausible. Milner simply cannot have really existed, except perhaps in a tale by Baron von Munchausen. And yet there he stood at the Scarborough races, looming gigantically over the wee mannikin Wilberforce. The sight of them together must have suggested a circus poster. Wilberforce was universally described as tiny and stood just over five feet with a child-sized torso. His chest was measured in later years at thirty-three inches.

Wilberforce had stayed in touch with Milner somewhat over the years and had been good enough to obtain tickets for him to the gallery in the House of Commons. And so now Wilberforce invited Milner to join them on their continental trip. Milner accepted, and they were off from the races, leaving Scarborough on October 20. Milner rode ahead in the post chaise with Wilberforce, and if one cannot help picturing it as tilting comically to one side, one is forgiven.

The Channel crossing was smooth, though Wilberforce was seasick nonetheless. Wilberforce had digestive troubles his entire life, though precisely what he had is difficult to say. He seems to have suffered from some form of ulcerative colitis. Once in France they went first to Lyon, which Wilberforce described as "sweetly situated, but a most dirty hole; particularly our inn, the St. Omers." Many other well-to-do English travelers were at Nice, and Wilberforce and his companions mixed with them over lavish dinners and card parties— the usual. As ever with the wealthy, there were fads, and in France during the 1780s, "animal magnetism" was all the rage. It seems to have been a precursor to any number of quackish trends such as mesmerism, phrenology, Jungian analysis, Gestalt therapy, EST, and V8 colonics. The chief "magnetist," Monsieur Tauley, essayed to work his invisible art on both Milner and Wilberforce, neither of whom succumbed, "owing, perhaps," Wilberforce says, "to our incredulity." But one Frederic North who was there swore by Tauley and was so affected by the man's extraordinary powers of magnetism that, according to Wilberforce, this fellow North "would fall down upon entering a room in which they practised on him; and he even maintained to me that they could affect the [bodily] frame, though in another room, or at a distance, and you were ignorant of their proceedings."

Wilberforce's son writes: "In all these scenes he was constantly accompanied by Milner, whose vivacity and sense, in union with most unpolished manners, continually amused his friends." What the lords and ladies made of the uncouth weaver's son, thrice their size and smarter than any fifteen of them put together, is anyone's guess. Wilberforce would later regale his friends with the story of Milner being presented at one of these gala gatherings to the young Prince William of Gloucester, then about nine. In his broad Yorkshire accent, Milner cooed, "Pretty boy, pretty boy," all the while stroking the young prince's head with an odd familiarity. It's a wonder the royal youth didn't run bawling from the room, afraid he was about to be consumed.

Wilberforce says that Milner "was free from every taint of vice, but not more attentive than others to religion. Though a clergyman, he never thought of reading prayers during their whole stay at Nice. He appeared in all respects like an ordinary man of the world, mixing, like myself, in all companies, and joining, as readily as others, in the prevalent Sunday parties. Indeed, when I engaged him as a companion in my tour, I knew not that he had any deeper principles."

The only clue Wilberforce might have had would have been gleaned while they were still at Scarborough. Wilberforce mentioned a Mr. Stillingfleet, who was the rector at Hotham, saying that he was a "good man, but one who carried things too far." "Not a bit too far," shot back Milner. When they continued the conversation that evening, Milner stayed firm in his opinion. Milner's disposition was always and indefatigably jocular, but on this subject he seemed entirely serious.

"This declaration greatly surprised me," says Wilberforce, "and it was agreed that at some future time we would talk the matter over. Had I known at first what his opinions were it would have decided me against making him the offer; so true is it that a gracious hand leads us in ways that we know not, and blesses us not only without, but even against, our plans and inclinations."

Like the rest of his crowd, Wilberforce took a powerfully dim view of anything touching the Methodism of his aunt and late uncle. Methodists all "carried things a bit too far" and were generally embarrassing and out of step with the age in which they lived. Wilberforce had obviously formed the opinion that it was possible to be good and moral without "overdoing things"—without all of that fusty theological gingerbread hanging from one's eaves. Most of his friends thought him to be very moral and upright indeed. Wilberforce even brought Pitt and Pepper Arden to the parish church in Wimbledon when they stayed at his house there. It was all good, up to a point. The old doctrines of Christianity and the Bible had served their purposes in their day, but the idea of believing them and preaching them in the late eighteenth century simply seemed willfully anachronistic and silly. Why drag one's feet against the inevitable pull of Progress? Had not the Enlightenment brought the sunshine of Reason to the world, and hadn't those felicitously reasonable beams evaporated the fetid swamps of backwater religious parochialism? Had not Athens at last defeated Jerusalem?

When he was in London, Wilberforce sometimes attended the Essex Street Chapel to hear the preaching of the Reverend Theophilus Lindsey, the "father" of modern-day Unitarianism. Lindsey had had the courage to leave the Church of England when he'd renounced its main doctrines—such as the divinity of Christ—but most of the clergy who had renounced these same doctrines had chosen to remain where they were. Consequently, one could attend parish churches all

over England—as Wilberforce did at Wimbledon—and never be
pestered by a sermon that jabbed at the congregation with the sharp
tenets of the Nicene Creed.

In their chaise across France, Wilberforce sometimes ridiculed
the faith of his youth, and Milner parried with him, upholding the
orthodox Christian faith of the Methodists but without ever suggesting that it was necessarily more to him than theological speculation.
It's possible that Milner, being a theologian and logician, saw the
inner logic of the doctrines that Wilberforce mocked and would have
defended them as he would have defended any mathematical theo-
rem, but that he himself didn't believe them with anything beyond
mere intellect. Perhaps Wilberforce's mockery pricked Milner's
conscience somewhat, for Milner assented intellectually to the doctrines Wilberforce attacked, but perhaps he'd put it all to one side, as
people sometimes do. One knows what is right, but holds it at arm's
length for a time, neither throwing it out, nor embracing it. Perhaps
as their discussion had inspired Wilberforce to think more deeply
about these matters it was now forcing Milner himself to ruminate
on them in a way that he had not done before.

It's also possible that Wilberforce's mockery was pure flippancy,
as so much mockery is, not rising to the level of serious debate but
merely takes sarcastic potshots from behind a rock, unwilling or
afraid to "come out and fight like a man," as it were. Which perhaps
accounts for Milner at one point declaring: "I am no match for you,
Wilberforce, in this running fire, but if you really want to discuss
these subjects seriously, I will gladly enter on them with you."

Wilberforce now received an affectionate letter from Pitt, imploring him to return to London in time for Pitt to introduce his Bill
on Parliamentary Reform. So it was decided that the ladies would
remain behind to continue enjoying the mild weather and sun, but
Wilberforce and Milner would depart. Wilberforce and Milner
planned to rejoin them at Nice in three months' time, when the parliamentary session would have ended. But for now they must away.

On February 5, 1785, however, just before they were to depart,
Wilberforce's eyes happened to light on a volume belonging to his
cousin, Bessie Smith, and he picked it up. It was titled *The Rise and
Progress of Religion in the Soul* and written by Philip Doddridge. Bessie

had borrowed the book from her mother, who had been given it by William Unwin, the evangelical clergyman in Essex who had befriended William Cowper. Wilberforce asked Milner his opinion of it. "It is one of the best books ever written," declared Milner. "Let us take it with us and read it on our journey." They did.

Doddridge had written the book in the early 1740s and died in 1751. He lived in a time when we would think that dourness was *de rigueur* for men of the cloth, especially those of theological seriousness, as Doddridge certainly was, but in fact he was widely known to have been charming and of a particularly cheerful temperament. An aged friend once said of him that "he never knew a man of so gay a temper as Doddridge." His published *Travel Letters* were well known in "polite society," and the book that Wilberforce and Milner would now turn to discussing was thought of as "reasoned" and "elegant"— ideally suited for someone with Wilberforce's fashionable antipathies toward the unsophisticated excesses of the Methodists.

And so our odd couple left Nice, via Antibes, with Doddridge's book. What one would give to hear their brilliant conversations in that chaise rumbling day after day northwestward across the entire country of France, just four years before it would explode in revolution. As the crow flies, the distance from the southern coast at Nice to the northern coast at Calais is over six hundred miles, but on the twisting and unpaved roads of the late eighteenth century it was twice that distance. Returning to London in time for the parliamentary session and Pitt's resolution necessitated a breakneck pace. "Milner and I," says Wilberforce, "attended by Dixon our courier, made the best of our way, setting out in the morning before it was light and travelling till after dark."

The snowfall was heavy as they crossed the French Alps. They traveled on, through eighteen days of snow, comfortably wrapped in their traveling rugs in the chaise, taking in the bright white, alpine scenery and discussing Doddridge's book as they went. The extraordinary felicity of this scene, of these incandescent minds meeting on this subject of eternal things, sailing in their horse-drawn coach through the mountains, seems like something out of a fairytale, one in which a gnome and a giant on a journey in a sphere of glass and silver discover the Well at the World's End, and drinking a draught therefrom learn the secret meaning at the heart of the universe. For Wilberforce and Milner it must at times have seemed like a wild but happy dream, one from which they never wanted to wake.

Sometimes when going uphill on an especially icy road, it became necessary for them to get out and walk behind the carriage to lighten the load for the two horses. Once, at a considerable altitude, they did just this, getting out and walking behind the carriage as the beleaguered horses pulled it up the icy grade—but suddenly the chaise began to slide sideways on the ice, the horses lost their footing, and the weight of the chaise began to drag them backward and toward the edge of a precipice. The postboy could not hold them, though he tried desperately. It was a scene of unfolding horror until Milner, the Yorkshire giant, sprang into action, himself grabbing the carriage and with impossible, cartoon-character strength arresting its slide toward the abyss, and then holding it steady for a time until the two spooked horses could regain their footing and again pull it onto the road.

At the top of that hill, Milner and Wilberforce got back into the carriage, wrapped themselves again in their rugs, and with the snowy alpine scenery unspooling past them, continued their discussion.

Samuel Wilberforce writes that the "strong friendship was matured, which lasted to the end of life, between the rough coarse philosopher and the genial and accomplished statesman." And so affected and pricked was Wilberforce by these enchanted discussions in the alpine snow that he was now determined to investigate the Scriptures for himself.

After the pair reached Calais, crossed the Channel, and arrived at last in London, Wilberforce seemed outwardly the same as ever, but surely something had occurred deep inside him, where it would remain hidden for a time: a seed had been pressed into the soil of his soil, and had been watered, and would soon burst and sprout green and grow beyond all possibility of concealing.

For now, all would be just the same as before. Wilberforce would take his meals several nights each week with Pitt; much effort would be spent on Pitt's reform bill and other measures; and, as ever, each day would end with a goodly amount of singing and dancing, usually through much of the night, and sometimes through all of it.

But in Wilberforce's private diary we can see the first hints that the ground is shifting, that the "Great Change," as he would always thereafter call his conversion, had begun. Of a wealthy friend he now writes: "Strange that the most generous men and religious, do not see that their duties increase with their fortune, and that they will be punished for spending it" on themselves in eating and drinking. He describes as "shocking" a dance at an opera performance of the story of Don Juan, but what particularly touches him is that the audience is too jaded to react at all. It's easy to dismiss these observations as moralistic, but what is compelling is the idea that Wilberforce had at this time all he wanted for the taking: money, entertainment, accolades, and friends in the highest places. The world that had embraced him as its dearest darling would shower him with whatever he liked. But he is now suddenly untouched by its charms. He seems for the first time to sense that there might be something more. Something is troubling him that he's only just beginning to sense, whose shape he can hardly yet make out in the dim light.

Wilberforce is having thoughts now that seem utterly strange and foreign. He is having, for example, pangs of fellow feeling very uncommon among the members of his privileged set. After an informal cabinet dinner at Pitt's, he writes in his diary that he was "often thinking that pompous T. and elegant C. would soon appear in the same row with the poor fellow who waited behind their chairs." Anyone who had been privy to his thoughts at this time would have wondered what had happened to the gay, carefree fellow of just a few months before—the one who had so viciously and sarcastically wiped the floor of Commons with Fox; who had thought nothing of shaving the truth here and there during his speech in the castle yard at York to "tear the enemy to pieces" and elevate himself to the highest parliamentary place in the land; who ate and drank and danced and sang till the wee hours of hundreds of mornings. Where had that fellow gone?

Wilberforce and Milner had planned to return to the Continent in May, but Parliament dragged on into June and was still not finished at month's end. So Wilberforce left even before the session had ended, with Milner again his companion. This time Wilberforce did not get sick crossing the Channel. He spoke to the ship's captain, who

lectured him about the scandal of wool and live sheep being continu-
ously smuggled in vast quantities across to Boulogne, an illegal trade
of which he himself was an eyewitness. Wilberforce passed the information to Pitt, suggesting that action on it would bring him the
undying affections of the entire cloth industry.

Wilberforce's plan now was to join the ladies in Genoa, the late-
ness of his departure having made it impossible to go to Nice, which
was now simply too hot to be borne by people who could afford to
find it unbearable—and they could. And so he and Milner began
the reverse journey southeastward toward the Mediterranean coast,
but this time via a different route. Wilberforce writes, "We went
thither by way of Switzerland, and I have never since ceased to recur
with peculiar delight to its enchanting scenery, especially to that of
Interlaken, which is a vast garden of the loveliest fertility and beauty
stretched out at the base of the giant Alps."

And now again, Milner and Wilberforce resumed their previous conversation, this time taking as their text not Doddridge, but a
Greek New Testament, whose doctrines they now examined. In the
course of this ongoing conversation, Wilberforce pressed upon Milner
his various "doubts, objections, and difficulties," and one by one the
massy weaver's son expounded his answers in his Yorkshire basso.

Wilberforce was throughout his life possessed of a rare and bracing intellectual honesty. At Cambridge, he had once been asked to
sign his name assenting to the articles of the Church of England.
This was viewed then as a formality, one of the college's ancient re-
quirements for receiving one's degree; everyone simply signed the
document and took their degree. But Wilberforce refused. He didn't
at that time agree with the official tenets of the Anglican Church,
or at least wasn't sure whether he did, and therefore couldn't bring
himself to sign it, which delayed his degree for several years. In an
age when, just as today, most people shrugged or winked their way
through such hypocrisies, Wilberforce would not.

But now his intellectual honesty would work in the other direction. With Milner as his interlocutor, he examined the same tenets
of orthodox Christianity to which a few years before he couldn't give
his assent. He seems to have wanted to know what was true, but
until now had been unable to find out to his satisfaction. He knew

if he discovered a truth to his satisfaction he would have no choice but to embrace it and act upon it. Just as he wouldn't sign the paper assenting to beliefs he didn't hold, he knew that if he held a belief he would be obliged to act upon it, and not just in small and isolated instances, as with that signature, but in all of his life. He knew that the tiniest mustard seed can grow and grow and become a tree in which the birds of the air make their nests. Ideas have far-reaching consequences, and one must be ever so careful about what one allows to lodge in one's brain. Now, as the conversation with Milner continued, Wilberforce could almost see the birds of the air looking domestically in his direction.

❧

As planned, they met Sally, Mrs. Wilberforce, and Bessie Smith in Genoa. On July 11, traveling as before with the two men in their post chaise and the ladies in a coach behind them, they made their way north to Turin and then, beyond that, to Geneva. During this trip, Wilberforce and Milner prosecuted their conversation with such intensity that the ladies took notice: Mrs. Wilberforce now complained of her son's less frequent visits to their carriage. Poor, ill-attended Mrs. Wilberforce! If only she had known that she was competing for her son's attentions with the man who was Stephen Hawking, Dick Cavett, and Andre the Giant all rolled into one.

Wilberforce writes: "By degrees, I imbibed [Milner's] sentiments, though they long remained merely as opinions assented to by my understanding, but not influencing my heart. At length I began to be impressed with a sense of their importance. Milner, though full of levity on all other subjects, never spoke on this but with the utmost seriousness, and all he said tended to increase my attention to religion."

At Interlaken, Wilberforce was awed and affected by the exquisite grandeur of the Jungfrau. His love of nature was a constant throughout his life, and surely the transcendent power of its beauty must now also have stirred his heart toward thinking of first things.

In early September they came to the Ardennes region of Belgium and stopped for six weeks at the eponymous town of Spa, a fashionable wet spot since the fourteenth century. Everyone was there, as they say, and everyone did what everyone always does and continues to do. But Wilberforce didn't. He couldn't. He did most of what everyone else did—he danced and sang and spent countless hours indulging in the endless meals that were then the fashion in high society. But something was happening to him, and while now at fashionable Spa amongst the fashionable set, his new feelings expressed themselves rather suddenly and specifically with regard to the theater and the Sabbath. These were two important shibboleths for the evangelicals and Methodists of the day, two areas where they stood out sharply from the rest of society.

"Mrs. Crewe cannot believe that I think it wrong to go to the play," he writes in his diary. "Surprised at hearing that halting on the Sunday was my wish, and not my mother's." It must have positively scandalized Mrs. Crewe, for she was one of the leading society hostesses of her day, a renowned beauty whose portrait had been painted by Joshua Reynolds. For the popular and witty and brilliant Mr. Wilberforce to wrinkle his nose at something must have been very upsetting indeed. In another person, she surely would have dismissed this reaction and made sport of it to the guests at one of her parties—what would the hopelessly sour Methodists denounce next?—but Mr. Wilberforce was a close friend of Mr. Pitt's and a member of five clubs, and he was extremely witty. Perhaps he would soon be mocking me for my behavior!

There was other scandalous behavior in which Mr. Wilberforce was engaged that October in Spa, though it wasn't likely that Mrs. Crewe would have known about it. "Began three or four days ago to get up very early," he writes. "In the solitude and self-conversation of the morning had thoughts, which I trust will come to something."

It is quite clear that Wilberforce has somehow moved solidly forward, but is doing so slowly and is counting the cost of every step. He writes: "As soon as I reflected seriously upon these subjects the deep guilt and black ingratitude of my past life forced itself upon me in the strongest colours, and I condemned myself for having wasted my precious time, and opportunities, and talents."

Wilberforce's "Great Change" did not happen overnight or in an instant. St. Paul might have been blinded by the light and changed in a single moment that could, in effect, be captured in a painting, but Wilberforce's transformation was much more gradual. His conversion was much closer to St. Augustine's, who came to intellectual clarity about the doctrines of Christian faith but was frustrated by his inability to conform his behavior to his beliefs. "I got a clear idea of the doctrines of Religion," Wilberforce wrote years later, "perhaps clearer than I have had since, but it was quite in my head. Well, I now fully believed the Gospel and was persuaded that if I died at any time I should perish everlastingly. And yet, such is man, I went on cheerful and gay."

In his diary, he writes: "What madness is the course I am pursuing. I believe all the great truths of the Christian religion, but I am not acting as though I did. Should I die in this state I must go into a place of misery." He saw that he had turned his back on God but, oddly, didn't know how to turn around. But later in the diary he says, "Yet I may become religious. Has God not promised His Holy Spirit on them that ask Him?"

"It was not so much the fear of punishment by which I was affected," he says, "as a sense of my great sinfulness in having so long neglected the unspeakable mercies of my God and Saviour; and such was the effect which this thought produced, that for months I was in a state of the deepest depression, from strong convictions of my guilt. Indeed nothing which I have ever read in the accounts of others, exceeded what I then felt."

It's clear from reading his journals and letters during this time that Wilberforce's mind was all over the place. Numerous lines were converging; his thoughts on culture and society figured into the overall picture too. In a letter to his friend Lord Muncaster from this time, he despairs over the entrenched selfishness he saw among the rich and privileged, who behaved, in his view, like drunken parents who have abandoned their dying children. For the first time he sounds the note that in a few years would become one of his two lifelong passions: "It is the universal corruption and profligacy of the times, which taking its rise amongst the rich and luxurious has now extended its baneful influence and spread its destructive poison through the whole body of the people."

Wilberforce seemed to think that accepting these truths and living by them meant leaving Parliament and spending the next fifty years repenting in perpetual misery and sackcloth. What could he do? Wilberforce felt that he must declare himself to the world, or at least to all of his friends. He seems to have formed the opinion that not to do so was to deny God, and he dared not do that, not anymore. His whole being ached with the anguish of having denied God these many years, of having gaily pleased himself and exalted himself while ignoring God and God's love, as well as ignoring the poor and the suffering all around him. He realized that his debt in this regard could never be paid, and as is often the case in such situations, he seems almost to have repented too much, to have been blind to God's grace toward him.

This was evidently the place Wilberforce had come to, a place of such guilt before God, of such misery at his own failings, that nothing short of being publicly pilloried would do. And so now he unburdened himself somewhat by declaring himself to his friends. One can only imagine what, in this overemotional state, he might have written to them, and one can only imagine what they would have thought upon reading his declaration. The rumor went about that dear, brilliant Wilberforce was "melancholy mad"—and wasn't he?

The most important friend in his life was William Pitt, and the letter Wilberforce wrote to Pitt, around November 24, must have been an agony to write. In the letter, he seems to tell the prime minister of the country that he, Wilberforce, his best friend and best political ally and confidant, must leave politics altogether, must turn away from all that he has known, and must, as it were, "live now for God."

Wilberforce had no one in his life who would understand or who could help him sort out his feelings, and it's likely that he suffered far more than he needed to. Milner was in Cambridge, and it seems that he too was wrestling with what they had discussed during those weeks in their carriage. All Wilberforce now had to guide him was what he had learned with Milner—those truths that were now to him self-evident and that had changed everything. But something was missing. It was as if what he had learned had eaten the very ground from under him but had not yet replaced it, and so he was falling and falling, wondering when he would hit bottom, wondering whether there was a bottom at all.

What he needed desperately was someone to whom he might unburden himself, someone who would understand and know what to do, someone with the wisdom to remind him of what he needed to be reminded of just now—of God's grace—of the upside of God's love. But this other side of God's love—the good news, as it were— he seems not to have heard at all. At least not yet. And so he was sequestered with his guilt, writhing that November in London and Wimbledon, dreading what lay ahead. It was apparently in the grip of these feelings, and while thinking along these lines, that Wilberforce wrote to Pitt around November 24.

In his diary that day we get a snapshot of his mental and spiritual state: "Heard the Bible read two hours—Pascal one hour and a quarter—meditation one hour and a quarter. . . . Pitt called and commended Butler's *Analogy*—resolved to write to him, and discover to him what I am occupied about: this will save me much embarrassment, and I hope give me more command both of my time and conduct."

Wilberforce's eyesight was so poor that he sometimes had readers who would read aloud to him. The idea of his sitting and hearing two full hours of Scripture and an hour and a quarter of the dense, philosophical *Pensées* followed by an hour and a quarter of prayer is certainly impressive and tells us that he was almost crazy with what he now knew.

On the twenty-fifth, he mentions attending services at St. Antholyn's. "Walked, and stage coach, to save the expense of a chaise." The wealthy best friend of the prime minister was now taking public transportation and walking out of guilt for all of the money he had wasted over the years, knowing that any money he saved could be better spent in caring for the poor. On the twenty-sixth: "Refused to go to Camden Place, and to Pitt's; but all religious thoughts go off in London—I hope by explaining my situation and feelings, to relieve myself from my embarrassment."

The next day, Sunday the twenty-seventh: "I must awake to my dangerous state, and never be at rest till I have made my peace with God. My heart is so hard, my blindness so great, that I cannot get a due hatred of sin, though I see I am all corrupt, and blinded to the perception of spiritual things."

November 29: "Pride is my greatest stumbling block; and there is danger in it in two ways—lest it should make me desist from a

christian life, through fear of the world, my friends, &c; or if I per-
severe, lest it should make me vain of so doing."

And then, at last, on the thirtieth, the worm turns. He thinks
of visiting John Newton, whom he hasn't seen since he was a boy.
It's hard to know exactly what this pilgrimage would have meant to
Wilberforce. Newton was a public figure, and had been for twenty
years. He was the foremost evangelical in London at that time. Whitefield had died fifteen years earlier, and John Wesley was now very old.
Newton was a unifying and stabilizing force in the Methodist world of
the eighteenth century. By all accounts, he was emotionally healthy and
theologically balanced; Newton was himself especially aware of God's
"amazing grace," and was therefore just the sort of person Wilberforce
needed to see at this time. It's telling to think that among the hundreds
of people Wilberforce knew, there wasn't a single Methodist friend to
be found. He had so completely isolated himself from that world that in
order to find someone who might understand his situation he had to go
back, as it were, to his own boyhood. Of course, he would have felt all
kinds of trepidation about the visit too. Newton was the man whom he
had thought of as a father, and who had thought of him as a son.

Screwing up his courage, Wilberforce wrote to his old friend on
December 2:

To Mr. Newton: ——

    ... I wish to have some serious conversation with you, and will
take the liberty of calling on you for that purpose, in half-an-hour;
when, if you cannot receive me, you will have the goodness to let me
have a letter put into my hands at the door, naming a time and place
for our meeting, the earlier the more agreeable to me. I have had ten
thousand doubts within myself, whether or not I should discover myself to you; but every argument against doing it has its foundation
in pride. I am sure you will hold yourself bound to let no one living
know of this application, or of my visit, till I release you from the
obligation.

p.s. Remember that I must be secret, and that the gallery of the House
is now so universally attended, that the face of a member of Parliament is pretty well known.

One can hardly help thinking of Nicodemus, the open-minded and open-hearted Pharisee who came to see Jesus at night, in secret, lest anyone learn that he had done so. Nicodemus felt there was something to this compelling rabbi, and he couldn't keep away from him—but he wasn't ready to tell anyone else. Not just yet. And neither was Wilberforce.

That very same day, December 2, Wilberforce received a reply from Pitt. Though Wilberforce's letter to Pitt is lost to history, Pitt's letter is not, and is reprinted here in its entirety. It gives us a strong hint of the contents of Wilberforce's letter, as well as an extraordinary picture of Pitt at this time and of the intimacy of their friendship:

My dear Wilberforce,

Bob Smith mentioned to me on Wednesday the letters he had received from you, which prepared me for that I received from you yesterday. I am indeed too deeply interested in whatever concerns you not to be very sensibly affected by what has the appearance of a new era in your life, and so important in its consequences for yourself and your friends. As to any public conduct which your opinions may ever lead you to, I will not disguise to you that few things could go nearer my heart than to find myself differing from you essentially on any great principle.

I trust and believe that it is a circumstance which can hardly occur. But if it ever should, and even if I should experience as much pain in such an event, as I have found hitherto encouragement and pleasure in the reverse, believe me it is impossible that it should shake the sentiments of affection and friendship which I bear towards you, and which I must be forgetful and insensible indeed if I ever could part with. They are sentiments engraved in my heart, and will never be effaced or weakened. If I knew how to state all I feel, and could hope that you are open to consider it, I should say a great deal more on the subject of the resolution you seem to have formed. You will not suspect me of thinking lightly of any moral or religious motives which guide you. As little will you believe that I think your understanding or judgment easily misled. But forgive me if I cannot help expressing my fear that you are nevertheless deluding yourself into principles which have but too much tendency to counteract your own object, and to render your virtues and your talents useless both to yourself and mankind. I am not, however, without hopes that my anxiety paints this too strongly. For you confess that the character of religion is not a gloomy one, and that it is not that of an enthusiast. But why then this preparation of solitude, which can hardly avoid tincturing the mind either with melancholy or superstition? If a Christian may act in the several relations of life, must he seclude himself for all to become so? Surely the principles as well as the practice of Christianity are simple, and lead not to meditation only but to action.

I will not, however, enlarge upon these subjects now. What I would ask of you, as a mark both of your friendship and of the candour which belongs to your mind, is to open yourself fully and without reserve to one, who, believe me, does not know how to separate your happiness from his own. You do not explain either the degree or the duration of the retirement which you have prescribed to yourself: you do not tell me how the future course of your life is to be directed, when you think the same privacy no longer necessary: nor, in short, what idea you have formed of the duties which you are from this time to practise. I am sure you will not wonder if I am inquisitive on such a subject. The only way in which you can satisfy me is by conversation. There ought to be no awkwardness or embarrassment to either of us, tho' there may be some anxiety: and if you will open to me fairly the whole state of your mind on these subjects, tho' I shall venture to state to you fairly the points where I fear we may differ, and to desire you to re-examine your own ideas where I think you are mistaken, I will not importune you with fruitless discussion on any opinion which you have deliberately formed. You will, I am sure, do justice to the motives and feelings which induce me to urge this so strongly to you. I think you will not refuse it: if you do not, name any hour at which I can call upon you to-morrow. I am going into Kent, and can take Wimbledon in my way. Reflect, I beg of you, that no principles are the worse for being discussed, and believe me that at all events the full knowledge of the nature and extent of your opinions and intentions will be to me a lasting satisfaction.

Believe me, affectionately and unalterably yours,
W. Pitt

On the following day, Saturday, December 3, Wilberforce and Pitt spoke for two hours. Wilberforce tried to convert his friend to his way of thinking, and failed, but withal the meeting seems to have put Wilberforce at some ease.

The next day, Sunday, December 4, Wilberforce delivered his letter himself to Newton's home at Charles Square in Hoxton, more than a mile from St. Mary Woolnoth's, Newton's church in London. Though Wilberforce obviously hopes to meet with Newton that day, Newton was unable to do so, but they planned to meet the following Wednesday, the seventh of December. And so that Wednesday Wilberforce traveled to Hoxton again, alone, and "after walking about the square once or twice before I could persuade myself, I called upon old Newton." The trepidation he seems to have felt about doing this is extraordinary. How his heart must have fluttered at the thought of seeing Newton again after all these years. Newton had been forty-eight when they last saw each other, and was now sixty.

We may only imagine the scene, the old man, the rough ex–sea captain who had so loved little Wilberforce as a boy, and who had entertained such hopes for him, only to see them dashed. And now, all these years later, to be surprised so, to see him again. There is something in the scene reminiscent of Pip's return to old Joe at the forge in Dickens's *Great Expectations*. So much is felt but unspoken in that moment when Joe beholds the little boy he once knew and then, in his humble rural accent, says, "You're a gentleman now, Pip."

Wilberforce writes that he was "much affected in conversing with him—something very pleasing and unaffected in him. He told me he always had entertained hopes and confidence that God would some time bring me to Him."

Wilberforce must have poured out his heart now to the one person who might understand his anguish and his difficult choices. But as so often is the case, Wilberforce discovered that what he had so terribly feared was a chimera, nothing as bad as he had thought. Newton didn't tell him what he had expected—that to follow God he would have to leave politics. On the contrary, Newton encouraged Wilberforce to stay where he was, saying that God could use him there. Most others in Newton's place would likely have insisted that Wilberforce pull away from the very place where his salt and light were most needed.

How good that Newton did not. Wilberforce writes afterward: "When I came away I found my mind in a calm, tranquil state, more humbled, and looking more devoutly up to God."

Years after this meeting Newton wrote to Wilberforce: "The joy that I felt and the hopes I conceived, when you called on me in the vestry of St. Mary's, I shall never forget."

We can imagine his desire to tell the others, John Thornton and Wilberforce's Aunt Hannah, who had doubtless been praying for him all those years, the bright and sensitive boy they had so loved and who had been taken from them under such painful circumstances. How they must have rejoiced to hear this news. And surely they now all thought of the story of the Prodigal Son. "For this my son was dead, and is alive again; he was lost, and is found."

Later that month Wilberforce received a letter from Thornton: "You may easier conceive than I can express the satisfaction I had from a few minutes' converse with Mr. Newton yesterday afternoon."

On January 11, Wilberforce went to London, to Newton's church, and after church brought Newton with him in his chaise down to Wimbledon. Newton stayed for dinner and slept overnight. Wilberforce wrote some years later that it was as if he'd been all those years in a dream from which at last now he had been awakened. It was as though, like Scrooge, he had been given a second chance, as though his own childhood had been somehow returned to him.

On the evening of the twelfth, someone Wilberforce knew saw him walking across Wimbledon Common with Newton, and suddenly Wilberforce realizes the gig is up. "Expect to hear myself now universally given out to be a Methodist," he writes. "May God grant it may be said with truth."

By that April, Wilberforce's life and mental state seem to have found some long-desired equilibrium. It had been a long and dark winter of the soul, but at last the spring had come. Newton writes to his friend

Cowper about Wilberforce: "I judge he is now decidedly on the right track. . . . I hope the Lord will make him a blessing both as a Christian and a statesman. How seldom do these characters coincide!! But they are not incompatible."

On Good Friday, April 14, Wilberforce "communicates"—takes communion—for the first time. And two days later, on his first Easter Sunday as a Christian, he does so again while visiting the Unwins in the village of Stock in Essex.

"I scarce recollect to have spent so pleasant a day as that which is now nearly over," he writes to his sister Sally.

> I was out before six, and made the fields my oratory, the sun shining as bright and as warm as at Midsummer. I think my own devotions become more fervent when offered in this way amidst the general chorus, with which all nature seems on such a morning to be swelling the song of praise and thanksgiving. Surely this sabbath, of all others, calls forth these feelings in a supreme degree; a frame of united love and triumph well becomes it, and holy confidence and unrestrained affection.

In his diary he puts it, as ever, more succinctly: "At Stock with the Unwins— day delightful, out almost all of it—communicated— very happy."

CHAPTER 5

YE MUST BE BORN AGAIN

Glory, glory, said the Bee,
Hallelujah, said the Flea.
Praise the Lord, remarked the Wren.
At springtime all is born-again.

—Anon.

When Wilberforce returned to the House of Commons in 1786, he was a different man. He had not yet officially discovered the two great causes to which he would give the rest of his life—what he would later famously call his two "great objects"—but he seems already to have been sauntering in their direction. He had lived so long for his own ambition that to live for God, as he now longed to do, was a foreign and strange proposition and would take time to sort out. Two changes manifested themselves right away: the first was a new attitude toward money, the second toward time. Before "the Great Change," Wilberforce had reckoned his money and time his own, to do with as he pleased, and had lived accordingly. But suddenly he knew that this could no longer be the case. The Scriptures were plain and could not be gainsaid on this most basic point: all that was his—his wealth, his talents, his time—was not really his. It all belonged to God and had been given to him to use for God's purposes and according to God's will. God had blessed him so that he, in turn, might bless others, especially those less fortunate than himself.

This new attitude toward money revealed itself most quickly and dramatically with regard to Lauriston House in Wimbledon. This was where Newton and John Thornton had so often visited when he lived there as a boy with his aunt and uncle, and it was this house that became his to use when he was a student at Cambridge. In the last five years, it had been the scene of his still-youthful escapades with his friends—where Pitt and Edwards and the Goostree's Gang escaped from the cares of their political ambitions and public lives; where the "Foinsters" foined into the wee hours of the morning; and where the boyish prime minister and his boyish chief adviser behaved like boys, sometimes upsetting the neighbors with their scandalous behavior. In the spring of 1786, while Parliament was in session, Wilberforce escaped to Lauriston House as often as possible, usually alone. But now, for the first time, he was aware of the cost of its upkeep. Did a single young man really need such a grand house and all of the servants necessary to keep it running? He realized he could probably feed a whole village of poor families with what it cost. And so now, whether rashly or wisely, or a bit of both, he decided to sell Lauriston House.

Wilberforce's attitude toward time changed even more dramatically. There was now an overwhelming sense for him of time lost, of having to play catch-up. He mourned as mostly wasted the years at Pocklington and Cambridge and afterward. It had all been an endless, meaningless round of theater performances that he now couldn't remember and long stays at country houses and dances and card parties and eating and drinking to excess and more eating and drinking to excess—and nothing to show for any of it.

In his diary on June 21 he writes: "To endeavour from this moment to amend my plan for time. I hope to live more than heretofore to God's glory and my fellow-creatures' good." The carping accusation sometimes leveled at Christians, that they are "so heavenly-minded as to be no earthly good," would be leveled at Wilberforce many times in the years to come, but of no one could it have been less true. His new perspective made him about as zealous to improve the social conditions of the world around him as anyone who has ever lived. As we shall see, in Wilberforce's day, it was devout Christians almost exclusively who were concerned with helping the poor, bringing them education and acting as their advocates, and who labored to end the slave trade, among other evils. But so successful would Wilberforce and these other Christians be at bringing a concern for the poor and a social conscience into the society at large that by the next century, during the Victorian era, this attitude would become culturally mainstream.

Regarding his own improvement, Wilberforce resolved to begin immediately by making up for the time lost at Cambridge, where he'd frittered away the years and opportunities in idleness. "Books to be read," he writes in his diary, "Locke's Essay—Marshall's Logic— Indian Reports." This resolve to read was no flippant New Year's resolution. For the next twelve summers, until his marriage, he would spend one or two months at some country home, assiduously studying nine or ten hours alone each day. He became renowned for reading everything—Montesquieu, Adam Smith, Blackstone, Pope—and for the rest of his life, his pockets were literally stuffed with literature on every subject. He would in his later years carry corked inkwells in his pockets too—for he was forever making notes and writing letters— and his clothing ever after bore the ebon blots of his obsession. Once, while he was kneeling with others in prayer, one fatally overstuffed pocket interrupted the devotional atmosphere by exploding under the strain of literature and pouring its contents upon the carpet.

When Parliament ended that July, Wilberforce left London to return north to Scarborough, where he would join his mother and sister again. Mrs. Wilberforce was terribly agitated at the rumors she'd been hearing about her son's return to Methodism; she had heard that he'd gone "melancholy mad"—and as far as she was concerned, what was Methodism if not melancholy madness itself? She heard that he now refused to go to the theater or concerts. *What could be worse?* And now he was coming up to Scarborough. It was at Scarborough, two summers before, that he had bumped into that lumbering oaf Isaac Milner, who had started all of this new trouble. Mrs. Wilberforce must have died a thousand deaths at the thought of her son's relapse into the embarrassing overearnestness of his youthful Methodism. He was twenty-six now—surely too far out of the woods to be lured back into them. He'd made a name for himself throughout the country and was known to be the closest friend and confidant of the prime minister. The Sykes family, with whom Wilberforce had grown up in York, and who had been a big part of his mother's plan to eradicate the Methodism in him during those early years, were also there now. It was all unbearable.

But Wilberforce did not arrive wearing a scowl and sackcloth. On the contrary, he seemed not only as well as ever, but somehow better. Though theologically "serious," as the term was then used, he was outwardly sunny in his disposition, even joyous. But most extraordinary—and evidence to Mrs. Wilberforce of a "Great Change" indeed, though one she certainly welcomed—was a marked absence of that irritability and harsh temper he had sometimes displayed, especially toward her. Others saw it too. Said Mrs. Sykes to Mrs. Wilberforce: "If this is madness, I hope he will bite us all."

In 1785 in the first months after the "Great Change," Wilberforce comes across as quite harsh on himself. In his diary, he continually takes himself to task for the smallest infractions and spends a great deal of time in self-examination. But Wilberforce knew his own weaknesses too well and realized that if he was really to change and to do the things he meant to do with his life, he must somehow gain control of himself. He knew that, if left to do as he liked, he might fritter away the rest of his life, just as he'd frittered away so many years already. He knew that he didn't want to go back to where he had been before, and he would take whatever steps were necessary to ensure that he continued on the new path he was now on.

And so he took stock of himself. He well knew his mind's natural tendency to be endlessly on a thousand subjects at once, to flit from this to that and to the next thing to no particular purpose—indeed, he called it his "butterfly mind." He also knew that his natural enthusiasm caused him to overeat and overdrink, and he knew that this in turn adversely affected his already fragile and sickly constitution, and he knew that such excess would often put him in bed and out of commission for weeks, unable to do the many things he wanted to do. He knew that his world-class wit could turn into the most vicious and wounding sarcasm, and that his ability to mimic others and joke and sing and generally be charming could be used merely to draw attention to himself, merely to exalt himself and to feed his personal and vain ambitions. Wilberforce had seen all too clearly who he was, what it had led him to, and where he had been headed. And now that he'd been given a second chance in life, as it were, he was deeply determined to chart a new course. He was determined not to go back.

Wilberforce alone knew how constitutionally weak he was with regard to self-discipline. And he knew that his years at Pocklington and Cambridge had powerfully reinforced his worst tendencies, feeding them when they should have been starved. While his friend Pitt had been at the very elbow of his brilliant and accomplished father, who had taken it upon himself to train his son rigorously from earliest youth to be a great orator and politician, Wilberforce had been fatherless and had been encouraged by his friends and his mother, and even by his tutors, to do exactly as he pleased. So where Pitt was now reaping the ample rewards of all those years of paternal sternness, Wilberforce was an undisciplined mess who had gotten where he was precisely and only because of the raw talent that he possessed but had never cultivated one whit. For the rest of his life, he would pay a price for those idle years. As brilliant as his oratory was, it was often criticized for being too extemporaneous, too unshaped in its arguments. All of this was shown to him now in these months; he saw, so to speak, the full horror of himself. God, in his mercy, had allowed Wilberforce to see himself as he truly was, and it was crushing. But Wilberforce knew God didn't mean to end there. On the other side of the worst of who he was, if he dared face that worst, was a God who would help him overcome his faults and do great things, the very things for which he had created him. It was not too late.

And so, quite like the young Ben Franklin fifty years earlier, Wilberforce now made lists of his vices and kept track of how often he failed and endeavored to improve his record. Wilberforce's journal is filled with the simplest exhortations to self. "Go to bed at eleven and wake at six," he writes. At one point he entered into a pact with Milner to "exercise the invaluable practice of telling each other what each party believes to be the other's chief faults and infirmities."

During this period, he did some things that challenge our modern sensibilities. He would sometimes walk with a pebble in his shoe, to

remind himself of the sufferings of Christ; given the ill-fitting foot-
wear of his day, the gesture seems redundant. He would also fast frequently, so much so that he appeared even more gaunt and ethereal
than usual. Perhaps the most dramatic of all of Wilberforce's gestures
during this period was his resignation in a single day from all five of
the exclusive social clubs to which he belonged. That too seems un-
necessarily severe, but we mustn't judge too harshly, for those who
have gone through anything like a dramatic conversion usually stagger
a bit too far in one direction before they correct their course and learn
where the best forward path lies. From Pitt's reply to Wilberforce's
letter and from other scraps of Wilberforce's writing, we see that at
first he was sure he needed to go away for an "indeterminate time" so
that he would no longer be distracted by the "world" and its noise. So
perhaps, for Wilberforce, merely resigning from five clubs was dramatically moderate.

The counsel of Pitt and Newton at this time were crucial. Newton
wrote Wilberforce a letter sometime later that seemed to sum up his
view of the situation. "It is hoped and believed," he famously wrote,
"that the Lord has raised you up for the good of His church and for
the good of the nation." Pitt, in his letter, had said something similar: "Surely the principles as well as the practice of Christianity are
simple and lead not to meditation only, but to action."

Thus December 1785—when both Newton and Pitt advised
Wilberforce to stay where he was, in politics, and to put his newfound
perspective to use in that sphere—was an historic moment. Before
this time, a serious Christian would have felt theological pressure to
leave "the world" and enter a life of Christian service. Wilberforce's
decision to remain in politics made the transfer of Christian ideas
into the previously "secular" realm of society possible for generations
of Christians to follow.

And so, in a letter to his mother at that time, when she was still
worried about his "melancholy madness" and the possibility that he
would do something drastically "otherworldly" and Methodist, such
as disappear from public life, Wilberforce could put her at ease.
Some, he writes to her, "are thrown into public, some have their lot
in private life. . . . [It] would merit no better name than desertion . . .
if I were thus to fly from the post where Providence has placed me."

CHAPTER 6

THE SECOND GREAT OBJECT: THE REFORMATION OF MANNERS

"God almighty has set before me
two great objects: the suppression of the Slave Trade
and the reformation of manners."

A mericans have an outsized tendency to romanticize the past, to see previous eras as magically halcyon and idyllic, and of no era would this be truer than the eighteenth century in Britain. Visions of powdered wigs and liveried coachmen dance in our heads. If forced to think of something negative about that time, we might come up with the charming anachronisms of chamber pots and wooden teeth. Perhaps someone will bring up the absence of anesthetics. But if the subject of slavery comes up, we will probably think of it as a grotesque aberration, as a single monstrous evil without much connection to an otherwise genteel and civilized society. That would be a gross mistake.

Entirely surprising to most of us, life in eighteenth-century Britain was particularly brutal, decadent, violent, and vulgar. Slavery was only the worst of a host of societal evils that included epidemic alcoholism, child prostitution, child labor, frequent public executions for petty crimes, public dissections and burnings of executed criminals, and unspeakable public cruelty to animals.

Of the many societal problems Wilberforce might have thought needed his attention, slavery would have been the least visible of all, and by a wide margin. In fact, the answer to how Britain could have allowed something as brutal as West Indian slavery to exist, and for so long, has much to do with its invisibility. Few British people ever saw the slightest hint of it, for only a tiny handful of the three million Africans who had been pressed into British slavery over the years had ever set foot on British shores. They were kidnapped and shipped straight to the West Indian sugar plantations thousands of miles away. The sugar and molasses from those plantations came to England, but who could have known of the nightmarish institution of human bondage that attended their making? Who would have known that much of the wealth in their nation's booming economy was created on the other side of the world by the most brutal mistreatment of other human beings, many of them women and children? Most British citizens had never seen anyone branded or whipped or subjected to thumbscrews. They had no idea that conditions on West Indian sugar plantations were so brutal that most of the slaves were literally worked to death in just a few years and most of the female slaves were too ill to bear children. Black faces were very rare in Britain in the late eighteenth century, especially before the 1770s, and any blacks one might have seen would probably have seemed to be treated rather well.

Just as most Americans today have never visited a slaughterhouse to investigate the grim details of how large animals become the shrink-wrapped frankfurters in their supermarkets, nor have ever witnessed the degradation and violence of life among the one and a half million people incarcerated in our prisons, so most Britons went about their lives with no idea of the universe of horrors that existed under the British flag or the nightmarish way of life of the slaves, whose existence was nonetheless intimately intertwined with their own way of life thousands of miles away.

To be sure, Wilberforce was not as unaware as most Britons about the slave trade. But right in front of his eyes and everywhere around him was a vast array of other societal evils. Upon coming to faith, Wilberforce was deeply moved by the social decay all around him and he knew that he wanted to do something about it. He also understood that the social evils in Britain itself at that time arose from precisely the same source as the evil of slavery and the slave trade.

When eighteenth-century British society had retreated from the historical Christianity it had earlier embraced, the Christian character of the nation—which had given Britain, among other things, a proud tradition of almshouses to help the poor, dating all the way back to the tenth century—had all but disappeared. The almshouses remained, and the outward trappings of religion remained, but robust Christianity, with its noble impulses to care for the suffering and less fortunate, was gone.

The retreat from serious Christian faith was not completely unreasonable, of course. Religious excesses in the seventeenth century had led to terrible violence and religious wars, so the subsequent avoidance of religious ardor was a natural reaction. France would experience the same reaction against religion, of course, but there the rejection was far more overt and would culminate just a few years later in the official and formal rejection of Christianity by the French Republic. But England was not, after all, France. And so, in keeping with its national character, Britain chose a more civilized and decorous path away from religion: it would staunchly retain the outward trappings and forms of religion—which were all well and good and would help keep the lower classes better behaved—but it would deny religion any real power. Religion would be defanged and declawed quietly, not killed in front of the mobs. Britain continued to use the terms and the symbols of its religion and would never make a vulgar Gallic show of executing clerics, but it would reject real religion nonetheless. If, before, the British faith had been like a great and noble lion, it would now become something more like a lapdog that never roared nor dared to bite, and that could be fed bits of cheese and petted when one was in the mood to do so.

And so keeping religion officially and outwardly in place, but holding it very lightly, became the hallmark of the age and accounted for the small hypocrisies one had sometimes to endure, as when Wilberforce at Cambridge had been required to assent to the tenets of the Church of England. No one believed such silly things anymore, but it would not do to say so openly and make a spectacle. One was not, after all, French.

By the time Wilberforce experienced his "Great Change," all of the social problems that would plague eighteenth-century Britain had come to full flower, having been unchecked by the social conscience of genuine Christian faith for nearly a hundred years. The unfortunate effects of religion's retreat were everywhere and in many ways evident and, of course, the poor suffered greatly.

Like the proverbial dead fish that rots first from the head, British society began to decay from the top; so our description of the situation must begin with the aristocracy. The British aristocracy at the end of the eighteenth century was, among other things, exquisitely selfish and gave no more thought to the conditions of those below them than the Charleston-dancing flapper and her dinner-jacketed suitors aboard a luxury liner would give to the Irish masses in steerage six decks below them. It simply wasn't fashionable to do so. The English nobility took its cues from its Gallic counterparts across the Channel and had been doing so for almost a century. The fabled excesses and decadence of the wealthy and noble classes of prerevolutionary France were mirrored expertly by their English counterparts.

King George III himself, it must be pointed out, stood out as a rare and notable exception to the advanced moral decay of those around him. He was deeply sensitive to his symbolic position as the head of the country and sincerely wished to set an example for the subjects he ruled. He was a faithful husband to his wife, Queen Charlotte, and a doting father who read the Bible to his daughters every night. But the moral seriousness, temperance, and uxoriousness that marked George III's character did not make the generational leap to his sons. There was an almost sublime bestiality to George's sons, a cadre of pleasure-choked buffoons who set the behavioral bar so low for the rest of society that one suspects they had perhaps thrown it into the basement.

The eldest son, the Prince of Wales, was the undisputed leader of the unfiltered pack and is believed, among other accomplishments, to have bedded seven thousand women; he is said to have snipped and kept a lock of hair from each of them. Had this eventual tonnage of hair been sold to wigmakers, it might have made a dent in his astronomical gambling debts, which, with other debts, amounted to £660,000 in 1796, a figure that in twenty-first-century dollars cannot be fathomed by anyone outside the Pentagon. (Thanks to his friends in Parliament, Charles James Fox and Richard Sheridan, the prince was routinely bailed out by the Royal Treasury.) But these hairy souvenirs, alas, were not sold but were merely cataloged by the future Monarch and Defender of the Faith in envelopes, each with the name of the lucky girl to whom it had belonged before her good fortune in being chosen as one of the seven thousand whom this discerning fellow found appealing and who had a pulse.

George was followed in the royal line by his brother Frederick, the Duke of York, who was followed by William, the Duke of Clarence. Clarence was adamantly pro-slavery, a vocal opponent of Wilberforce and abolition to the end. He was nicknamed "Cocoa-nut" for the shape and presumptive contents of the royal *tête*. The Duke of Wellington would later refer to the sons of George III as "the damnedest millstones about the neck of any Government that can be imagined."

A little further down the social ladder was Parliament, where alcoholism was epidemic—and terrifically fashionable. Two of the leading political figures of the day, Fox and Sheridan, were often drunk in the House of Commons, which is to say, while on the job *and* in public. Even Pitt, whom most thought a paragon of propriety, showed up drunk on the floor of Parliament, as did Lord Melville, the power-hungry Scotchman whose canny realpolitik in 1792 would keep the slave trade going for another fifteen years.

The historian Trevelyan wrote that a "statesman of the Georgian era was sailing on a sea of claret from one comfortable official haven to another. . . . No one can study the public or personal history of the eighteenth century without being impressed by the truly immense space which drinking occupied in the mental horizon of the young and the consequences of drinking in that of the old." Alcoholism was as bad or worse among the poor. Their drink of choice was not claret but gin, of which entire swamps were drained. Hogarth's famous engravings of "Gin Lane" depicting a drunken mother neglecting her baby, besides other horrors, is today thought to be a disturbingly accurate picture of the brutal debauchery among the poor of that era. The only contemporary equivalent for us would be the urban crack epidemic of the 1980s, but the gin craze and the social decay it spawned lasted not for one or two decades but for a century. The hopelessness of the poor at that time and the sordid misery of their lives were unrelieved by government or by private agencies. It was into this vast abyss that Wilberforce now looked.

Alongside the hopelessness and vulgarity, there was a widespread brutality to life in the "enlightened" eighteenth century. Public hangings were a popular form of entertainment, and if the rowdy, drunken crowds were lucky, the hanged criminal's body might be burned afterward as a further entertainment—or warning, depending on one's point of view. There were sometimes public dissections of hanged criminals too, such as from this 1790 account from a Sussex newspaper: "We do not hear that the young surgeons attempted to give lectures on the body but every one who chose to be present at the dissection was admitted whether led by curiosity or by the love of anatomy. In short the whole process was performed in public from the first incision to the boiling of the bones." The macabre aspect of these burnings and dissections is self-evident, but what gave the practice a particularly horrific twist is that the lower classes believed that such burnings and dissections would deprive the executed dead of the possibility of a bodily resurrection and of heaven. They believed that in watching these burnings and dissections, they had an actual window into hell itself.

The British ruling classes thought the crowds who gathered for these spectacles were irredeemably vulgar. But many also believed the public executions were an important deterrent to crime. Still many others cynically thought that the lower classes were simply brutish by nature and needed these entertainments as an outlet for their "passions"—and that if denied such outlets they would commit more crimes and perhaps even get ideas about social equality, such as were now brewing among the French. So it was best to keep the masses distracted and entertained in their squalor. Many thought God had ordained the poor's situation, that it was part of the natural order, and that they should therefore be kept where they were, in their misery. To help them was tantamount to shaking one's fist at God. Raising their sights from the vulgar spectacle of things like public hangings could rock the boat of civil society and mustn't be attempted. It also bears saying that public executions were hardly rare events. In eighteenth-century England, the number of crimes punishable by death was staggering. Sanctioned public hangings in England continued into the mid-nineteenth century. Charles Dickens remonstrated against them, rightly saying that the atmosphere of these hangings, far from being conducive to social order, coarsened the souls of those present. The last official public hanging in England was in 1868.

When there were no human executions to witness, a taste for grotesque spectacle could be satisfied by choosing from among every imaginable variety of cruelty to animals, the most popular of which was bull-baiting. This practice usually involved parading a bull through a town before staking it with a chain in a pit or designated area. A copious quantity of pepper was usually blown into the poor beast's nose, "to render him the more furious," and then dogs—usually one by one, but sometimes several at once—would be released to attack the bull and attempt to seize its sensitive nose and face in their jaws. The bull, for his part, would attempt to throw the attacking dog in the air with his horns. The fabled strength of a bull when applied to the weight of a dog would often result in the dog flying very high indeed. Dogs thrown high enough would break their necks or backs upon landing. If not permanently crippled, they would crawl back to have at the bull again, this being a large part of the spectacle.

Bulldogs were specially bred for bull-baiting, hence their name. Being mostly head and jaws with little body behind, a bulldog with his jaws fastened onto a bull's vulnerable snout would be nearly impossible to throw off. Then, according to a contemporary account,

> the bull bellows and bounds and kicks, all to shake off the dog. In the end, either the dog tears out the piece he has laid on, and falls, or else remains fixed to him with an obstinacy that would never end, did they not pull him off. To call him away, would be in vain; to give him a hundred blows, would be as much so; you might cut him to pieces, joint by joint, before he would let loose. What is to be done then? While some hold the bull, others thrust staves into the dog's mouth, and open it by main force.

A man who had seen a bull-baiting as a boy described it as "the most barbarous act I ever saw. It was a young bull and had very little notion of tossing the dogs, which tore his ears and the skin off his face in shreds, and his mournful cries were awful. I was up a tree, and was afraid the earth would open and swallow us all up."

There were ghastly variations upon the theme: one bull's hoofs were cut off so he might fend for himself on stumps. Bear-baiting was popular as well, also with endless repugnant variations. William Cobbett, the Enlightenment apologist and radical journalist who loathed Wilberforce and abolition, was an outspoken advocate of bear-baiting. History even gives us one perverse account of a pony being baited—with an ape tied to its back. According to a Spanish nobleman in attendance, "to see the animal kicking amongst the dogs, with the screaming of the ape, beholding the curs hanging from the ears and neck of the pony, is very laughable."

Finally, in this world of cruelty, vulgarity, and hopelessness, we come to prostitution, which was so rampant one can scarcely imagine it. No less than 25 percent of all unmarried women in London were prostitutes. There were brothels that exclusively offered the services of girls under fourteen, and the average age of a prostitute in London during those years was sixteen.

All of these things were swimming around in Wilberforce's mind as he began to think and pray about how his newfound faith would express itself in his life and work. It wouldn't be entirely clear to him until 1787, but in the meantime, as a first step in the right direction, Wilberforce championed two bills, both of which failed. One was for parliamentary reform and the other was a strange and ghoulish bill combining two macabre issues: putting an end to the burning of women at the stake, and selling the corpses of hanged criminals for dissection. In 1786 there was still a law on the books that women should be burned at the stake for petty treason—such as murdering a husband. By that time the women were no longer burned alive, but were mercifully first hanged. But their corpses were publicly burned immediately afterward. Wilberforce didn't think that the spectacle of incinerating a recently living woman's corpse much contributed to the good of society, and he put his bill forward to abolish it. The bill would probably have passed if he hadn't committed the rookie error of linking it to a second issue, one that involved body snatchers and corpse dissection. It was as if he had fatally loaded an otherwise good bill with too much political "pork," only far more disgusting.

The corpse side of the story begins with a law passed in 1752 that made it possible for the corpses of executed murderers to be sold to surgeons, who needed fresh corpses for dissection. Before this time, there had been a black market in corpses. But even after the 1752 law was passed, there weren't enough corpses to feed the surgeons' hunger for them, and they again turned to body snatchers. How these illegally obtained corpses came to be corpses the surgeons knew not; they could hardly be expected to have a taste for such legal arcana; they simply wanted a nice fresh supply of corpses, and that was the end of it. The bill that Wilberforce put forward was aimed at hitting the body snatchers where they lived—or exhumed—and it proposed that the corpses of criminals executed for lesser offenses than murder could now be sold. Thus, arsonists, burglars, robbers, and rapists would now be eligible to further the cause of medical research. Or so Wilberforce had thought.

The grotesque and long-winded "Bill for Regulating the Disposal after Execution of the Bodies of Criminals Executed for Certain Offences, and for Changing the Sentence pronounced upon Female Convicts in certain cases of High and Petty Treason" was passed in Commons. But the House of Lords, led by Lord Loughborough, defeated it. As far as he was concerned, both parts of the bill were bad business, for if the women being burned in front of the jeering crowds were already dead, what was all the blessed kerfuffle? The ghoulish spectacle and acrid smell were indeed intended as a deterrent to crime, and while hanging women was something of a deterrent, it was not quite enough. When the hanged troublemaker was burned too, the anti-murder message became that much clearer. Loughborough also thought that legalizing the sale of the corpses of nonmurderers was a grave error, putting murder on an equal footing in the public eye with mere stealing, which might encourage murder. As both were capital offenses, murder required a further penalty, and dissection fit the bill quite nicely. Stealing got one hanged—but after a murderer was executed, he shouldn't have it quite so easy. He should, in a word, be *publicly dissected.*

❦

As Wilberforce was figuring out what he would do with the rest of his life, moving toward finding purpose and meaning beyond

personal ambition, it's extraordinary to see that the two "great objects" he would declare his lifelong goals at the end of 1787 were arising simultaneously. How he came to take up abolition, and the story
of abolition itself, we will tell in the next and following chapters; but
first, let's look at that part of 1787 in which his other "great object"
was suggesting itself to him.

In a letter to his friend Christopher Wyvill, Wilberforce writes:

> The barbarous custom of hanging has been tried too long,
> and with the success which might have been expected from
> it. The most effectual way to prevent greater crimes is by
> punishing the smaller, and by endeavouring to repress that
> general spirit of licentiousness, which is the parent of every
> species of vice. I know that by regulating the external con-
> duct we do not at first change the hearts of men, but even
> they are ultimately to be wrought upon by these means,
> and we should at least so far remove the obtrusiveness of
> the temptation, that it may not provoke the appetite, which
> might otherwise be dormant and inactive.

These words, tossed off in a letter to a friend, are fresh and profound in their insight. Wilberforce is saying at the end of the eighteenth century something similar to what John Q. Wilson and George
Kelling would become famous for saying two centuries later in their
famous "Broken Windows" essay in the *Atlantic Monthly*. Wilson and
Kelling made the argument that if law enforcement effectively assumes that a certain area is a crime zone and therefore does not prosecute smaller crimes, this encourages an atmosphere that leads to
much greater crimes and overall lawlessness. This theory was put into
practice in New York City, which turned in a few years from having
one of the highest crime rates in the nation into having one of the
lowest. The smallest crimes—subway fare-beating, aggressive pan-
handling, and so on—which would have formerly been ignored so
that law enforcement could focus on more serious crimes, were now
aggressively pursued. The message this change sent out was that no
crimes would be tolerated, and extraordinarily, murder and all other
serious crimes plummeted.

Wilberforce grasped this idea over two centuries ago, and at the age of twenty-seven. Even more impressive, he then set out to implement the idea throughout Britain—and the British Empire. It's not too much to say that this single observation was the lever by which little Wilberforce replaced an entire world of brutality and misery with another of civility and hope, one that we now refer to as the Victorian era.

CHAPTER 7

THE PROCLAMATION SOCIETY

". . . making goodness fashionable."

Wilberforce's plan for the "reformation of manners"—or at least the beginning of it—centered on a document with the delightfully old-fashioned title of "The Proclamation for the Encouragement of Piety and Virtue and for the Preventing of Vice, Profaneness and Immorality." It was already a bit out-of-date by Wilberforce's time, but every king or queen, upon ascending to the throne, had traditionally issued such a royal proclamation, and no sooner had any of them done so than it would be instantly and assiduously ignored. When King George III issued his royal proclamation in 1760, that's precisely what happened. Such proclamations were mere formalities, part of the larger hypocrisy of eighteenth-century society, which gave rouged lip service to Christianity, and simultaneously dismissed it with all of the requisite winks and mandatory nods.

But Wilberforce had an idea. An old book titled *History of the Society for the Reformation of Manners in the Year 1692* had somehow found its way into his hands. In it he learned that when William and Mary acceded to the British throne in 1692, their royal proclamation had in fact had a widespread and genuine effect on society. For along with the usually toothless proclamation, the king and queen had formed a "Proclamation Society"—by which society was thereby deputized to put into effect what the royal proclamation had proclaimed. And it had worked. Wilberforce's clever plan now was to persuade George III to reissue his royal proclamation. It had, after all, been twenty-seven years since he had first issued it. And now, when he issued it again, Wilberforce and his friends would put together proclamation societies that would do what the Proclamation Society had done a century earlier during William and Mary's reign.

Wilberforce's chief ally in this plan was Bishop Beilby Porteus, the recently installed bishop of London. Porteus had been the personal chaplain to the king and was as well connected in the right circles as one would imagine the bishop of London to be. Porteus helped Wilberforce strategize and lent credibility to the effort, for it could not be seen as a Methodist venture. Porteus suggested that Wilberforce first put the idea to Pitt, which he did, and Pitt, who was entirely in favor of it, took the idea to the archbishop of Canterbury, who gave it his blessing. Pitt also brought it before Queen Charlotte, who lent her royal and weighty approval. Wilberforce's ability to be a political bridge between the Methodists and mainstream Church of England leaders such as Porteus was here demonstrated for the first time, and that ability was at the very heart of his tremendous effectiveness in accomplishing both of his "great objects."

Things were quickly surging forward, and Wilberforce was powerfully heartened. In a May 29 letter to a friend, he writes:

> It would give you no little pleasure could you hear how warmly the Archbishop of Canterbury expresses himself . . . the interest he takes in the good work does him great credit, and he assures me that one still greater [the king himself] to whom he has opened the subject in form, and suggested the measures above mentioned, is deeply impressed with the necessity of opposing the torrent of profaneness which every day makes more rapid advance. What think you of my having myself received a formal invitation to cards for Sunday evening from a person high in the King's service?

What made this royal proclamation—and the formation of proclamation societies—so important was that it furthered two parts of Wilberforce's plan: his "broken windows" analysis of the condition of the poor, and his quest to "make goodness fashionable." It helped the "broken windows" part of his plan by addressing the fact that the Crown almost never brought suit against anyone. Only the victims of a crime usually brought suit to get recompense. Whenever there was a crime against *society at large* or against the community, no one prosecuted and absolutely nothing was done. So-called disorderly houses of prostitution and gambling were veritable petri dishes of crime, and many were given licenses year after year. If a brothel opened up in a neighborhood illegally, nothing was done about it. Crime in that area would naturally increase, and residents would suffer but be unable to do much of anything. But now this would change, because the local proclamation society would themselves prosecute. It was as if a vast archipelago of crimes and offenses had been unreachable on foot or via horse, and some resourceful scamp had suddenly thought of police boats. The problem was instantly solved. A whole host of horrors were suddenly no longer beyond the ameliorating reach of the law.

The reissuing of the royal proclamation and establishment of proclamation societies would further the "making goodness fashionable" aspect of Wilberforce's plan by promulgating the idea that all leaders in society are responsible for being moral exemplars. In Georgian England, this idea would have engendered smirks and howls, just as it would today. But Wilberforce, the consummate politician, pushed it forward with proto-Keaton-esque deadpan, knowing full well what he was doing. When a local proclamation society was formed, prominent members would be invited to take part. They would give in to the social pressure to accept, and would soon find themselves in a rather interesting position, for their own moral standards would be seen in light of their participation in the society. It was a subversive and politically brilliant strategy.

The proclamation specifically said that those in high places of honor or authority were obliged to set a good example and were to be involved in reforming those who were leading "dissolute and debauched lives." Those in high law enforcement positions, such as judges and sheriffs, were supposed to be "very vigilant and strict in the discovery and eventual prosecution of all persons who should be guilty of excessive drinking, blasphemy, profane swearing and cursing, lewdness, or other immoral and dissolute practices," and they were also to suppress "loose and licentious" booklets and pamphlets and so on.

The royal proclamation was issued on June 1, 1787. Although Wilberforce had pushed everything forward, he remained very much in the background. There was nothing to be gained, and much to be lost, from his association with the endeavor, for the slightest whiff of Methodism would be enough to spook most of those getting involved. It all had to seem entirely "respectable." Wilberforce never presented it as a religious or Christian effort. It was an effort to ameliorate social conditions, pure and simple. Wilberforce simply focused on reducing crime and on lifting the generally depressed and depressing social climate in which so many of the poor lived. Had he been motivated by his previous "darling ambition"—to promote himself—he would never have been able to succeed.

Once the proclamation had been issued, Wilberforce quickly set about the more important business of putting together a proclamation society. This would give teeth to the whole affair. On June 7 he went to Whitehall, met with the Duke of Montague, and invited him to be the society's president. Montague was not at all religious, but seeing the good common sense of Wilberforce's efforts, he accepted. As did Montague's brother, Lord Ailesbury, whom Wilberforce visited on June 13 and invited to become a member.

In a society that seemed to have accepted rampant crime and brutal living as the sad but inevitable lot of the poorest neighborhoods, it must have been a tonic to see a bright, ambitious politician with fresh ideas. "It gives me pleasure," the Duke of Manchester wrote, "to find that you join in the ideas of many humane and thinking men, in reprobating the frequency of our executions and the sanguinary severity of our laws. . . . If you and other young men who are rising in the political sphere would undertake the arduous task of revising our code of criminal law in its severity, I mean largely the number of capital punishments, I am satisfied it would go far toward bettering the people of this country."

By June 1787, Wilberforce had already taken many steps on the very long journey ahead toward the "reformation of manners." In fact, it wasn't until October 28 that he coined that phrase, when he famously penned in his diary: "God almighty has set before me two great objects: the suppression of the slave trade and the reformation of manners."

Though written privately in a diary and unknown for decades, these words may as well have been affixed to the door of Westminster Abbey, or Parliament. The momentousness of their writing can scarcely be appreciated. Wilberforce, writing these words at age twenty-eight, was either insane, idiotic, or inspired by the very Subject of his two-object sentence. Achieving either of the "great objects" was humanly impossible, but the extraordinary testimony of history is that Wilberforce was indeed instrumental in accomplishing both of them during his lifetime.

To our modern ears, the phrase "reformation of manners" sounds merely quaint, but what Wilberforce meant by the phrase was different from what we think when we hear it. By "manners" he did not mean anything having to do with etiquette but rather what we would call "habits" or "attitudes"; there was also a distinctly moral aspect to his use of the phrase, though not in the puritanical sense. He wished to bring civility and self-respect into a society that had long since spiraled down into vice and misery; he wanted, among other things, to stem the epidemic of teenage mothers prostituting themselves to pay for their gin habit. It was exceedingly progressive of him to see such actions not merely as crimes but as symptoms of a larger social condition that required the extraordinary intervention of those in power.

There were effectively only two responses to the condition of the poor in Wilberforce's day. One was to look down on them scornfully, moralistically judging them as inferior and unworthy of help. The other was to ignore them entirely, to see their plight as inevitable, part of the unavoidable price of "modern civilization." But Wilberforce would introduce a third way of responding to the situation. This response would neither judge the poor and suffering nor ignore them, but rather would reach out to them and help them up, so to speak.

So Wilberforce spent the summer of 1787 bumping hither and yon across the land to meet with such members of high society as might be drawn to the idea. Not everyone was inclined to help or encourage him. Earl Fitzwilliam laughed at Wilberforce, saying that moral dissolution was the result of the nation's wealth: "I promised him a speedy return of purity of morals in our own homes, if none of us had a shilling to spend in debauchery out of doors."

Another nobleman was even less encouraging. "So you wish to be a reformer of men's morals," he said. "Look then, and see there what is the end of such reformers," and he pointed to a painting of the Crucifixion. The moment must have been a profound challenge for Wilberforce, for it captured in painful vividness the problems he faced. Here was a wealthy nobleman who had seen fit to display in his home a painting of the Crucifixion and who would have even somehow considered himself a "Christian" of sorts. But his theology was so stunted that for him the Crucifixion was precisely what it was to Pontius Pilate—a stern warning against do-gooders and upstarts like Jesus of Nazareth who went about stirring up trouble with all their foolish talk of morality.

But generally the response was favorable. As Wilberforce collected interested parties, he encouraged them to form local proclamation societies, and he discovered that there was an appetite for his scheme. The societies flourished.

That fall, again not feeling very well, Wilberforce went to Bath to take the waters. While there, he met Hannah More, who, like Isaac Milner—and like Granville Sharp, whom we will meet soon—would seem utterly contrived if someone had invented her. Like Milner, Hannah More would become one of Wilberforce's closest friends for life. She would be front and center in the cause of abolition, and front and center in this second "great object," the reformation of manners.

When Wilberforce met her at Bath in the fall of 1787, Hannah More was already a huge celebrity in Britain. She was a famous playwright whose *Percy* starred her friend David Garrick and was the most successful tragedy of that era. Exceedingly clever and talented and now, at thirty-nine, still attractive and flirtatiously witty, she was not only the most popular writer of her day—during her lifetime her books outsold Jane Austen's many times over—but one of the most talented. Her friend Samuel Johnson hailed her as "the most skilled versificatrix in the English Language." In Samuel Richardson's famous painting *The Nine Muses,* which hangs in the National Gallery, she is pictured as Melpomene, the Muse of Tragedy. But Garrick, the most famous actor of the eighteenth century, proclaimed her the very incarnation of all nine muses, and he and his wife lived with More for many years in a kind of mutual adoration society.

More was a Christian, though not quite a Methodist until about the time that Wilberforce met her. But even after her faith deepened and she became known as the "Queen of the Methodists," she remained close with such literary figures of the day as the "sacrilegious charmer" Horace Walpole. Walpole was a celebrated cynic and rake who invented the Gothic novel, had an early homosexual affair with the poet Thomas Gray, lived in a Gothic home he designed himself, wrote a definitive, though extremely catty, memoir of the Georgian period, and who coined the word serendipity. That More was simultaneously close with Walpole and John Newton tells us something about the breadth of her personality and the generosity of her theology.

More was fifteen years older than Wilberforce, and she swam in the very center of cultural life in 1770s London, the distaff pole of which was an exclusive group called the "Blue Stockings" or "Bas Bleu." These women had been convened since the 1750s by Lady Montague for the purposes of literary and intellectual conversation. In *Hannah More and Her Circle,* Mary Alden Hopkins describes them as a group of

> elderly ladies who talked better than they danced and elderly gentlemen who could overlook a woman's age and wrinkles if she had a good brain served by a lively tongue. . . . Dr. Johnson was, of course, the big fish for whom all hostesses angled and Boswell came with him when he was in London. Old Bubble-and-Squeak Sheridan would come if Johnson was not to be present, while his son Richard Brinsley Sheridan would come anyway. Sir Joshua Reynolds was sometimes

present. Edward Gibbon was too important to omit but the ladies did not much like him.

More was a prolific writer who never met a genre she didn't like. Her aphorisms, like the rest of her work, ran the gamut from seriously theological ("Love never reasons, but profusely gives; it gives like a thoughtless prodigal its all, and then trembles lest it has done too little.") to moralistic ("Luxury! more perilous to youth than storms or quicksand, poverty or chains.") to viciously witty ("Going to the opera, like getting drunk, is a sin that carries its own punishment with it.").

More had always been a Christian, but around the time that Wilberforce met her something deeper was stirring. The death of Garrick in 1779 had turned her away from her interest in the theater, and the death of Dr. Johnson in 1785 seemed to signal the end of an era in her life. She soon became friends with Beilby Porteus, Lady Middleton, and John Newton, all of whom fanned the flames of her devotion. At Wilberforce's instigation, she and her four less famous sisters started and ran the Mendip Schools for poor children, which at one point educated one thousand children, and she wrote scores of religious and moral tracts. Though she never married, she took the honorific "Mrs.," as was sometimes done at that time. Cobbett meanly dubbed her "the Old Bishop in Petticoats."

More's interests, like Wilberforce's, seemed boundless. She had a particular knack for collecting interesting rural figures whom she thought she could help. There was the penniless milkmaid with a real talent for writing verse—More dubbed her "Lactilla." And there was Louisa, the celebrated "Mad Maid of the Haystack," a mysterious innocent who was "discovered" by a friend of More's out riding in the country. About twenty-five and obviously mad, she lived inside a haystack whose environs she had decorated with trinkets. She hardly spoke, but wept when German was spoken, so was naturally believed to be the lost daughter of the German emperor. More and her sisters tried to help Louisa and eventually had her placed in a lunatic asylum at Hannam. Even John Wesley visited the "Mad Maid" twice. In his journal of September 1785, he writes: "I went over to Hannam once more and saw poor disconsolate Louisa, still wrapping herself up naked in her blanket, and not caring to speak to anyone; the late pretty tale of her being the Emperor's daughter, is doubtless a mere catch-penny; and her four and twenty examinations are as credible as Mahomet's journey through seventy thousand heavens."

Hannah More was greatly taken with Wilberforce on their first meeting at Bath, where they would meet so many more times over the years. "That young gentleman's character," she wrote of him, "is one of the most extraordinary I ever knew for talents, virtue and piety." And he was taken with her too. It was as if they had discovered they were the oldest of friends, and soon they were. More's concern for the poor, mingled with her presence in circles of the highest society, made her a powerful figure for advocating many of the moral reforms that Wilberforce would soon be championing, and the list of things they worked on together throughout their lifelong friendship—More died just a few months after Wilberforce—is endless. Her book *Thoughts on the Importance of the Manners of the Great to General Society,* aimed at her contemporaries, was the first in a series of writings that were widely read and to great effect.

But the next step in Wilberforce's "reformation of manners" was to convene the first proclamation society. They convened in November of that year. Charles Middleton was there, as was Edward Eliot, with whom Wilberforce had become very close. Elliot had married Pitt's sister Harriot, who had died the previous year in childbirth. Her death caused Eliot to turn to Wilberforce, and God, for solace. The two became best friends and prayed together for years, and together with Hannah More he became one of Wilberforce's staunchest allies in this second "great object." Others invited to this first meeting of the proclamation society were six dukes, eleven "lesser peers," a handful of commoners like Wilberforce, and umpteen bishops.

"Nothing is to be announced to the world of society," Wilberforce instructed them, "only that the gentlemen mentioned have felt the necessity of attending to His Majesty's call and have agreed to assist in carrying the Proclamation into effect." Wilberforce was, as it were, crazy like a fox. Many were approached on this subject, including Lord North, to give it the widest possible appeal and the widest possible appearance of general approval among the upper classes. Charles James Fox was not approached, understandably.

Wilberforce may have been crazy like a fox, but Fox himself was so often drunk as the proverbial skunk that Wilberforce wisely decided to forego badgering him about becoming involved. Even if Fox had initially assented to lend his name to the cause, it seems rather likely that he may have eventually weaseled out of any real commitment anyway, and it is always possible that, given his affection for dissolute living, he may even have become a mole for the opposition.

CHAPTER 8

THE FIRST GREAT OBJECT:
ABOLISHING THE SLAVE TRADE

"... that hideous traffic, so disgraceful
to the British character."

Exactly how William Wilberforce came to embrace the abolition of the British slave trade as the first of his two great causes, and the one that would forever attach itself to his name in history, we don't know. We know that the subject of the slave trade had first been presented to him when he was a boy, no later than when he was eleven or twelve and living with his aunt and uncle, for it was then that he met John Newton and grew close to him. Newton had written his autobiographical *Authentic Narrative* a decade before, and there can be little doubt that even if the young Wilberforce hadn't read it, he would have heard Newton talk about his days as a slave-ship captain many times during those early years. We also know that at age fourteen Wilberforce wrote a school essay in which he decried the business of slavery. And Wilberforce told his sons that as early as 1780, the year he first entered Parliament at age twenty-one, "I had been strongly interested for the West Indian slaves, and I expressed my hope, that I should redress the wrongs of those wretched beings." He remembered, in 1783, at the home of his Cambridge friend Gerard Edwards, discussing the subject with James Ramsay, a former naval surgeon who would figure prominently in Wilberforce's eventual decision to take up the abolitionist banner.

But the precise concatenation of events that launched Wilberforce in his historical quest is as impossible to sort out as whether the proverbial chicken can be said to have laid the proverbial egg or to have been hatched from it. But we know of one interesting character who played a key part. His name was Granville Sharp and he was unquestionably one of the foremost chickens—or eggs—involved. He was also something of a nut.

❧

There is no use beating around the bush: Granville Sharp really was *quite* nutty. But he was one of those nuts who was so nutty that in talking with him he could make you wonder if it was in fact you who were the nut and not he. Which is to say, perhaps he wasn't quite so very nutty after all.

Granville Sharp was a renowned musician in the mid-eighteenth century. There will be no jokes about his marrying a Miss Flat, nor about their having seven children named Doey, Ray, Mimi, and so on. Sharp's entire family were musicians, and most of them lived inside a large barge that was towed all over England's waterways. The Sharps would fortnightly perform their music for royals and other privileged persons whilst wearing tricorn hats and buckled shoes and were exceedingly famous in their day. There is a well-known painting in the National Gallery of all sixteen of them posed atop their barge. They were rather a talented group. Granville's brother, who played with them, also held the title of Official Surgeon to the King. Still, Granville stood out among them, being indefatigably brilliant and possessed of a tenacious streak both wider and longer than the Thames, upon which the family's barge sometimes traveled.

While still a young man, Sharp, a devout Christian, had been accused by a Unitarian of believing in the Trinity because he didn't know the original language of the New Testament. Quicker than you could say, "It's Greek to me," Sharp taught himself Greek, refuted the linguistically and theologically confused Unitarian, and then wrote a definitive pamphlet, titled "Remarks on the Use of the Definitive

Article in the Greek Text of the New Testament," in which he corrected some long-standing translation errors in the Bibles of the
period (they've been corrected ever since). Sharp was similarly challenged on the Hebrew of the Old Testament, and before you could
shout, *"L'chaim!"* he had conquered a second ancient tongue in no
time flat and was likely rolling up his sleeves to subdue the wily cu-
neiform lingo of the Babylonians when history interrupted in 1765.

That was the year when Sharp's tenacity and Christianity would
converge once more, this time in a matter not of linguistics but of
law. What precipitated this convergence was not a mistaken Unitarian but a bloodied African who staggered one day that year toward
Sharp on a London street after having been pistol-whipped until the
pistol broke apart; the young man was nearly blinded and had lost
the use of his legs. Sharp immediately brought him to his brother,
the king's surgeon. They got him admitted to a hospital, where he
spent four months recovering, and afterward they found him a job.
The man's name was Jonathan Strong. He was about seventeen years
old and had belonged to a Barbados lawyer named Lisle, who had
brought him to London from the Caribbean. But two years later Lisle
was suddenly surprised to see his miraculously resurrected—and
again quite valuable—former property, and he decided now would
be an excellent time to cash in his long-lost chips, happily rediscov-
ered. Lisle reckoned that Strong would bring about £30, and while
he busied himself finding a buyer, he had Strong kidnapped by two
men and brought to jail, where he would be held until Lisle could
return. But somehow Strong got word to Sharp, and Sharp immediately went to the Lord Mayor, who agreed that Strong should indeed
be set free. Lisle was none too pleased, but perceiving Sharp's inex-
haustible reserves of tenacity—the piercing eyes, aquiline nose, and
sunken cheeks fairly shouted as much—Lisle decided to back off.
Strong was freed.

But this episode had engaged Sharp's curiosity, and he now began
a study of English law. What he found on the subject of slavery disturbed him. It seemed that sometime during the reign of William
and Mary a Justice Holt had wisely ruled that "one may be a villeyn in
England, but not a slave." So indeed, for a time, slavery was forbidden
on English shores. But Holt's ruling was overturned just a few years

later, in 1729, and ever since then it had been legal to keep slaves in England. Sharp had studied only one book of law before this episode, but that one book was the Bible, which the doughty genius believed to be both the infallible Word of God and the urtext of all English law. He knew that all English law sprang from this just and noble soil, and any rulings that said slaves could be owned in England were simply mistaken and must needs be weeded out of that soil with all alacrity. Sharp even consulted the venerable William Blackstone on this subject (not the book but the author himself), weighed the great authority's opinion on the legal balance, and—authority or no—found him wanting. And so Sharp himself would deal with these erroneous rulings as he had dealt with those pesky mistranslated Greek verbs: he'd find them, pull them up by their roots, and toss them behind him, along with the other jetsam of errata, in his frothy, churning wake.

Granville Sharp was one of those Christian fanatics who took the injunction to love one's neighbor literally—who loved his neighbors even when they were inconvenient African neighbors trying to reclaim their freedom. Of course, word of his literal interpretation traveled quickly, and slaves who had heard of Sharp and his work sought him out. Granville Sharp was of course thrilled to be doing the Lord's work in freeing these poor souls—and each case provided a fresh opportunity to do the wider good of improving the vexingly weedy British legal system.

In 1772 things came to a head, for it was in this year that Sharp's eagle gaze fell upon what looked like a deep taproot among the smaller weeds. This taproot was the so-called Somerset case, and it would in a very concentrated way put the whole unjust tangle plainly before a judge. The case concerned an African man named Somerset who had been brought from Virginia to London as a slave and who now, through Sharp, was demanding his freedom. The judge, one Lord Mansfield, didn't want to rule on the case, because he knew what its implications would be. The nature of the case was such that if Mansfield declared this fellow free on English soil, the fourteen thousand other slaves in England would effectively be legally freed too—and, as Mansfield saw it, it would create an unmanageable mess by spawning every kind of lamentable social ill. Mansfield was right that ending slavery precipitously would create any number of social ills, but Granville Sharp was enough of a crackpot to think of slavery itself as a social ill, not to mention an abomination to God. So he was willing enough to risk the other social ills and would surely be one of the evangelicals who did all they could to ameliorate them as they arose.

And so Sharp, the neophyte legal eagle, wanted to force Mansfield to rule on the case. For him, the whole point of taking on the case was to get a definitive ruling. Sharp was every judge's worst nightmare come to life, and as one might have predicted, Mansfield was indeed forced against his will to rule on the case.

Mansfield was no fool, however. His ruling was fussily careful to declare that only the one African, Somerset, was freed. But somehow, in the public mind, this detail was lost, or didn't matter. For all intents and purposes, slavery had been abolished in England! And to some very real extent, because of the public perception, it had.

The celebration over this ruling was widespread, and the abolitionist cause now happily boiled over into the British consciousness in a way that would have been unthinkable a short time before. Adam Smith, Charles Wesley, and Dr. Johnson publicly declared themselves against slavery, and the poet William Cowper happily greeted the Somerset verdict with a shouted hurrah in lapidary verse:

> Slaves cannot breathe in England; if their lungs
> Receive our air, that moment they are free.

The Somerset case was in some ways a very great victory, but every victory only whetted Sharp's appetite for the next battle. He knew that while England's slaves might now have been freed, the British slave trade every day still "legally" carried endless thousands of slaves from Africa to the British colonies in the West Indies. What those poor souls suffered was manifestly against the law of God. Sharp knew that the slave trade had to be abolished, and that slavery itself, in the vast precincts of the British Empire, must be abolished too. God had not given Granville Sharp a beakishly sharp nose for trouble for nothing, and now it was to these wider and much more horrible injustices that this indefatigable Christian fanatic turned his nose and attentions.

Throughout the 1770s, little had happened in any concerted way regarding the abolition of slavery or the slave trade, but public attention to slavery had been galvanized, and slowly a movement was beginning to come together. In 1774 John Wesley, one of the first to come out publicly against the trade, wrote a popular pamphlet titled "Thoughts on Slavery." That same year Granville Sharp met Olaudah Equiano, a freed slave who was one of the most colorful figures of the entire abolitionist movement. Equiano was eleven when he was sold into slavery, having grown up in what is today Nigeria. He was able to purchase his own freedom and traveled all over the world, including a trip on which he came within six hundred miles of the North Pole on a Royal Navy polar expedition that included a certain rather reckless fourteen-year-old boy who grew up to become Lord Nelson. Equiano eventually wrote a fascinating autobiography, *The Interesting Narrative of the Life of Olaudah Equiano, or Gustavus Vassa, the African*. His story, which was published in 1789, did much to educate the British people about the actual experiences and horrors of the slave trade and slavery itself, and it provided a powerful argument against the idea that Africans were different from any other people. The book showed its author to be a deeply sensitive, extremely intelligent human being, and an exceedingly devout Christian.

The acutely Christian character of the British abolitionist movement is undeniable, for its leaders were all consciously acting out of the principles of their deeply held faith. For the pronounced enemies of abolition, however, the notion of human equality had no objective basis and was a mere tautology, a snake swallowing its tail. Though many who fought abolition were outspokenly atheistic, many others were nominally Christian. For this the leaders of the Church of England, not merely the people in its pews, were to blame. The Church of England at the time had a great deal of money invested in West Indian plantations and did not make any connection between the tenets of the Christian faith and abolition. Making that connection fell to outsiders—to the Methodists and other so-called Dissenters, such as the Quakers and Moravians. It's hard to avoid the harsh conclusion that the Church of England at the time was little more than a pseudo-Christian purveyor of government-sponsored, institutionalized hypocrisy.

◦◦◦

Perhaps the greatest accomplishment of the Somerset case was that it captured the public's attention and drew increasing numbers to the cause. But eleven years later, that cause had not made any significant forward progress. In 1783 another grim milestone in the abolitionist movement was marked, and it would further galvanize the abolitionists and begin to draw them together for their siege on this great human evil. It was on March 18 of that year that Olaudah Equiano came to Granville Sharp with a bloodcurdling tale of something that had happened more than a year before. It was just now making its way into the newspapers, and the agonizing and unbearable details that Equiano related to Sharp had come out in the course of the trial. The British public could hardly believe what it was reading.

But before we turn to the evils perpetrated aboard the ill-fated *Zong,* we need to put the event in context and describe an infinitely more typical evil, the one that has come to be called the "Middle Passage."

The Middle Passage across the Atlantic was front and center in the slave trade's catalog of horrors. It was so named because it was the middle leg of the infamous "triangle trade." On the first leg, European goods were transported to Africa and there unloaded; on the second, the ship was filled with its human cargo, who during this "middle passage" were transported to the West Indies, to be sold there; and on its final leg the ship carried West Indian goods back to Europe. The Middle Passage illustrates in a nutshell what much of the British public would eventually see as an intolerable horror, one that needed to be ended at any cost.

One famous account of the Middle Passage comes to us via Alexander Falconbridge, a ship's surgeon in the trade, and it is worth quoting at length inasmuch as its words form the nightmarish central image of the slave trade.

"The men Negroes," wrote Falconbridge,

on being brought aboard the ship, are immediately fastened together, two and two, by handcuffs on their wrists and by irons rivetted on their legs. . . . They are frequently stowed so close, as to admit of no other position than lying on their sides. Nor will the height between decks, unless directly under the grating, permit the indulgence of an erect posture.

[On these decks] are placed three or four large buckets, of a conical form, nearly two feet in diameter at the bottom and only one foot at the top and in depth of about twenty-eight inches, to which, when necessary, the Negroes have recourse. It often happens that those who are placed at a distance from the buckets, in endeavoring to get to them, tumble over their companions, in consequence of their being shackled. These accidents, although unavoidable, are productive of continual quarrels in which some of them are always bruised. In this distressed situation, unable to proceed and prevented from getting to the tubs, they desist from the attempt; and as the necessities of nature are not to be resisted, ease themselves as they lie. This becomes a fresh source of boils and disturbances and tends to render the condition of the poor captive wretches still more uncomfortable. The nuisance arising from these circumstances is not infrequently increased by the tubs being much too small for the purpose intended and their being usually emptied but once every day. . . .

The hardships and inconveniences suffered by the Negroes during the passage are scarcely to be enumerated or conceived. They are far more violently affected by seasickness than Europeans. It frequently terminates in death, especially among the women. But the exclusion of fresh air is among the most intolerable. For the purpose of admitting this needful refreshment, most of the ships in the slave trade are provided, between the decks, with five or six air-ports on each side of the ship, of about five inches in length and four in breadth. But whenever the sea is rough and the rain heavy it becomes necessary to shut these and every other conveyance by which the air is admitted. The fresh air being thus excluded, the Negroes' rooms soon grow intolerable hot. The confined air, rendered noxious by the effluvia exhaled from their bodies and being repeatedly breathed, soon produces fevers and [diarrhea] which generally carries off great numbers of them.

During the voyages I made, I was frequently witness to the fatal effects of this exclusion of fresh air. I will give one instance, as it serves to convey some idea, though a very faint one, of their terrible sufferings. . . . Some wet and blowing weather having occasioned the port-holes to be shut and the grating to be covered, [diarrheas] and fevers among the Negroes ensued. While they were in this situation, I frequently went down among them till at length their room became so extremely hot as to be only bearable for a very short time. But the excessive heat was not the only thing that rendered their situation intolerable. The deck, that is the floor of their rooms, was so covered with the blood and mucus which had proceeded from them in consequence of the [diarrhea], that it resembled a slaughter-house. It is not in the power of the human imagination to picture a situation more dreadful or disgusting. Numbers of the slaves having fainted, they were carried upon deck where several of them died and the rest with great difficulty were restored. It had nearly proved fatal to me also. The climate was too warm to admit the wearing of any clothing but a shirt and that I had pulled off before I went down. . . . In a quarter of an hour I was so overcome with the heat, stench and foul air that I nearly fainted, and it was only with assistance I could get back on deck. The consequence was that I soon after fell sick of the same disorder from which I did not recover for several months.

Of course, the slaves were in these conditions for weeks at a time. Falconbridge told of a worse situation on a Liverpool ship that, though smaller than the one just described, took on six hundred slaves, who "were so crowded that they were obliged to lie one upon another. This caused such a mortality among them that without meeting with unusually bad weather or having a longer voyage than common, nearly one half of them died before the ship arrived in the West Indies."

Falconbridge's description of where the sick and dying were put is a further horror:

> The place allotted for the sick Negroes is under the half deck, where they lie on the bare planks. By this means those who are emaciated frequently have their skin and even their flesh entirely rubbed off, by the motion of the ship, from the prominent parts of the shoulders, elbows and hips so as to render the bones quite bare. And some of them, by constantly lying in the blood and mucus that had flowed from those afflicted with the flux and which is generally so violent as to prevent their being kept clean, having their flesh much sooner rubbed off than those who have only to contend with the mere friction of the ship. The excruciating pain which the poor sufferers feel from being obliged to continue in such a dreadful situation, frequently for several weeks, in case they happen to live so long, is not to be conceived or described.

And finally, the point of all of this was to sell human beings. We can hardly be surprised that the men who were responsible for the sins of capturing and transporting these poor souls might engage in unscrupulous tactics in selling them. Falconbridge described "various deceptions at use in the disposal of sick slaves":

> Many of these must excite in every humane mind the liveliest sensations of horror. I have been well informed that a Liverpool captain boasted of his having cheated some Jews by the following stratagem. A lot of slaves afflicted with the flux, being about to be landed for sale, he directed the ship's surgeons to stop the anus of each of them with oakum. Thus prepared they were landed and taken to the accustomed place of sale, where, being unable to stand but for a very short time they were usually permitted to sit. The buyers, when they examine them, oblige them to stand up in order to see if there be any discharge; and when they do not perceive this appearance they consider it as a symptom of recovery. In the present instance, such an appearance being

prevented, the bargain was struck and the slaves were accordingly sold. But it was not long before discovery ensued. The excruciating pain which the prevention of a discharge of such an acrimonious nature occasioned, not being able to be borne by the poor wretches, the temporary obstruction was removed and the deluded purchasers were speedily convinced of the imposition.

CHAPTER 9

THE *ZONG* INCIDENT

Anne liceat invitos in servitutem dare?

T he news that Olaudah Equiano breathlessly brought to Granville Sharp concerned the following.

On September 6, 1781, the *Zong,* a slave ship of 107 tons, set sail from the coast of Africa headed for Jamaica. Beneath its decks were crammed 470 slaves, horribly packed together as in the method described by Falconbridge. Even before beginning this overlong journey, many of the captured had been held in the ship's hold for weeks before it actually sailed. Slave ships would cruise up and down the African coast, buying slaves wherever they could, and often the process took weeks before the traders felt that they had enough and could set sail across the Atlantic. When they did finally make the crossing, the woefully inexperienced captain of the *Zong,* one Luke Collingwood, made so many navigational errors that the nightmarish trip took four months, far longer than usual.

As the weeks of the extra-long voyage dragged on, many more slaves died than was usual. At the three-month mark, sixty of them had died—a rather high mortality rate, but certainly not among the worst. Dead slaves, incidentally, were forced overboard, and it was a known fact that, uncoincidentally, sharks in great numbers were found in the sea lanes plied by these slave ships. Many of those who hadn't died, however, looked as though they soon would. Captain Collingwood's navigational failures would cost him a pretty penny, because most of the payment for slave-ship captains was a percentage of the ship's overall profits. Every slave who died would bring zero profits—and surely many more would die before they made landfall. In addition, any sick or half-dead slave delivered to Jamaica would bring close to no money, and many of the hundreds of slaves who were still alive belowdecks fell into this category.

Collingwood knew that just as any slave who died "naturally" brought no money, any slave who was killed in an insurrection also brought no money—for insurrection was considered the fault of the captain, whose job it was to keep his captives properly chained and subdued. But perhaps there still was a legal way around his difficulties: Collingwood knew that if a slave died in what was called a "Peril of the Sea"—meaning something beyond the captain's control—then the monetary value of that slave was covered by the insurance underwriters. The price for each slave was set at £30, something in the neighborhood of $4,000 of today's money. It was at this point that Collingwood came up with a novel piece of thinking. It was certainly grotesque, even by the brutal standards of the day, but it was perfectly legal and had a compelling logic to it, though it had never been tried before.

Collingwood gathered his officers and explained the situation. He then ordered them to haul the sickest slaves out of the hold, remove their shackles, and throw them—the sick slaves, not the expensive shackles—overboard. Each drowned soul would turn a pure profit. Once you'd killed them, they couldn't die on board and rob you of the price for which you would sell them in Jamaica. Collingwood knew that maritime law allowed a captain to jettison some of his cargo if he felt it was necessary in order to save the remainder. He instructed the sailors, if ever asked, to say that the ship had been running low on water owing to the length of the journey. Throwing some dying slaves overboard so that the others could survive simply made good business sense.

At first some of the crew refused to carry out the order, for even men inured to evils unthinkable to us today could see the plain horror of what had been suggested. But slave-ship captains were not running a democracy. The sailors knew that disobeying a captain on his ship might well result in any number of consequences as horrible to them as drowning some dying Africans. And so, that day, as the *Zong* sailed toward Jamaica, the crew threw fifty-four of the sickest captives into the endless ocean. Because these slaves were so sick, some of them drowned immediately. Others were surely not so fortunate. That night in his bunk, turning the events of the day over in his mind, Collingwood must have been quite satisfied to think that he'd improved the ship's profits by £1,620.

The next day—or the day after, it's not clear—another batch of sick slaves, though obviously not as sick as the previous batch, were selected and brought out of the hold and onto the deck. One cannot begin to imagine what was going through the minds of these Africans, many of whom had absolutely no idea where they were headed or why they had been captured. Part of the worst horror of the slave's initial experiences had to do with his or her sheer fear of the unknown. Were these men or demons who had enchained them and treated them thus? Had they left the land of the living? Most of them had never seen an ocean before. Forty-two of them were now selected, taken on deck, and forcibly thrown into the ocean, increasing the *Zong*'s guaranteed profits by a further £1,260.

On the third day, thirty-six more slaves were selected to be a part of Collingwood's plan to improve the investors' profits. But this last group was the liveliest yet. Perhaps they had deduced their fate beforehand. In any case, they fought back. Consequently, twenty-six of them had to be shackled before they were thrown overboard to drown. But ten of them escaped being shackled and leapt overboard on their own, without chains. One of these sick men who had jumped overboard had enough strength to grab on to a rope hanging over the ship's side and then climb back on board, undetected. It was he who furnished many of the details of these events.

As Collingwood had predicted, the *Zong*'s underwriters covered the unfortunate loss of "cargo." But what he hadn't predicted was that they afterward decided to contest the claims in court. The chief mate, guilt-ridden over his role in the events, testified for the insurance company and all was revealed, including the fact that it had rained plenty during the voyage and the water rationing rationale was a simple fiction. But somehow the court still found in favor of Collingwood and the *Zong*. The insurers filed an appeal, and at this point Granville Sharp entered the scene. He wanted to file a criminal action for murder against those involved, realizing that the events aboard the *Zong* presented an unprecedented opportunity to, at last, now turn the British law against the slave traders.

Amazingly, the judge was again Lord Mansfield, who had equivocated in the Somerset case some eleven years before. What must he have thought to again see Granville Sharp in his courtroom? Regrettably, Granville this time did not get the better of Mansfield. Mansfield coolly ruled that nothing at all had been amiss in what took place aboard the *Zong*. From the point of view of the law, he said, it was just "as if horses had been thrown overboard." Case closed.

But Granville Sharp couldn't be accused of taking his cues from intellectually lazy judges. The deliberate drowning of 131 human beings, and for profit, was a grotesque abomination against God, not to say an unconscionable blot on the British legal system. Sharp would do whatever he could, and the first thing he did now was write a host of letters to numerous clergymen across the country, informing them of the monstrous details of the case. Some of them preached about it in their sermons, and thus word of the murders and the subsequent legal travesty spread. When news of the *Zong* incident reached a very prominent Anglican minister named Peter Peckard, he was profoundly affected. Peckard had been made vice chancellor of Cambridge in 1785, and his growing horror of the slave trade—abetted by his fresh knowledge of the *Zong* incident—caused him to do something that would have very far-reaching results indeed. The vice chancellor set the topic for the university's annual Latin essay prize, a contest so terribly prestigious that the winner usually beamed with pride all the way to his grave. Peckard now indulged his growing abolitionist passion and in 1785 set the question at: *Anne liceat invitos in servitutem dare?* Is it lawful to enslave others against their will? The winning essay answering this provocative question would play a huge role in the cause of abolition.

That year the winner was a divinity student on scholarship named Thomas Clarkson, of St. John's College, which Wilberforce had attended a few years earlier. Clarkson was a devout, twenty-

five-year-old Christian who had not previously been especially interested in the subject of slavery and its lawfulness. But in the process of
throwing himself into the subject with the extreme zeal that is born
of academic ambition, the young scholar discovered things about the
slave trade that he might rather not have known. The maimed parade
of horrors that passed through Clarkson's mind during this period
changed him utterly. In the course of chasing an academic distinction, he came to know what few men in his day knew: the full scope
of the monstrous traffic in human flesh that had continued for millennia and that was flourishing just then in the British Empire.

When his studies had been completed, Clarkson left Cambridge on
horseback and headed for London, where he planned to pursue a career
in the Church. But thoughts of what he had learned tortured him as he
rode. He tried and tried to put the nauseous, sadistic images out of his
mind, and failed. He rode on. While riding through Herefordshire, at a
spot near Wades Mill, he got off his horse and sat down by the side of the
road, overwhelmed. It was a moment he would remember for the rest
of his long life. For it was there and then, on the side of the road, that it
first occurred to Thomas Clarkson that if the things he had uncovered
and written about in his prize-winning essay were a reality in the world
in which he now sat, it was time someone put an end to them.

Clarkson resolved then to translate his Latin essay into English
and distribute it. In the course of his efforts he soon met some of the
others who had been working in this cause for years, among them
Granville Sharp and Olaudah Equiano. A critical moment in the
abolitionist cause was quickly approaching. Like-minded men and
women were finding each other, sharing their stories, and beginning
to formulate strategies. Clarkson also soon met James Ramsay, who
knew Wilberforce and who two years earlier at the Teston home of
the Middletons had been instrumental in bringing the cause of the
slaves to Wilberforce's attention.

❧

The year 1783 was an important year for abolition. It was the year
Wilberforce had first spoken with Ramsay, and the year the *Zong* case
had riveted the public to the issue of the slave trade and drawn them

into it as never before. It was also the year that Quaker abolitionists formed a six-member committee "for the relief and liberation of the negro slaves in the West Indies and for the discouragement of the Slave Trade on the coast of Africa." Granville Sharp soon became involved with them, as did Equiano. Something like a movement was on the verge of being born. Those involved in it, however, lacked two crucial assets: a solid knowledge of slavery in the West Indies and some kind of real political influence. We know that Sharp, being Sharp, and the Quakers, being Quakers, prayed. And waited for God's answer.

The two men who would provide what was missing were William Wilberforce and Dr. James Ramsay, and the man who would connect them to each other was Wilberforce's old friend from St. John's College, Gerard Edwards. While still very young, Edwards, a member of the old Goostree's Gang, had married the daughter of Lady Middleton and Captain Sir Charles Middleton, who was the comptroller of the Royal Navy. The Middletons' Kent country home in Teston was called Barham Court, and Wilberforce went there many times in the early 1780s to visit Edwards. The Middletons were Methodists, and it's interesting to think that years after his early lapse from Methodism, and some years before meeting Milner and rediscovering his faith, Wilberforce was often in the home of these serious Christians.

Sir Charles and Lady Margaret Middleton were two more vital players in the movement to end the slave trade in the British Empire. It's hard not to wonder at the thin threads by which world-changing movements sometimes hang. Lady Middleton seems to have been one of those threads. Margaret Gambier was a young girl when she found faith through the ministry of George Whitefield. She was the niece of a Navy captain, and one of this captain's lieutenants was Charles Middleton, who met Margaret in the 1750s and married her in 1761. Middleton said that "all I possess of religion" was a tribute to his wife. An accomplished painter and musician, she was friends with the painter Joshua Reynolds, the actor David Garrick, and Dr. Johnson. Margaret Middleton was also friends with Hannah More and was influential in drawing the writer to a deeper faith and to the abolitionist cause.

As the story goes, Sir Charles Middleton was in the British West Indies in 1759 when he ordered the surgeon on his ship, the *Arundel,* to

Painting by John Russell, oil on canvas, 1770, courtesy of National Portrait Gallery, London

Wilberforce in "Van Dyke" costume at age eleven (1770) at the Wimbledon home of his aunt and uncle, Hannah and William Wilberforce. John Russell, the artist, called him "sweet young Wilberforce" and said that already at this age he "had the appearance of conversion upon his soul."

Portrait of the abolitionist as a young man: Wilberforce at age twenty-nine.

A widely reproduced 1810 portrait of Wilberforce, age fifty-one, three years after the abolition of the slave trade.

The English poet William Cowper (1731–1800) was one of Wilberforce's favorites. He happily lent his poetical talents to the abolitionist cause with "The Negro's Lament." Cowper's close friend John Newton suggested that he write hymns to alleviate his depression; between them, they wrote nearly three hundred.

John Newton, the "old African blasphemer," former slave-ship captain, and author of the hymn "Amazing Grace." He knew Wilberforce as a boy, and Wilberforce "reverenced him as a father." Years later, after Wilberforce's "Great Change," Newton counseled him to remain in politics, "for the good of the nation."

George Whitefield (1714–70), a one-man salvation army, had an incalculable influence on eighteenth-century England and America. He could preach to thirty thousand at a time, a figure verified by his Philadelphian friend Benjamin Franklin.

Reprinted in A. B. Hyde, *The Story of Methodism Throughout the World* (Springfield, MA: Willey & Co., 1889).

The great eighteenth-century evangelist John Wesley (1703–1791) is pictured three days before his death, writing his famous letter to Wilberforce: "Unless God has raised you up for this very thing, you will be worn out by the opposition of men and devils. But if God be for you, who can be against you?"

JOHN WESLEY ON HIS DEATH-BED WRITING THE LETTER TO WILBERFORCE.

High-society doyenne, salon hostess, and cultural arbiter Madame de Staël (1766–1817) was greatly taken with Wilberforce, pronouncing him "the wittiest man in all of England."

In 1783 Wilberforce sojourned to France with Pitt and Eliot. At Fontainebleu, he met the ill-fated monarch Louis XVI and described him as a "clumsy, strange figure in immense boots."

"Mrs." Hannah More (1745–1833) in a 1789 portrait. One of Wilberforce's closest allies in both of his "great objects," More stood at the center of the London literary world. She was hailed by Samuel Johnson as "the most skilled versificatrix in the English Language" and later denounced by Cobbett as "the Old Bishop in Petticoats" for her religious writings.

Granville Sharp (1735–1813) was every enemy of justice's worst nightmare and one of the prime movers in the abolitionist cause. A devout Christian, linguistic genius, and accomplished musician, Sharp could play two flutes at once and often signed his name G#.

King George III (1738–1820) was a model of uxoriousness, standing in sharp contrast to most nobles of his era, especially his sons. He and his wife, Queen Charlotte, seem to have had a genuinely happy marriage and were the parents of fifteen children, the most of any British monarch. George was initially friendly toward Wilberforce's abolitionist efforts and would ask him, "How are your negroes?" but later cooled toward him for his stand against the French war.

His Dandified Lese Majesty King George IV (1762–1830), here pictured
bursting the seams of social propriety.

William Pitt the Younger (1759–1806), a close friend of Wilberforce's, became Britain's youngest prime minister at age twenty-four. Though he urged Wilberforce to take up the cause of abolition in Parliament, Pitt did not live to see its success.

Hickel's painting of Pitt addressing the House of Commons on the French declaration of war in 1793. Wilberforce sits behind Pitt, in the second row, just to the right of the supporting column. Charles James Fox, with hat and cane, sits directly across from Pitt, in the first row of the Opposition bench.

Charles James Fox (1749–1806) was an eloquent friend of abolition, but politically opportunistic and ambitiously dissolute. For his role in leading the Prince of Wales—later George IV—astray, and for his pioneering work in late eighteenth-century British decadence in general, Fox was King George III's bitterest enemy and formed the macaronic Whig half of that living taxidermic prank called the "Fox-North Coalition." Though seemingly destined to be portrayed in film by the great British actor Robert Morley, the honor would elude him.

Lord Frederick North (1732–92). An embattled, spheroidal figure, pictured before achieving final circumference, North led Britain's hard-line approach toward the American colonies and is chiefly known as the man who lost them. Wilberforce was early on renowned for his ability to "set a table at a roar" with his spot-on mimicry of North but was persuaded to desist from this habit by an elder colleague. North was nicknamed Boreas—"North wind"—for his deep voice, and upon hearing of Cornwallis's defeat at Yorktown, he is supposed to have said, "Oh, it is all over! It is all over!"

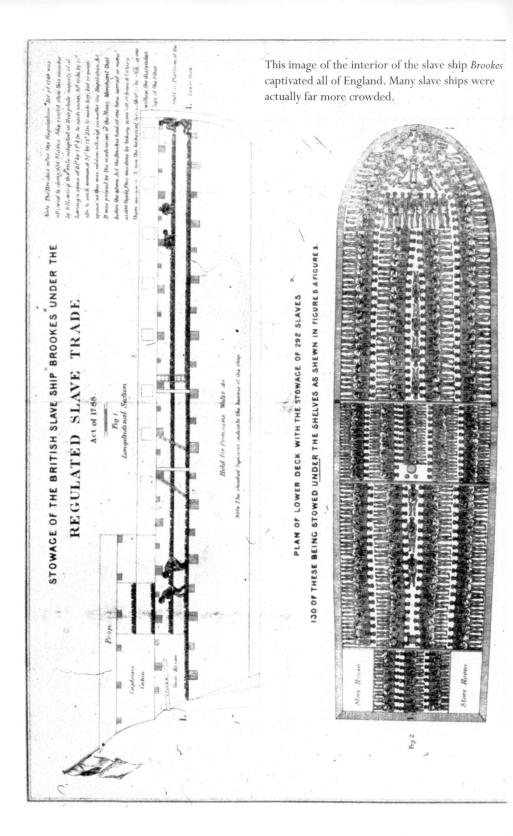

This image of the interior of the slave ship *Brookes* captivated all of England. Many slave ships were actually far more crowded.

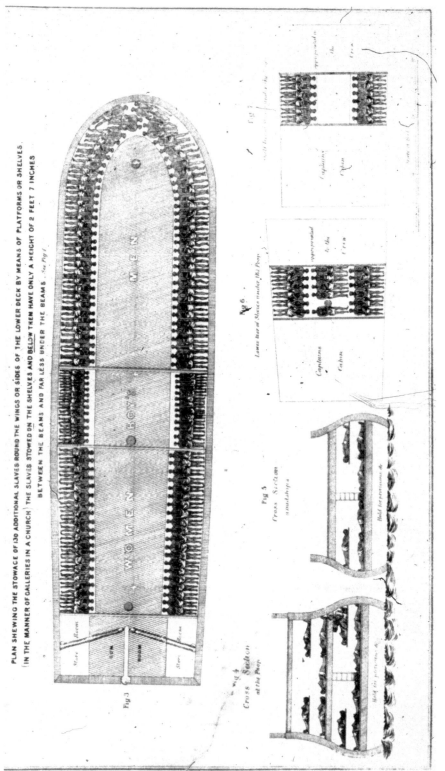

PLAN SHEWING THE STOWAGE OF 130 ADDITIONAL SLAVES ROUND THE WINGS OR SIDES OF THE LOWER DECK BY MEANS OF PLATFORMS OR SHELVES. (IN THE MANNER OF GALLERIES IN A CHURCH) THE SLAVES STOWED ON THE SHELVES AND BELOW THEM HAVE ONLY A HEIGHT OF 2 FEET 7 INCHES BETWEEN THE BEAMS AND FAR LESS UNDER THE BEAMS. See Fig 1.

MEN

BOYS

WOMEN

Store Room

Stores Room

Fig 3

Fig 4
Cross Section
at the Poop

Fig 5
Cross Section
amidships

Hold for provisions &c

Hold for provisions &c

Fig 6
Lower Tier of Slaves under the Poop.

Captains
Cabin

Fig 7

Captains
Cabin

In Austa Malinda French, *Slavery in South Carolina and the Ex-Slaves; or, The Port Royal Mission* (New York: Negro University Press, 1969), (image is in the public domain)

The "legal" drowning of 132 Africans, thrown overboard from the infamous slave ship *Zong,* sparked the abolitionist movement in England. Lord Mansfield, the judge, said it was "just as if horses were killed."

The Colonial Williamsburg Foundation

The image that stopped a thousand ships. Josiah Wedgwood's poignant antislavery cameo was reproduced on brooches, hat pins, cuff links, watch fobs, bracelets, and even in sealing wax on letters. It popularized the message of abolition throughout Britain and presaged the logos, campaign buttons, and bumper stickers of our own day.

board a slave ship, the *Swift,* which had just been recaptured from the French. The surgeon was James Ramsay, and what he and Middleton saw in the reeking hold of the *Swift* that day shocked and horrified them both. We are safe in assuming that it was not much different from the scenes described by Alexander Falconbridge. An injury soon after this caused Ramsay to leave the Navy and seek employment onshore. He settled on the island of St. Christopher (today called St. Kitt's) and was ordained as an Anglican clergyman, serving as rector to two parishes. He was also at that time medical supervisor for the sugar plantations. The horrors this sensitive soul witnessed during this time burned a deep and prayerful desire in him to do all he could to help the slaves. He welcomed them into his church and held Bible studies for them, which very quickly earned him the undying hatred of the island's white plantation owners. Little could he have known during these years that he would one day be a crucial link in the abolitionist movement.

In 1781 Ramsay's old commander, Sir Charles, invited him to leave the West Indies and become the vicar of the Teston parish church, which was just down the hill from the Middletons' home, Barham Court. Ramsay accepted the position and returned to England. At Teston, he spoke often and passionately with the Middletons about the horrors of slavery. After Lady Middleton and Bishop Porteus both urged him to set his experiences and thoughts down on paper, Ramsay began writing his book-length *Essay on the Treatment and Conversion of Slaves in the British Sugar Colonies.* It was in 1783, while Ramsay was writing this essay, that Wilberforce first met him through Gerard Edwards. Doubtless hoping that Wilberforce, as an up-and-coming MP, would do something, Ramsay engaged him in a serious discussion of the West Indian slaves. Ramsay feared the consequences of publishing what he was writing—and rightly so, as we will hear—but he published it nonetheless. Its publication in 1784 produced much the same effect as turning a hose on a nest of hornets. All hell was loosed upon Ramsay, and the battle in earnest had now, at long last, begun.

In 1786 abolition's cause again moved forward. This was the year Clarkson's essay was published. The Quaker publishers sent a copy to Ramsay, whose essay they had also published. Clarkson had never heard of Ramsay, but after Ramsay read the essay, he invited Clarkson to stay with him at Teston.

In July 1786 the Middletons invited both Bishop Porteus and Benjamin La Trobe to Teston. Lady Middleton had wanted them to meet, for La Trobe was a leader of the "Moravian Brethren," who were the only missionaries to the slaves. The Moravians were extraordinary Christians who, like the Quakers in that day and like Wesley's Methodists, ignored the high-toned sneering of the theologically compromised Church of England religious leaders, and quietly did what their faith in God called them to do. Porteus was that rare exception among Anglican bishops, being theologically orthodox.

It was at a dinner that summer at Teston that Clarkson publicly for the first time declared his decision to give himself full-time to the cause of ending slavery, and he would from that point forward be unflagging in his efforts to stir up public zeal by distributing copies of his essay.

Lady Middleton's prominent role in promoting the cause of abolition is undeniable. Ramsay and Sir Charles Middleton had begun to see that some sort of parliamentary action would be needed to accomplish anything, but it was Lady Middleton who pushed things forward at a breakfast that autumn. Speaking to her husband in front of some others, she said: "Indeed, I think, Sir Charles, you ought to bring the subject before the House, and demand a Parliamentary enquiry into the nature of that hideous traffic, so disgraceful to the British character."

Middleton didn't think himself the right man, for his gifts as an orator were not what they would need to be to advocate for something as unpopular as abolition, but his wife's comment led to a wider discussion of who in Parliament might be the right man for the job. Not surprisingly, Wilberforce's name came up. Shortly thereafter, Middleton wrote him a letter, but the reply was not dispositive. Wilberforce said he felt the great importance of the subject and didn't think himself equal to it; he would not positively rule it out, however, and promised to visit the Middletons sometime soon to discuss it. He visited Barham Court in the early winter of 1786–87.

At about that time, Wilberforce had put Lauriston House, his Wimbledon villa, on the market and had bought a house located at

4 Palace Yard, just across the King's Entrance to the House of Lords. It would be like commuting to his own backyard.

It was here, one day early in the new year 1787, at 4 Palace Yard, that Thomas Clarkson came to call, leaving behind a copy of his essay. A few days later he called again, and he and Wilberforce met. If ever there was an important moment in the abolitionist movement, the first meeting of these two men must be one. Each recalled it somewhat differently. Wilberforce had thought a number of times before then about the slave trade and had a few months before received the Middletons' letter. That seems to have been the first time the question was put to him directly about whether he would take up the cause in Parliament. He had also met with the Middletons very recently to discuss the subject, and there can be no question that during that time at Teston their goal was to persuade him to take up the cause.

Clarkson was under the impression that he had brought abolition to Wilberforce's attention with his essay. Though that was not the case, there can be no question that Clarkson was a prime mover. He called on Wilberforce many times in the next months, they exchanged information, and Clarkson reported back to the Quakers on his conversations. It seems clear that Wilberforce was already seriously considering parliamentary action at this time. It also seems clear that Clarkson didn't realize there were other forces besides himself at work, and so he felt compelled to push Wilberforce to agree publicly that he would move things forward in Commons.

With the idea of getting a firm and public promise of parliamentary action, Clarkson invited Wilberforce to a dinner on March 13 at the home of a wealthy Lincolnshire landowner, Bennet Langdon, who was six-foot-six and storklike in appearance. Langdon had been a friend of Dr. Johnson's, and at the dinner that evening were Johnson's Boswell, the painter Joshua Reynolds, Sir Charles Middleton, and two other MPs. Wilberforce was asked during the evening whether he would put forward a motion for abolition. He responded, somewhat typically, with a politician's firm maybe—in effect, a yes with two escape clauses. He said he would do so provided no one more suitable could be found, and once he had had more time to gather his facts.

But Clarkson—hearing the assent more than the equivocation— reported to his Quaker colleagues that Wilberforce had made a public avowal of his commitment to take action on the issue, and it has often been treated as though that dinner was the place where Wilberforce made that decision. It doesn't seem to have been. Wilberforce was famous for considering every side of an issue, often to a fault. He would do this out loud while speaking in Parliament, seeming to dandle every decision like an infant. But surely this issue was more important than any other issue he would decide, and he wasn't about to be bullied or badgered into a decision on how to spend the rest of his life, or most of it. He would need to know God's mind, as he would put it, and this is what he was trying to determine in all of these essentially noncommittal conversations. Wilberforce was painfully conscious of having wasted years doing little or nothing, and he was steadily coming to the conclusion that abolition was indeed that single cause to which God was calling him in Parliament, and the very thing to which he would apply himself, ending the years of having failed to apply himself to anything meaningful. But Wilberforce was not about to leap into the fray thoughtlessly; he would first "count the cost," and at the March 13 dinner at Langdon's house he was still in the process of doing so.

Nevertheless, the pressure to decide mounted. Exactly one month after the dinner at Langdon's, Bishop Porteus wrote to Wilberforce to say that the information in Ramsay's incendiary essay was correct—a Mr. Stuart, very reputable, had corroborated it. If anything, according to this Stuart, Ramsay's version had been conservative in its descriptions of the horrors of West Indian slavery. All was seemingly now in hand to bring the issue into Parliament decisively, with a strong case for abolition. But still another month would pass before Wilberforce would gird his loins and wade into the waters of the Rubicon.

Wilberforce family tradition set the date at which he irrevocably made up his mind as May 12. Wilberforce was that day visiting Pitt at his great country home, Holwood Estate, and while he and Pitt were taking a walk they stopped to sit down and rest beneath a vast and ancient oak. The national symbolism of the venerable English oak was apt, an aegis over them as they spoke, its great age and size framing them in a kind of historical context. With them was Pitt's first cousin, William Grenville, who would succeed Pitt as prime minister; his

inclusion in this conversation would eventually seem powerfully prescient and providential. Pitt had also been pushing Wilberforce to
make a decision, saying how ideally suited he was for the task. It's
possible that Pitt, having had time to observe the seriousness of his
friend's "Great Change," feared somehow losing Wilberforce and
wanted to be sure to find something that would keep his dearest friend
and ablest ally by his side in Parliament.

"Do not lose time," Pitt famously said, "or the ground will be occupied by another." It's somehow funny to think that Pitt didn't understand that he was dealing with a different man than the one whose
principal motivation had been personal ambition. But what Pitt said
was true enough, for if, as Wilberforce thought, God Himself was
calling him to this task and he shrank from it, God too could find
another to do it, and surely would.

"I well remember," Wilberforce wrote years later, "after a conversation in the open air at the root of an old tree at Holwood, just
above the steep descent into the vale of Keston, I resolved to give
notice on a fit occasion in the house of Commons of my intention to
bring the subject forward."

And thus, history: three men, each named William, each twenty-
seven years old, talking at the base of an ancient oak tree on a hill in
May: one prime minister, one prime-minister-to-be, and one who
would stand from that moment forward at the center of something so
big and beyond any single man that a tree whose life had begun several
centuries earlier, and would continue for nearly two more, was the
humble creature chosen to bear mute witness to the conversation.

CHAPTER 10

ABOLITION OR BUST

" . . . one mass of iniquity
from the beginning to the end."

Now that Wilberforce had openly declared himself—and a bright standard had been raised on the battlefield and could be seen above the fray—the many abolitionist soldiers straggling here and wandering there suddenly had a focus. A battle plan had been drawn up, leaders had been chosen, and victory had been clearly defined as the abolition of the slave trade by a bill in Parliament. The abolitionist movement was in full fan.

On May 22, 1787, Granville Sharp chaired the newly formed Committee for the Abolition of the Slave Trade. Its members decided that as much information as possible on the trade had to be gathered immediately, before it became known that there would be a parliamentary inquiry. Stealth was the order of the day; once it became known there was going to be a parliamentary inquiry, the slave trade interests would do all they could to keep information from getting out, and they could do much. But now there was still time, and Clarkson planned an extensive fact-finding mission to England's slave ports that summer. For his courage in this adventure he deserves eternal praise. It's no surprise to think that there were many

in places like Liverpool and Bristol who hated anyone remotely associated with abolition, much less this fiend Clarkson whose damnable
Latin essay had started much of the trouble that was now beginning
to brew. His life would be threatened on numerous occasions in the
months ahead, but the more he saw of the horrors of the slave trade,
the more his zeal to end it increased. "On whatever branch of the
system I turned my eyes, I found it equally barbarous," he wrote.
"The trade was, in short, one mass of iniquity from the beginning
to the end."

Everywhere he turned there were fresh horrors. He climbed
aboard slave ships and measured the spaces allotted for the slaves; he
purchased the ghastliest implements of restraint and torture, from
manacles and shackles to thumbscrews and branding irons. There
was a device used to pry open the mouths of slaves who refused to
eat. Clarkson spoke to anyone who would talk on the subject and
amassed endless tales of cruelty, with specifics. All he uncovered
simply goaded him to uncover more. The relentless Clarkson is one
of those figures whose efforts seem genuinely inconceivable: before
he was through he had interviewed twenty thousand sailors.

One of the things that became quite clear to Clarkson and to
Wilberforce was that the slave trade, like all evil systems, corrupted
and ruined the lives of all who touched it. It seemed that nearly everyone involved in it had somehow been duped into it: many were
kidnapped and pressed into it against their will, while others were
forced into it to pay debts, which somehow never got paid. The whole
slave trade was like some kind of seaborne gulag in which one level
of prisoners (called sailors) were brutalized physically and mentally
by psychotic and pathologically cruel captains, and another level of
prisoners (called slaves) were brutalized physically and mentally by
both of the above. As Wilberforce, Clarkson, Sharp, and the others sifted through their findings, the most surprising evidence they
uncovered was that the trade degraded and harmed the sailors, the
white Englishmen. The lie that the traders and the West Indian planters put forward was that the slave trade was an excellent way to train
young men for the Navy—a claim that made service on a slave ship
sound like an issue of national security. Everything Clarkson uncovered, however, showed the opposite: the white sailors involved were

nearly always miserable and would have done anything to escape, but they feared the lash themselves and were powerless.

It was also the case that the sailors on board slave ships died of the same diseases that killed the slaves, and just as often. All of these facts were quite simply unknown to the British populace, and it was hoped that this evidence would move them, as well as those politicians who were still open-minded on the subject, who were not in the pocket of the planters. As Clarkson's work progressed, he came to the inconceivable conclusion that the mortality rate among the English sailors on board slave ships was 25 percent annually. The sailors themselves, of course, came to know what their odds were, but by then it was too late. They could no more escape from the system than could the slaves. This and other horrors were the dirty secrets of the trade, and to uncover them was an ugly and dangerous business.

Wilberforce knew that the appalling conditions under which white Englishmen worked in the slave trade would be a powerful argument for ending it, a way to convince the public and members of Parliament that it was anything but what its proponents claimed, a vital and excellent training ground for British sailors. Wilberforce said that far from being a "nursery of seamen, [it] may rather be termed their grave."

In Liverpool, Clarkson came upon the unimaginable but verified story of a slave captain who had flogged his own steward for two and a quarter hours. Not surprisingly, the man died. Stories like this piled up until the strain began to tell on Clarkson. "I was agonised to think that this Trade could last another day," he wrote. "I was in a state of agitation from morning to night."

During his travels, Clarkson came upon Alexander Falconbridge, part of whose account of the Middle Passage we have already read. Falconbridge was only too willing to tell Clarkson of the horrors he'd witnessed, and he accompanied Clarkson for much of the summer. Falconbridge always carried a pistol, for he knew far better than the young Clarkson what malevolent forces they were up against in their work.

It needs to be explained why those in the abolition movement were not intent on abolishing slavery altogether, but merely the slave trade. There is no simple answer, but part of the answer has to do with strategy. To come out openly for the abolition of slavery at that point was seen as a bridge too far. To discuss even ending the trade was at that early point seen as economic insanity. It fell to Wilberforce to demonstrate that abolition was the right thing to do not only morally but also economically—or at least to show that eventually it would be the right answer economically, that Britain could bear the short-term costs involved, and that these costs would be justifiable in the longer term.

It was also believed—naively, we now realize—that abolishing the trade would force the planters in the West Indies to treat their slaves better. There being no fresh supply, they would be forced to take care not to work their slaves to death, as they had certainly been doing; they would also be forced to see that the women were healthy enough to bear children and to care for them. The lives of the slaves on the West Indian sugar plantations, if it can be believed, were far worse than the lives of most of the slaves in colonial America. Raising sugar cane and harvesting it was one of the most brutal activities imaginable. The planters indeed worked their slaves to death—and then bought new ones. Wilberforce and the others thought that this practice would change as soon as the trade ended. They were mistaken, but this was the belief behind their initial political strategy.

It was also thought that the slaves were not quite ready for complete emancipation, that they would need to be brought to that point gradually. There was something to be said for this idea from a strictly pragmatic point of view—just as there was something to be said for Mansfield's fear that his ruling in the Somerset case would free fourteen thousand British slaves who would then be unable to care for themselves. But the morality of such pragmatism can hardly be defended.

❦

One way in which Wilberforce thought abolition could most quickly be brought about was through an international agreement with the other countries that participated in the slave trade, principal among them, France. Without an agreement with France, the cause would be hopeless, because the first argument put forward in Parliament against abolition would be that all of the trade that Britain abolished would simply be picked up by the French, their ancient enemy. The British could not think about abandoning something so vital to their economy—or so the pro-slavery forces would argue—if France wouldn't do the same. So Wilberforce and Pitt did all they could to bring that about.

William Eden, the statesman who had been sent to the American colonies during England's dispute with them, was now already in France, and at Wilberforce's and Pitt's behest, he entered into discussions on abolition with de Montmorin, the French foreign minister. Montmorin asked for more information on the trade, and in response Wilberforce wrote him a long letter on November 23. He poured out a torrent of the details they had discovered and debunked some of the propaganda and misinformation that was believed about the trade. For one thing, he disavowed the false claims that most of the slaves sent to the West Indies were criminals saved from execution, or that they were war captives, also probably being saved from execution. If one sincerely believed this, as so many people did, the idea of slavery was hardly worth batting an eye over; it certainly wasn't worth risking the nation's economy. But it was vile propaganda. How many women and children could have been war captives slated for execution? Even when the slaves really were "war captives," it turned out that the "wars" had been started on the flimsiest pretexts by African chiefs crazed with greed and looking for any reason to capture people and sell them at huge profits. The corruption was everywhere. The Africans quickly realized that European slavers were completely unscrupulous and desperate to fill their ships as quickly as possible. The slave traders weren't going to question African tribal leaders about whether the "captives" they were selling had been captured in a conflict that met St. Augustine's standards for a "just war."

One of the things that came out of Wilberforce's investigations was that the slave trade had ravaged and ruined the African economy, and he came to believe that a debt was therefore owed to the African continent. Wilberforce spent the rest of his life trying to help Africa. This is not to say that the behavior of Africans on the issue of the slave trade was morally superior to that of the white Europeans. Everyone was grotesquely guilty, all down the line, including the African chiefs who kidnapped and brutalized anyone they could and who death-marched them to the coasts, where they were sold to others in the trade, who in turn sold them to slave-ship captains, who in turn sold them to West Indian planters, who in turn worked them to death. The captured Africans suffered and died in shocking percentages during every part of the journey from their homes. But Wilberforce rightly saw that it was the Europeans who had instigated this inhuman system and who had heaped endless fuel upon its satanic fires. He would do all he could to repay this debt to the continent of Africa.

By December the strategy regarding France was suddenly changed. Wilberforce now believed that once the British slave trade was abolished the French would come alongside. And at this point he felt that abolition would happen very soon indeed. "As to our probability of success, I assure you I entertain no doubt of it," he wrote to Eden. "The evidence, the glaring justice of the proposition itself; Mr. Pitt's support of the measure, and the Temper of the House, the disposition of which I know rather better than I wished at so early a period, through the indiscreet zeal of some very worthy people who have been rather too chattering and communicative."

Wilberforce was young, and the abolition movement was young too—newborn, in fact, and bursting with energy and naïveté. One old-timer who tried to communicate his less sanguine view of their prospects was the eighty-four-year-old John Wesley. Wesley wrote a letter to Granville Sharp in October 1787. "Ever since I heard of it first, I felt a perfect detestation of the horrid trade," he said, ". . . therefore I cannot but do everything in my power, to forward the glorious Design of your Society. . . . All the opposition which can be made by men who are not encumbered by either Honour, Conscience or Humanity and will rush on . . . through every possible means, to secure their great Goddess Interest." Wesley knew well the viciousness that Sharp and the others were sure to encounter. "In all these difficulties, What a comfort it is to consider (unfashionable as it is) that there is a God! Yea, and that (as little as men think of it!), He still has all power, both in Heaven and on Earth! To Him I commit you and your Glorious Cause, and am, sir, Your affectionate servant, John Wesley."

Wesley had suffered much and knew that those called to battle the evils of the world would suffer. Wilberforce, at twenty-eight, was a supremely brilliant, talented, wealthy, well-connected young man. He had just become a Christian and knew nothing of the battles he would face for his faith and his beliefs. He was as yet untested and could hardly imagine that he would be vilified for trying to improve the lot of his fellow man. He hadn't yet seen that respectable gentlemen and noblemen, when presented with evils and cruelties more horrible than they had ever dreamed, would nonetheless yawn and shrug and turn away, or that, given what seemed an exceedingly clear choice between good and evil, they would choose evil. Such a response was inconceivable to Wilberforce, who was by nature a cheerful and good soul. Because of his own good nature, he could hardly believe that others wouldn't leap to do what was right when they finally knew the facts. He was mistaken.

Wilberforce had read Jesus's words in John's Gospel: "that the light has come into the world, and men loved darkness rather than light, because their deeds were evil. For everyone practicing evil hates the light and does not come to the light, lest his deeds should be exposed." But he had not yet experienced them.

Wilberforce did not yet know that he lived on a planet that was, in Luther's famous phrase, "with devils filled"—that he was part of a rearguard action well behind enemy lines. And so, optimistically, in the final days of December 1787, Wilberforce rose in Commons to announce that early in the new year he would put forward a motion for abolition. He could feel things churning toward victory. The veteran Fox assured him of his support, as did many others. And the people across the land would speak too! Petitions from towns all over England, each covered with thousands of signatures denouncing the trade, were just then being amassed, and they would speak volumes to Parliament of the good sense of the British people. Who then would dare stand athwart this juggernaut and shout, "Stop!"—who?

Well, for one thing, the French now sniffed suspiciously. They suddenly feared that they were being lured into abolition with no

guarantees that the British would follow suit. But Wilberforce's sunniness could not be quenched so easily. "Assure yourself," he wrote
to Eden in January 1788, "that there is no doubt of our success." Two
centuries later, we wince. The sunniness continued. In a letter to a
constituent, he writes: "I perceive with joy that [the Africans'] cause
begins to interest the public, and I trust a flame is kindled that will
not be extinguished till it has done its work."

The line between courageous faith and foolish idealism is, almost
by definition, one angstrom wide. Wilberforce was quite right that
a flame had been kindled and would not go out until it had done its
work, but he had no idea that it would be twenty tortuous years in
the burning before its work was done. And if the "work" in question
was not the abolition of the slave trade but the abolition of slavery itself, the flame would continue burning for another forty-five years.

Then, on February 19, the first serious setback came: Wilberforce
nearly died. He had been ill the previous summer, and had, in fact,
been sick in bed when Clarkson stopped by just before leaving for
his investigative tour. But Wilberforce had recovered. Toward the
beginning of January, six weeks before, he'd been sick again, but had
recovered again and resumed his breakneck pace, both with abolition
and with his proclamation efforts. He'd hoped to introduce the motion for abolition in early February but then realized it would probably be another month or so before they were ready. But now, on the
nineteenth, halting all forward motion, he had a definitive relapse.
He suffered from fevers, exhaustion, and had no appetite. On February 23, he saw a very famous doctor, James Pitcairne, who could
do nothing. Isaac Milner, Wilberforce's truest friend till the end of
his life, canceled his Cambridge lectures and raced to Wilberforce's
side, where he now plied his skills as a medical doctor.

Soon Wilberforce felt well enough to resume some work, and on
March 4 he went to John Thornton's house in Clapham. Having sold
Lauriston House in Wimbledon, he now stayed at Clapham whenever
he needed the fresh air of the country, the "country" in those days being
a mere four miles from downtown London. But when Wilberforce returned to London, still not feeling well, the doctors insisted that he go
to Bath for the waters. They seem to have believed that in fact there
was no hope, that Wilberforce was dying. The waters at Bath might

change his condition, and if not, at least he would be more comfortable there. But in London on March 8, before he had the chance to leave for Bath, Wilberforce collapsed completely. The doctors diagnosed an "absolute decay of all the digestive tracts." The fevers and diarrheas were recurrent, and the worst was assumed: he would die soon.

Wilberforce's sister and mother were summoned, and another famous doctor, Richard Warren, entered the scene. Dr. Warren's pronouncement was dour: "That little fellow with his callico guts cannot possibly survive a twelve-month." But Warren was known to be a pessimist, so other doctors were consulted too. Their combined thoughts on Wilberforce's longevity were even less cheery. "He has not the stamina," they declared, "to last a fortnight." But this little fellow, "with his callico guts," would go on, as we know, to make monkeys of them all, living another four and a half decades. Indeed, already by March 27 it was clear that the grave had been averted and he was somewhat on the mend. But what had happened? What had plucked our fragile hero from Charon's boat just as it was about to set sail across the black water? It seems that the lifesaver was a new miracle drug, one that was much prescribed in the last decades of the eighteenth century, though it has since fallen out of favor in professional medical circles. And the password is? Opium.

The doctors of Wilberforce's day were quick to prescribe opiates and laudanum, its liquid form, and they did so now. Wilberforce would take it for the rest of his life. There is no question that it alleviated his symptoms now and at many other times in the future. Nor is there any dispute that it had generally deleterious effects on his overall health over the years, eventually making his bad eyesight much worse and, to some extent, affecting his mind. But unlike most people who took it regularly, Wilberforce did not appear to become addicted to it; he quite admirably managed to keep his dosage from increasing over the decades.

And so, feeling better, Wilberforce at last, on April 8, made the trip to Bath. The opiates had improved his symptoms but not their cause, which is thought to have been ulcerative colitis. Before Wilberforce left London for Bath, Pitt promised his ailing friend that he would make a motion for abolition in his absence, something that greatly endeared him to Wilberforce. Wilberforce remained at Bath for a month, drinking and taking, we cannot doubt, the miraculously ameliorative waters that have been there enjoyed by persons of good taste since antiquity.

Meanwhile, Pitt and Bishop Porteus supervised the Privy Council inquiry into abolition. On May 9, Pitt made a resolution that the House should officially investigate the trade in the following session. He cannily gave a speech feigning some neutrality on the issue, but said that he hoped Wilberforce would soon recover and be able to "resume his charge." Fox was not so careful, nor did he need to be. "I have no scruple to declare at the onset," he said, "that my opinion of this momentous business is that the Slave Trade ought not to be regulated but destroyed." Edmund Burke also pronounced himself for abolition. That two members of Parliament so politically distant from each other could both come together against the slave trade was certainly impressive.

The West Indian interests in Parliament were clearly squirming in their buff-colored breeches but said nothing, nor did they even vote against Pitt's resolution. They would keep their powder dry, having obviously decided to return to the question at a more opportune time.

Wilberforce had by now quitted the miraculous waters of Bath for Cambridge and the genuinely restorative company of his mountainous medicine man, Isaac Milner. Wilberforce stayed at his old college, St. John's, for the month. "Lived more regularly and quietly than I had done for a long time," he writes in his diary. "Chiefly with Milner in the evenings."

Back in Parliament, on May 26, William Dolben, the MP for Oxford, now served up a steaming heap of trouble for the slave interests. It seems that Dolben had visited a slave ship docked on the Thames and was deeply disturbed to see with his own eyes the cramped spaces allotted for the slaves. The horror of what he saw prompted him to put forward a bill to regulate the number of slaves a ship could carry, based on its reported tonnage. For the first time now, the slave interests would show their colors. They knew that the noose, however slowly, was tightening around their necks. Any inquiry into the dark corners of their despicable world was sure to turn opinion against them. They had previously said that the slaves

were afforded plenty of room—and they had come up with the first
of many ingenious and bold lies. They had said that the ships' holds
were larger than what was reported, claiming that the sizes were deliberately *under*-reported in order to pay lower port dues. But now,
because of Dolben, this clever invention had been exposed. Parliament now also learned that at least 5 to 10 percent of all slaves died
during the Middle Passage, and evidence was duly presented of a
voyage on which fully one-third of all the slaves had died. In time the
reality would be shown to be even worse than these numbers con-
veyed, but the House of Commons was hearing these things for the
very first time and was quite affected. It was as if Dolben's bill had
suddenly shone a light into a damp, never-before-disturbed snake pit
to reveal a writhing mass of surprised serpents therein.

The slave interests acquitted themselves particularly poorly at
this time. They were desperate and from this point on would say
and do anything to forestall the inevitable, without scruple. They
behaved like children who switch stories every time the current
story is contradicted with new facts, unaware of their own self-
incrimination. And they really *would* say anything. Indeed, Dolben
now quoted Liverpool shipowners who had claimed that the most
crowded ships were actually healthier. And now the plantation interests said that any regulation whatsoever of the British slave trade
would only put British-owned slaves—and money—into the hands
of French slavers. This was the most desperate ploy of all—playing
the "French card."

But it didn't work; it backfired. Pitt was so disgusted by what he
was hearing that he now rose to give an inspiring and impassioned
speech, saying that if the slave trade could not be conducted in a manner different than what he had been hearing, he would certainly give
his vote for abolition. He called the trade "shocking to humanity"
and "abominable to be carried on by any country," and said that it
"reflects the greatest dishonour on the British senate and the British
nation. The Trade, as the petitioners propose to carry it on, without
any regulation, is contrary to every humane, to every Christian principle, to every sentiment that ought to inspire the breast of man." Pitt
was rather like George Washington in that he represented the very
best of the late-eighteenth-century classical ideal. Holding the Roman

virtues in the highest regard was probably as close as he came to religion, but he was as devoted a practitioner of that religion as one might
find. When he spoke of sentiments "that ought to inspire the breast
of man," he meant it most earnestly. The barbarians had been served
notice. But barbarians are not usually dissuaded with noble words.

Wilberforce spent much of that summer and autumn of 1788 at
Rayrigg, the house he had rented in the glorious Lake District since
1780. His mother and his sister came too, and in his months there
he regained much of his strength. "I never enjoyed the country more
than during this visit," he later wrote, "when in the early morning I
used to row out alone, and find an oratory under one of the woody
islands in the middle of the lake." He would read his Bible there and
pray "early in the fine autumn mornings when the lake used to be
as calm as so much glass, and all the mountains, shrouded with va-
pours, compassed me round like so many sleeping lions and the sun
shining on the varied enclosure in the nearer foreground used to
present a scene I never saw surpassed."

CHAPTER 11

~~~~

ROUND ONE

"We can no longer plead ignorance . . ."

I t was on the fifth of November in 1788, during dinner at Windsor Castle, that the fabled madness of King George III made its first appearance. At the premiere of this lifelong tragedy, the bewigged monarch leapt up from the royal table for the purpose of dashing the head of his eldest son, the Prince of Wales, against the nearest wall. The element of surprise afforded by leaping granted success to the royal endeavor, but despite this decidedly unpleasant corrective, the naughty prince continued to behave quite as he had previously done. Both of these unfortunate things, the king's madness and the prince's unflaggingly ugly character, caused a great political crisis—especially for William Pitt. Pitt knew that if the king became unfit for office or died of whatever it was that now afflicted him, the prince would become king and would surely cashier Pitt and install his profligate pal Fox as prime minister. He would also call a general election in which the Whigs would doubtless triumph. And if the king lived but continued in his illness, Pitt would be obliged to appoint a regent in the king's stead—and that regent would surely have to be the Prince of Wales. And he would be able to cause almost as much trouble as regent as he would as king.

Dr. Warren, who had made the "callico guts" remark while treating Wilberforce, now led the crackerjack medical team for His Majesty, and without benefit of the complicated modern technologies available to doctors today, Warren and his team nonetheless managed to be breathtakingly incompetent. Warren's bulletin to Pitt on the king's condition for November 22 is a small masterpiece of hermetical evasion: "H.M. is entirely deranged this morning in a quite good humoured way." Two days later, another occluded gem: "His Majesty passed the whole day in a perfectly maniacal state."

To be more specific, the king believed he could see Germany through a telescope. George was, of course, of the House of Hanover, and it may have cheered him to think he could so easily check in on his ancestral *Heimat*. Also, whilst out of doors, the king one day mistook a tree for His Majesty the King of Prussia and with all of the dignity attendant upon one sovereign greeting another proceeded to shake the royal tree's "hand," a low-hanging, though fingerless, bough.

It seems from what we now know that King George's mysterious and terrible illness was the genetic disorder porphyria, one of whose symptoms is temporary insanity. Porphyria is a hereditary disease that is triggered and exacerbated by arsenic (a lock of George's hair was discovered by chance in a British museum in 2003, and analysis showed that it contained poisonous levels of arsenic), which was present in a laxative called "Dr. James's Powder," which the king's team of doctors had prescribed in liberal quantities for his illness. Dr. Warren and his team, however, confidently diagnosed "the flying gout"—a disease that seems to have been made up—and prescribed mustard plasters and Dr. James's Powder. Also, as a matter of course, the monarch's scalp was shaved so that the harmful "humours" might more easily be drawn out of the regal cranium.

Pitt now found himself in a particularly difficult situation. The best he could do was stall for time, hoping the king would recover. Pitt stalled for as long as he could, but time ran out and he was finally forced to make plans for a regency government. He hoped to limit severely the powers of the regent, and the ensuing political battle between him and the prince—and the prince's friend, Fox—was not pleasant. Fox and the prince had in their debaucheries together grown bloated and fat and grotesquely alike—two whales in a pod, as it were. They openly resented the morally upright Pitt and were anxious to take power and show him the door. On February 27, 1789, as if to weigh in on the political situation, the king regained his sanity, and Pitt triumphed. The king's sanity would come and go over the next several years, but for now it was definitely back, and like a kidney stone, the crisis passed.

Wilberforce was at his friend Pitt's side throughout this period, standing with him and admiring him for his leadership. To his friend Wyvill, he wrote: "I wish you were constantly as I am witness to that simple and earnest regard for the public welfare, by which he is so uniformly actuated; great as I know is your attachment to him, you would love him more and more."

Wilberforce's dear Aunt Hannah, whose deep faith had had such an effect on him as a boy, died during this period, in the last week of 1788. Early in 1789, Wilberforce made the acquaintance of another devout Christian who would marry into the Wilberforce family in a few years' time. James Stephen was a Scottish lawyer who would figure very prominently in Wilberforce's future, becoming one of his closest friends and allies and—by marrying Sally Wilberforce Clarke after her first husband died—his brother-in-law. Stephen seemed to arrive just in time to help Wilberforce prepare for the coming debate in Commons. As a lawyer in Barbados, he knew a great deal about the grim realities of the West Indian slave business; he had seen all there was to see. Stephen's revulsion at slavery was bottomless, and he was a man of unsurpassed moral passion on the issue. That passion and his eloquence on the subject would serve the abolitionists well in the years to come. Stephen was also, among other things, the creative genius whose unorthodox idea in 1806 would simultaneously make abolition of the slave trade possible and inadvertently start the War of 1812.

James Stephen's connection with West Indian slavery began in 1783, the year he arrived in that part of the world. At an elegant dinner shortly after his arrival, the table conversation concerned a soon-to-be-held and hotly debated murder trial. Four black slaves were accused of having murdered a white doctor, and the single witness for the prosecution was a frightened-looking fifteen-year-old female slave who gave the impression that she had little choice but to say what she now said, accusing the four of the crime. It should be pointed out that the word of a black slave in court was usually worthless. But this time, rather curiously, it was worth four human lives. Stephen attended the trial and became totally convinced of the four slaves' innocence. Nonetheless, they were all four pronounced guilty and, even more shockingly, sentenced to death by burning. Two of the four somehow escaped this execution, but the other two were burned alive, just as the sentence dictated—chained to a stake in the ground, doused with fuel, and ignited. One of the two, Stephen had heard, pulled the stake from the ground in his agonies and managed to extinguish the flames. The stake was replaced, and he was again doused and ignited. "Both," Stephen wrote, "were literally roasted to death."

Stephen's seething hatred of slavery began with this grisly introduction and grew with several years more of indescribably awful observations. He once said, "I would rather be on friendly terms with a man who had strangled my infant son than support an administration guilty of slackness in suppressing the Slave Trade." He was not given to hyperbole and dearly loved his son. Like Wilberforce, Stephen was a devout Christian, and he promised Wilberforce that upon his return to St. Kitt's he would provide as much information as possible against the trade. He had to be extremely secretive, for he had a family and a law practice there, and they would not permanently leave St. Kitt's for England until 1794.

The battle for abolition now surged forward when in April 1789 the Privy Council committee released its report to Parliament. It was 850 pages long, and there were only three weeks to digest it before the debate began. But the more Wilberforce read of the facts of the damnable trade, the more he was convinced that anyone aware of them as he was would see that abolition was the only conceivable position to take. The facts had not been known, but now would be. But when the West Indian interests perceived that a push would be made for abolition, they quickly changed their tune again, saying that regulation of the trade was the answer. They would take what they could get and twist and turn however necessary to stall for time.

In April, Wilberforce went again to Barham Court, the home of Lord and Lady Middleton in Teston. James Ramsay and Thomas Clarkson were there too, and Hannah More visited. Thinking of the

Magna Carta, she offered her hope that Teston would be "the Run-nymede of the negroes, and that the great charter of African liberty will be there completed."

Much was going on now. John Newton was asked whether he could persuade his dear friend William Cowper to write a poem. He could and did, and Cowper happily complied. "The Negro's Com-plaint" was not the poet's greatest artistic creation, but it solidly ad-vanced the ideas of abolition throughout England at that time. Chief of these, for Cowper and all of the Christians engaged in this holy cause, was the rank hypocrisy of a nation that dared call itself Christian and used the pomp and circumstance of Christian religion whenever these suited it, but that willfully disobeyed God's plainest commands by brutally oppressing hundreds of thousands of other human beings. One stanza of Cowper's poem reads:

> Is there, as ye sometimes tell us,
>   Is there One who reigns on high?
> Has He bid you buy and sell us
>   Speaking from His throne, the sky?
> Ask Him, if your knotted scourges,
>   Matches, blood-extorting screws,
> Are the means that duty urges
>   Agents of His will to use?

Josiah Wedgwood too was asked to bring his artistry to bear on the cause. He created an image that was probably the first iconic image ever used in a human rights campaign—the first logo, as it were. The image is of a kneeling African, chained hand and foot, looking up imploringly and asking: "Am I not a man and a brother?" This image was reproduced on snuffboxes and made into cameos that women wore pinned to their dresses and in their hair. It was also made into a letter-sealing fob, like a signet ring, so that even the wax seals on letters would draw attention to the cause.

Another powerful image and icon was circulated at this time. Equiano had spotted the plate of a ship's interior, depicting how slaves should be positioned to maximize their numbers, and he ob-tained a copy and showed it to Clarkson. It was a kind of silent, static nightmare of understatement. Clarkson reworked the illustration slightly, to exacting standards, and precisely depicted the interior, with measurements, of a specific slave ship, the *Brookes,* proudly owned by the wealthy Brookes family of Liverpool. This arresting image horrified the entire nation; it was reproduced endlessly and posted everywhere. Under Dolben's improved regulations, the *Brookes* was allowed to legally carry 482 slaves, and that was the number precisely pictured. To anyone unfamiliar with the slave trade, it would have been inconceivable that so many human beings could be crammed together as the illustration depicted—and inconceivable that the depicted horror was allowable under the new and more humane regulations that the slave interests had fought a few months before. Before these recent regulations, the same ship had carried as many as 740 slaves. This image was abolition's trump card: 482 human beings, thus. At first, one sees something that looks like a schematic, but it's difficult to know what one is looking at. It could be anything: insects, hash marks, hieroglyphics. Then suddenly the tiny figures become human beings—there is just enough detail to each figure to make the image work, like an illusion that is at once optical and moral. The level of detail of each figure adds to the slowly dawning horror, and then one notices that many of them are smaller than the others—they are children—and then one realizes that those things must be the latrine buckets, and those men must lie next to them. To look at the image is to crawl to the edge of the abyss and to stare, agape, at the horror.

Wilberforce's moment was now approaching. On May 12 it came. Interestingly enough, this was two years to the day after Wilberforce had vowed under the oak tree with Pitt and Grenville to move forward on abolition. In preparation for his speech, Wilberforce had absorbed as much of the 850 pages of the committee's report as possible. He would now stand and speak as only he could, extemporaneously for three and a half hours, going over each of the points he had enumerated for himself on a few sheets of paper (which are preserved in Oxford's Bodleian Library). At last his moment had come to move for the abolition of the odious slave trade. The time for the realization of the first "great object" was at hand. Wilberforce rose in his place at 5:00 p.m. and began.

Referring to the Middle Passage, he said: "So much misery con-
densed in so little room is more than the human imagination has
ever before conceived." It was the Middle Passage, he said, that had
brought him to where he now stood. "So enormous, so dreadful,
so irremediable did its wickedness appear, that my own mind was
completely made up for the abolition. A trade founded in iniquity,
and carried on as this was, must be abolished, let the price be what it
might—let the consequences be what they would, I from this time
determined that I would never rest till I had [secured] its abolition."

On and on he went, detailing every aspect of the evil process
whereby living men, women, and children were turned into chat-
tel. What was perhaps most remarkable about Wilberforce's speech
was the general tone of it. He might so easily have launched a blis-
tering philippic against the damnable scum who made this wicked
trade in tender human flesh possible and who still wished to keep it
alive and thriving for as long as their gaping pockets could be filled.
But he didn't. Wilberforce's faith had given him first and foremost a
painful but very real knowledge of his own sinfulness, and when he
now spoke, he did so with remarkable generosity and graciousness:
"I mean not to accuse anyone," he said, "but to take the shame upon
myself, in common indeed with the whole Parliament of Great Britain, for having suffered this horrid trade to be carried on under their
authority. We are all guilty—we ought all to plead guilty, and not
to exculpate ourselves by throwing the blame on others." Certainly
this was as much a political calculation as anything, but it was not
disingenuous. Wilberforce believed to the bottom the truth of what
he was saying.

When Wilberforce countered with his well-marshaled facts
what others had given as evidence during the hearings of the previous months, he did not mention the names of those whose despicable
inanities he was rebutting. The temptation to do so must have been
extraordinary—especially with regard to a man named Norris, a
Liverpudlian of some standing who probably had been hired by the
slave trade promoters to do their dirtiest work. Among other things,
Norris had met with Clarkson, pretending to be pro-abolition, and
fed him a raft of false information. He then later testified at the Privy
Council hearings and rebutted what he had told Clarkson in order to

confuse things and make Clarkson look foolish. He also floated despicable lies about Clarkson, among them that Clarkson had himself applied for the post of captain of a slave ship.

But the most memorable example of Norris's false testimony concerned his glowing descriptions of the slaves' lives aboard the slave ships. He went so far as to describe their daily regimen of "dancing," as though their merriment during these voyages could scarcely be contained. Wilberforce now dealt in his speech with much of Norris's testimony. He explained that the slaves did indeed dance on the decks of these floating arks of hell, not of their own merry accord but rather under the literal threat of the sailor's lash. They were forced to dance and even to sing for the amusement of the sailors and for their own exercise. The image of these broken husks of humanity forced to dance and sing when they wanted nothing more than to die and depart forever from the nightmare in which they were wide awake is hard to bear.

Norris wasn't the only one to provide absurd descriptions of the cheeriness of slave life on these ships. One former slave-ship captain gave this description:

> If the Weather is sultry, and there appears the least Perspiration upon their Skins, when they come upon Deck, there are Two men attending with Cloths to rub them perfectly dry, and another to give them a little Cordial. . . . They are then supplied with Pipes and Tobacco . . . they are amused with Instruments of Music peculiar to their own country . . . and when tired of music and Dancing, they then go to Games of Chance.

In his speech, Wilberforce did not humiliate the wicked men who had given these descriptions as he might have, and if ever anyone had been given the gifts with which to verbally smash his opponents like eggs, Wilberforce had. Instead, he coolly countered each of these false accounts with facts and facts and more facts. Not much more than facts was needed.

John Newton, the "old African blasphemer," testified too. His testimony before the Privy Council had been especially damning of the trade. Newton had great moral stature and was of course personally familiar with the trade in every detail. He explained, for instance, that many of the slaves were half-mad already when they came aboard the slave ships, having been brutalized for weeks and months or years by African slave traders. Most of them had never seen an ocean or white men, and they often earnestly believed that these white men—whether humans or demons, they knew not—were intent on eating them. Equiano too, in his account of being transferred from his brutal African captors to his brutal English captors, echoed this fear and these sentiments. For all who endured these horrors it must indeed have seemed as though they had fallen through the rotten floor of this world, and into hell itself.

The slave trade interests put forward astonishing misinformation regarding the world from which these lucky slaves had been saved, painting the slavers as saviors of these wretches rather than as their oppressors. One pamphlet, titled "Slavery No Oppression," was typical of its kind:

> It is well known that the eastern and western coasts of Africa are inhabited by stupid and unenlightened hordes; immersed in the most gross and impenetrable gloom of barbarism, dark in mind as in body, prodigiously populous, impatient of all control, unteachably lazy, ferocious as their own congenial tigers, nor in any respect superior to these rapacious beasts in intellectual advancement but distinguished only by a rude and imperfect organ of speech, which is abusively employed in the utterance of dissonant and inarticulate jargon. Such a people must be often involved in predatory battles, to obtain a cruel and precarious subsistence by the robbery and destruction of one another. The traffic has proved a fortunate event for their miserable captives.

Wilberforce used facts to counter every argument, both the ridiculous and the serious, that was put forward by the anti-abolitionists. He also told the House that the French were eager to abolish the trade as well, giving recent details of the diplomatic efforts to bring about an agreement with France and other countries engaged in the trade; he explained that Africa possessed a great many natural resources and other goods that would take the place of the trade in slaves and benefit both the British and African economies; and he spoke of the deleterious effects the trade had on British sailors. He made every argument, but in the end he said that although it was good and sound policy to abolish the trade—economically and in every other sense—it was ultimately not policy and economics that drove him to argue for abolition:

> Policy, Sir, is not my principle, and I am not ashamed to say it. There is a principle above everything that is political. And when I reflect on the command that says, "Thou shalt do no murder," believing the authority to be divine, how can I dare set up any reasonings of my own against it? And, Sir, when we think of eternity, and of the future consequences of all human conduct, what is here in this life which should make any man contradict the principles of his own conscience, the principles of justice, the laws of religion, and of God?
>
> Sir, the nature and all the circumstances of this Trade are now laid open to us. We can no longer plead ignorance, we cannot evade it, it is now an object placed before us, we cannot pass it. We may spurn it, we may kick it out of our way, but we cannot turn aside so as to avoid seeing it. For it is brought now so directly before our eyes that this House must decide, and must justify to all the world, and to their own consciences, the rectitudes of their grounds and of the principles of their decision. . . . Let not Parliament be the only body that is insensible to national justice.

By every account it was one of the finest speeches of Wilberforce's life, and those who judged such things thought it had elevated him into the marmoreal pantheon of immortals. Edmund Burke, perhaps the finest orator in that golden age of orators, thought the speech's "principles so admirable, laid down with so much order and force," that the speech was "equal to anything he had ever heard of in modern oratory; and perhaps not excelled by anything to be met with in Demosthenes."

Bishop Porteus raved about the speech too. Everyone did. It was as glorious a presentation of the incontrovertible facts and unanswerable arguments as anyone might have imagined, and it was an answer to Wilberforce's many prayers and all the prayers of those who stood behind him against the evil of the slave trade, from Equiano to Newton to Hannah More to the Middletons to Ramsay to Clarkson to Sharp and the Quakers to Charles Eliot to Isaac Milner to John Wesley. As Wesley had prophesied, however, the stony hearts of the members of Parliament, wedded to the "great Goddess Interest," were unmoved. And in the end, abolition failed.

And how exactly did it fail? The debate ended with that quintessentially nondecisive "decision"—a decision to "hear more evidence," as if more evidence needed to be heard. In the meantime, the West Indian slave trade, with its Boschian horrors, would continue just as ever; tens of thousands of slaves more would be kidnapped from African shores, suffocated in reeking holds for two or three months, driven to madness and despair, and then unloaded and sold and pressed into a life of such particular hardship that it would kill them—and all with the considered blessing of both houses of His Majesty's Parliament, which now adjourned for the summer.

CHAPTER 12

ROUND TWO

". . . as Athanasius contra mundum"

On July 14, 1789, the Bastille fell, and France at last dove headlong into violence. So paramount in Wilberforce's mind was abolition that despite the worsening situation he still planned to travel there to meet with French abolitionists. His friends, however— Gisborne in particular—were horrified at the idea. They knew that a wealthy and prominent English statesman might be lucky to get away with merely being killed in such a place, swarming as it was with blood-thirsty "egalitarianism." Wilberforce relented, but with regret. He had intended to meet with the charming abbé who had six summers before rescued him and Pitt and Eliot from their idle idyll with the Rheims grocer, but now he knew he could not and sent a letter apologizing.

Clarkson traveled to Paris in Wilberforce's place. Once there, the heady atmosphere of human rights ascendant intoxicated him and Clarkson felt that abolition in France was now simply inevitable. "I should not be surprised if the French were to do themselves the honour of voting away this diabolical traffic in a night," he wrote to Wilberforce. But he soon learned that his own idealistic views of the revolution were a far cry from the political reality. It seemed that the French revolutionaries suddenly wanted nothing to do with abolition; they felt that it could alienate some of the French port cities from their cause. Utopia died for Clarkson in that moment, and French abolition seemed not just unlikely but impossible.

Clarkson then met with the mulatto leaders of the French colony of Saint-Domingue (later the Republic of Haiti). Saint-Domingue had a population that was 90 percent African slaves and 10 percent French whites who lived in perpetual fear of a slave insurrection and were therefore particularly brutal to anyone who might foment one, which of course made the slaves all the more brutal toward the French during any uprisings. Clarkson learned that such had recently been the case: a gruesomely violent slave uprising had been brutally put down. Its leader had been "broken on the wheel," a torture so diabolical that we shall decline its description here. After this uprising, there could be no more talk of patience or moderation or political compromises. It was now all-out war for the French antislavery forces. They would not turn back until everyone was dead or free. For Clarkson, and surely for many others, this development was devastating. The abolitionist cause had been severely set back.

Back in England, there was other bad news for abolition. Wilberforce was at Teston with the Middletons that July when he got news that James Ramsay had died in London. Ramsay was only fifty-five, and somewhat ill, but so viciously and relentlessly had he been attacked by the pro—slave trade forces, with such a bombardment of cruel lies, that it literally seems to have killed him. His death must have been sobering to the Middletons, who had encouraged him to enter this fray, and to Wilberforce too. All of them might now have seen that they were indeed not battling against mere flesh and blood, but as the Scriptures averred, against "powers and principalities" in high places, against "thrones and dominions."

John Wesley's caution to Sharp must have returned with fresh meaning now. Wesley and his brother Charles had traveled hundreds of thousands of miles on horseback all across England, preaching the Christian Gospel and helping the poor, who in those days had neither a government nor a private sector friendly to their plight. For their pains, the Wesleys were denounced by almost all of the Church of England ministers and persecuted awfully and in every kind of way. This continued from 1740 until around 1780. Some of the Wesleys' "lay preachers" were even killed by mobs or kidnapped by naval press gangs.

∞

On August 21, Wilberforce traveled with his sister Sally to Cowslip Green to visit Hannah More and her sisters. Hannah's sister Martha, knowing Wilberforce loved natural scenery, insisted that he take a trip to the nearby Cheddar Gorge, which afforded some of the finest scenery in England. Cheddar Gorge is the largest gorge in the United Kingdom, and the site of many caves. But during his visit Wilberforce was less moved by the scenery than by the inhabitants of the area, whose poverty was extreme and, to Wilberforce, shocking. They had no school at all, nor any church. Some of the miserable souls did not even live in hovels but scratched out an existence in the caves themselves. On his return to the Mores', Wilberforce was clearly of a mind to be alone with his thoughts on what he had just witnessed. He retired to his room to pray, did not touch his food, and later emerged with a clear purpose: "Miss Hannah More," he said, "something must be done for Cheddar."

They discussed various schemes until the hour grew late. At last Wilberforce declared, "If you will be at the trouble, I will be at the expense." And he meant it. Whatever they would do to help the poor there, he would fund it. Wilberforce insisted that Hannah not be shy in asking for his money. To do so, he said, would only be pride disguised as false humility. Over his lifetime, Wilberforce gave away more money than we can imagine, and he now wrote the first of many generous checks to launch the Mores' work among the poor of that area. Hannah More soon started the first schools in the area, and Wilberforce would continue to fund them for many years.

In September, Wilberforce traveled to Buxton; his friend Dr. Hey had recommended a spa there. Buxton offered a new and decidedly queer way of "taking" the waters It was called "skin rotations" and was a type of "massage bath" in which one lay prone upon a flat, table-like trough of copper. Quantities of the miraculous local waters were then expertly spritzed upon the patient's afflicted parts. Wilberforce afterward traveled to Yoxall Lodge, the home of the Gisbornes, and there spent two weeks before returning to Buxton for further spritz-ing. Incredibly, these "skin rotations" seemed to help him, and he would return to Buxton each autumn for several years.

January 1790 found Wilberforce back at 4 Palace Yard for the new session of Parliament. During this session, as had been decided at the end of the previous one, Parliament would hear more evidence on the slave trade. In a deft maneuver, Wilberforce ensured that only a select com-mittee would hear evidence instead of all of Parliament. From his seat on this select committee, Wilberforce was directly involved in question-ing each of the witnesses. Norris again was questioned, and he violently threatened Wilberforce when his credibility was publicly brought into question—which, given his reprehensible statements, it certainly would have been. Evidence for the trade ended in April, and then evidence against the trade began and ran all the way through early June.

Again Wilberforce went to Buxton. At Buxton was Henry Thornton, the son of John Thornton, as well as the Sykes family, with whom he had grown up at Hull. Marianne Sykes, who was there with her family, would later marry Henry Thornton. It is striking how these circles of friends would spend time together at Bath and Buxton and their various homes. Henry Thornton had become Wilberforce's dearest friend, and Wilberforce had done much in encouraging his faith. We know of the generosity and goodness of Henry's father, John Thornton, but Henry thought his father's faith a bit severe and off-putting. Wilberforce, whom he'd come to know at Clapham, gave him a more charming and attractive model of Christian faith. Wilberforce biographer John Pollock writes that Henry "had been a little repelled by the ardour of his uncouth father, some of whose as-sociates pursued business methods out of tune with the easy pieties on their lips. Henry found his bachelor cousin 'Wilber' different."

In early 1791, we find Wilberforce again at Yoxall Lodge in Staf-fordshire, where he worked endlessly in preparing for the next session of Parliament. Wilberforce's mother and Marianne Sykes followed him there but wouldn't see much of him. It was at Yoxall Lodge that the names Macaulay, Wilberforce, and Babington would become inter-twined. Thomas Gisborne, as we remember, was Wilberforce's "sap" of a neighbor at St. John's College who had studied diligently while Wilberforce had chosen the path of greatest insouciance. Gisborne was now a renowned preacher and country parson and a dear friend of Wilberforce's. Mrs. Gisborne's brother, Thomas Babington, was also at Yoxall Lodge at this time. He had been at Cambridge with Wilberforce and Gisborne and was one of Henry Thornton's close friends.

Wilberforce now had to distill the ten thousand folio pages of evidence amassed during the months of testimony and make it digestible. Consolidating these vast acreages of pages and endless miles of scrawled penmanship was a formidable task.

In a letter to her mother, Marianne Sykes wrote that Babington and Wilberforce

> have never appeared downstairs lately except to take a hasty dinner and for a half an hour after we have supped. The Slave Trade has occupied them for nine hours daily. Mr. Babington told them last night that he has 14 hundred folio pages to read to detect the contradictions and to collect the answers which corroborate Mr. Wilberforce's assertions in his speeches. . . . The two friends begin to look very ill, but they are in excellent spirits and at this moment I hear them laughing at some absurd questions in the examination proposed by a friend of Mr. Wilberforce's.

Wilberforce was said to have had a "strong sense of the ludicrous," and we cannot doubt that he did. But the two centuries that separate us from him seem to fall away and make it immediately palpable in Miss Sykes's firsthand recollection of this laughter at some long-forgotten absurdity. She writes in the letter that Wilberforce is quite different than he was in 1784, before his "Great Change." "He is now never riotous nor noisy," she says, "but always very cheerful, and sometimes lively but he talks a great deal more upon serious subjects than he used to do."

After Yoxall, Wilberforce returned to London. The debate on abolition during this parliamentary session was at last opened on April 18, 1791. Wilberforce rose at 5:00 p.m. and spoke on the subject for four hours. His attitude was humble. He wrote that he looked to God in this battle now "for wisdom and strength and the power of persuasion, and may I surrender myself to him as to the event with perfect submission and ascribe to him all the praise if I succeed, and if I fail say from the heart thy will be done."

He spoke well, as ever. "Whatever may be its success, I attach my happiness to their cause and shall never relinquish it," he declared. "Supported as I have been, indeed, such a desertion would be most despicable. I have already gained for the wretched Africans the recognition of their claim to the rank of human beings, and I doubt not but the Parliament of Great Britain will no longer withhold from them the rights of human nature!"

Someday this would be true, but not yet. The vote was taken at 3:30 a.m.: noes 163, ayes 88. Once again, abolition had been defeated in England.

Less than two months before this terrible defeat, however, on February 24 of that year, Wilberforce received a letter that must have seemed to him in the moment he opened it an historic document. It was from John Wesley, then eighty-seven, and only a few days from death. It was probably the last letter he wrote:

Dear Sir:

> *Unless the divine power has raised you up to be as Athanasius contra mundum, I see not how you can go through your glorious enterprise in opposing that execrable villainy which is the scandal of religion, of England, and of human nature. Unless God has raised you up for this very thing, you will be worn out by the opposition of men and devils. But if God be for you, who can be against you? Are all of them together stronger than God? O be not weary of well doing! Go on, in the name of God and in the power of his might, till even American slavery (the vilest that ever saw the sun) shall vanish away before it.*
>
> *Reading this morning a tract wrote by a poor African, I was particularly struck by that circumstance that a man who has a black skin, being wronged or outraged by a white man, can have no redress; it being a "law" in our colonies that the oath of a black against a white goes for nothing. What villainy is this?*

> *That he who has guided you from youth up may continue to strengthen you in this and all things, is the prayer of, dear sir,*
>
> > *Your affectionate servant,*
> > *John Wesley*

Wilberforce would have remembered the words of this letter many times in the years and battles ahead, not least during the defeat that April. What an encouragement it must have been to read these words from the battle-scarred veteran, who had fought the good fight, and run with patience the race, and had kept the faith. Just before entering his rest, he had, as it were, extended his hand to his spiritual son and handed him the baton for this particular leg of the race *contra mundum*. And so William Wilberforce now ran, cheered on by a great and growing cloud of witnesses.

CHAPTER 13

THE GOOD FIGHT

". . . gradually."

The defeat of April 1791 was painful at the time, but as the years passed it would seem even more crushing in retrospect. What one could not see in 1791 was that the political prospects for abolition were then at a high-water mark. Those prospects would not be as good again for quite some time. An opportunity had been lost, and politically speaking, things would for a time move backward.

The popular attitude toward abolition was another story. Among the nonpolitical classes, abolition was more and more accepted. As the British people, for the first time in history, began to find their voice, they became suddenly aware that they themselves, the people, existed. What had happened in the American colonies and was now happening in France had everything to do with this trend toward human rights and democratization.

The change in popular sentiment toward abolition had been rapid. Just a few years before, there had been widespread and genuine ignorance of the horrors of the slave trade, but now suddenly the trade and all of its varied horrors were on everyone's lips. Posters of the *Brookes* were everywhere, as were images of Josiah Wedgwood's imploring African in chains. Cowper's poem "The Negro's Complaint" was not only well known as a poem, but had been set to music and was sung in the streets; also that year, a nineteen-year-old poet named Samuel Taylor Coleridge won a gold medal at Cambridge for his "Ode Against the Slave Trade." A boycott of West Indian sugar had become widespread, helped in some part by the false belief that it literally contained the blood of those who had harvested it. And because during the American Revolution the British gave freedom to any American black slaves who would fight on the British side, many blacks had gained their freedom and moved to England, where they now lived. Black faces, previously exceedingly rare, were suddenly quite numerous in England, and their presence humanized the issue and literally brought it home.

Just as the move toward democratization and government reform served the cause of abolition, so the cause of abolition helped the British people begin to exercise their budding political powers when petitions against the slave trade were collected. In the months after the 1791 defeat of abolition, 517 petitions for abolition (and only four against) arrived in Parliament. Each arrived rolled up, like a scroll. When unrolled, these documents could be seen to be covered with the signatures of thousands of British subjects who had never before known that their names or opinions could possibly matter in any real way. Almost all of these names of British subjects were entering the houses of Parliament for the first time. The very idea that humble citizens could have a say in what happened on their great island was unprecedented. But they could, and now did, petitioning their representatives in Parliament.

But the swelling movement toward democratization and human rights cut both ways. As much as the developments in France encouraged egalitarian thinking in England, so too every bloody excess in France and the French colonies were associated with the English movement toward reform of any kind, and especially with abolition. The ferment and agitation in France had moved things along quite nicely for a time, but now the backlash would begin.

That same year, and perhaps just in time, Henry Thornton had invited Wilberforce to move with him into Battersea Rise, Thornton's home in Clapham. Thornton called it a "chummery"—a place where bachelors lived together. They would live together for the next four years, sharing the upkeep of the place. Edward Eliot would live next door, in a house called Broomfield Lodge, and Charles Grant would live in yet a third house. Thus began the Clapham Community, which has also been called the Clapham Sect, the Clapham Circle, the Clapham Saints, the Claphamites, and other things, good and bad. But the grand experiment that history remembers as "Clapham" didn't happen by chance. Henry Thornton very much intended to create a place where he and his like-minded friends could encourage each other and enjoy each other's company, away from the soot and bustle of London. Clapham was only four miles away, but it was a world apart; inasmuch as Wilberforce's battles over abolition had become more difficult, it became important to have this place where he could get away. He needed the comfort of friends who thought as he did and would fight and pray alongside him. Henry Venn, the son of John Venn, was persuaded to be the resident clergyman, and each Sunday he preached there, to rave reviews. Granville Sharp lived in Clapham village, and others of their tribe would visit and stay. When he was not at Clapham, Wilberforce was usually at Bath, where he kept company with many from the same gang, and certainly with Hannah More, whose world-class wit invariably lightened his spirits.

Again now, in the new parliamentary session of 1792, Wilberforce gave notice that he would move for abolition. He would do so until abolition passed; that much he knew. The popular tide for abolition was continuing to swell, with petitions coming in from every corner of the country. But what was happening in France, in all of its ugliness, had at the same time created a countercurrent and a backlash in the British political class—who, of course, were the ones who voted in Parliament. There was no question that they were now rather quickly developing a distinct distaste for reform and for abolition.

Liberty no longer sounded innocent and beautiful, as it once had, not now that the Parisian mobs had gone so far as to imprison their monarch in the Bastille. Before the French Revolution, it had seemed an attractive romantic ideal, and at worst had seemed harmless. During the American Revolution, the American patriots had carried tall sticks with mobcaps on top—the Phrygian cap that signified freedom—and this image had been echoed in France. There was a charming freshness to it, and a kind of unassailable dignity. But now, as Lord North and the king and the other "High Tories" had warned all along, things had turned monstrous. The iconic beautiful young woman who represented *Liberté,* sometimes baring one breast, was being transformed in the minds of many British politicians into a bloodthirsty and goggle-eyed harpy, a demonic hag, a Frenchified Kali figure whose bloodlust threatened all law and order. The revolutionary forces had become drunk with power and had to be stopped and anything that smacked of "liberty" or "democracy" must be pushed back.

And so it was that, in this spirit, the abolition movement now, for all intents and purposes, came to a halt. The tide had shifted. For the political elite, it was a simple matter of defending British civilization. Proponents of abolition couldn't know the future, and their hopes for victory were as alive as ever. Indeed, everything seemed to move forward toward the long-hoped-for goal, but it was as if the backlash increased just ahead of the movement forward.

When the Christian abolition movement in England became allied in the popular consciousness with what was happening in France, the damage was incalculable. Every one of the leaders in the abolitionist movement was a Christian, but Thomas Paine in America and the mobs across the Channel were passionately anti-Christian; indeed, much of what Paine wrote was aggressively blasphemous, even by today's standards. So the moral authority that abolition had enjoyed for a few years was quickly bled away, and the staunch British politicians, especially Tory conservatives such as Burke, reverted to pure defensiveness. They felt compelled to protect British culture and civilization at all costs and had ceased feeling safe in moving toward any kind of reform—for the moment anyway. It was a great tragedy. But what could Wilberforce do?

For one thing, he might perhaps have reined in Thomas Clarkson, whose naive flirtations with the Jacobins were noticed by the opposition and swiftly taken on as evidence that abolition was dangerous.

Isaac Milner, after a long conversation with Clarkson, wrote to Wilberforce: "I wish him better health, and better notions in politics." It was bad enough that France's Revolutionary National Convention had elected Wilberforce—along with George Washington, Joseph Priestly, Thomas Paine, and Jeremy Bentham—as citizens of France. Wilberforce was able to quickly deflect this "honor" by joining a committee aimed at helping the French emigrant clergy, of whom, naturally, there were many, inasmuch as emigrating was one of the few ways in which they might still preserve their lives. One of these priests who fled was the kindly Abbé Lageard, who had hosted Pitt, Wilberforce, and Eliot during their sojourn at Rheims just a few years before.

Perhaps even more damaging to the abolitionist cause were the bloody massacres in Saint-Domingue. Wilberforce was at that point urged to put off his motion for abolition. But he elected not to; he would go forward, despite the opposition. And now again, in 1792, Wilberforce rose and moved for abolition of the execrable slave trade. In his opening speech on the night of April 2, he uttered a famous line of high emotion: "Africa! Africa! Your sufferings have been the theme that has arrested and engages my heart—your sufferings no tongue can express; no language impart." And again Fox and Pitt buttressed him, on the left and on the right, with their legendary eloquence.

But this time the Scotchman Henry Dundas, sensing the atmosphere of the chamber, began talking about regulating the trade—as though regulation of the villainous practice were the same as abolishing it. He talked of forcing the plantation owners to treat the slaves better, of giving them incentives to do so. He spoke of this as the "moderate" or "middle" way that would solve everyone's problems, and he implored the pro–slave trade members to heed what he was saying.

When he was through, Fox rose and flew at Dundas with all of his considerable oratorical skills, mocking the idea of moderation in such things as murder and atrocity. "I believe [the slave trade] to be impolitic," Fox said.

> I know it to be inhuman. I am certain it is unjust. I find it so inhuman and unjust that, if the colonies cannot be cultivated without it, they ought not to be cultivated at all. . . .

As long as I have a voice to speak, this question shall never
be at rest.... and if I and my friends should die before they
have attained their glorious object, I hope there will never
be wanting men alive to do their duty, who will continue to
labour till the evil shall be wholly done away.

It was a powerful peroration from Fox, a crackling bonfire of
truth and clarity, and it was much needed. His words shone a great
deal of light onto the moral cowardice of "regulation" and the lazy
wickedness of "moderation." But the canny Scotchman was not
troubled. Dundas had thrown water on fires before and knew that
one needn't extinguish the whole fire; sometimes simply creating
enough smoke would do all that was needed. Everyone would leave,
and then the idiot fire could burn and illuminate the blessed nothing-
ness around it all night long! So now Dundas rose and deftly splashed
the single word *gradually* into Fox's bonfire. It was very coolly done.
Yes to abolition—yes! But not too hastily—no! True leadership demanded prudence. So yes—but *gradually*. Wilberforce would have
thought of the slaves writhing in the Middle Passage, defeated, hu-
miliated, pining for death. *Gradually*. It was as though these three syl-
lables, soporific and falsely irenic, had bubbled up through Dundas's
mouth from the dead belly of hell itself. Everyone seized on it. And
why wouldn't they? Gradual abolition was abolition and it was *not*
abolition—what more could a politician dream of? The slave trade
would be soundly and formally condemned for the first time, and yet
nothing would have actually been done about it—extraordinary.

After Dundas's insertion of the word gradually, it was Pitt's turn.
They had debated all through the night. It was still black outside, but
it was already after five o'clock in the morning when Pitt rose and
began. He spoke for an hour and in that hour gave one of the greatest speeches of his life. Anyone who had ever doubted his commitment to abolition could not doubt it again. "How shall we hope to
obtain," he asked, "if it be possible, forgiveness from Heaven for the
enormous evils we have committed if we refuse to make use of those
means which the mercy of Providence has still reserved for us for
wiping away the shame and guilt with which we are now covered?...
Shall we not count the days and hours that are suffered to intervene

and to delay the accomplishment of such a work?" His rhetoric rose and rose magnificently.

And then something extraordinary happened. As Pitt ascended now to the very summit of his speech, the golden anthem of dawn burst from the horizon through the chamber's windows, and the great room swelled like a sail filled with morning. It was a transcendent moment, one remembered for decades by those who were there, and by all accounts Pitt stepped into the moment brilliantly, as though he had himself ordered the sunlight for his own purposes. From his vast storehouses of classical verse, he put his hand in an instant to an apt couplet from Virgil that spoke of light dispelling the gloom of darkness over Africa. It was a glorious ending, and those who would know said that it lifted him truly for the first time into the rarefied oratorical company of his famous father.

But when Pitt sat down, the political desire to compromise and defer had somehow not been utterly chased from the room. It had seemed to be dispelled by Pitt's magnificent oratory and the sun's golden entrance. But it had in fact never left. It had been crouched outside the door all that time like a hungry dog, content to wait as long as necessary to get what it desires. When Pitt sat down, it saw its chance and slipped in—and before anyone knew what had happened it had taken the sausage from the table, as it were, and disappeared. And so a motion was passed, 230 to 85, in favor of gradual abolition. All Wilberforce could do was wonder how it had happened and stare at the empty plate on the table where the sausage had lain. Three weeks later, "gradual" was determined to mean by January 1796.

Many expressed their hearty congratulations to Wilberforce that abolition had finally been "approved," but for Wilberforce it was confusing. Was this indeed some kind of triumph, after all, for which to be grateful, or was it an abject and heartbreaking failure to do what they had tried and tried to do since 1787, when it seemed that abolition might happen immediately? Each year since then, fifty thousand human beings had been torn from the lives they might have lived, and the families and friends they might have had, and the dreams they might have dreamed, and had been introduced to the tortures of the Middle Passage and sentenced for life to the inhuman, hopeless gulag of West Indian slavery. Wilberforce thought of all of these children of God in their suffering, and he felt the terrible weight of each year's failure. And now four more years of this evil nightmare were to continue.

Absurdly, congratulations from his colleagues flowed in. How could he rejoice? What comfort could Wilberforce possibly take? Four years was an eternity, nor was there any guarantee in this "gradual" bill that abolition would be passed in four years either. And as it turned out it would not. Around this time William Cowper wrote a poem to encourage Wilberforce. He surely could have used it. It was titled "Sonnet to William Wilberforce, Esq."

> Thy country, Wilberforce, with just disdain,
> Hears thee, by cruel men and impious, call'd
> Fanatic, for thy zeal to loose th' enthrall'd
> From exile, public sale, and slav'ry's chain.
> Friend of the poor, the wrong'd, the fetter-gall'd,
> Fear not lest labour such as thine be vain!
> Thou hast achiev'd a part; hast gain'd the ear
> Of Britain's senate to thy glorious cause;
> Hope smiles, joy springs, and tho' cold caution pause
> And weave delay, the better hour is near,
> That shall remunerate thy toils severe
> By peace for Afric, fenc'd with British laws.
> Enjoy what thou hast won, esteem and love
> From all the just on earth, and all the blest above!

CHAPTER 14

WHAT WILBERFORCE ENDURED

"I am permanently hurt about the Slave Trade."

Not everyone who wrote verse used their poetical talents to praise Wilberforce. James Boswell, the famous biographer of Dr. Johnson, who had indeed praised Wilberforce in 1784, when the "shrimp" had "become a whale," and who had attended that seminal dinner at the storklike Bennet Langdon's home in 1787, had nonetheless turned sharply against abolition—and bluntly against Wilberforce. Nor was he shy about expressing it. Probably the only similarity between Cowper's noble tribute and Boswell's foaming doggerel-bites-man attack is the rhymed couplets:

> Go Wilberforce with narrow skull,
> Go home and preach away at Hull.
> No longer in the Senate cackle
> In strains that suit the tabernacle;
> I hate your little whittling sneer,
> Your pert and self-sufficient leer.
> Mischief to trade sits on your lip.
> Insects will gnaw the noblest ship.

> Go, Wilberforce, begone, for shame,
> Thou dwarf with big resounding name.

Other notable figures felt similarly, including the great English hero Lord Nelson, though unlike Boswell he did not denounce Wilberforce in verse, likely thinking it effeminate. "I was bred in the good old school," he said, "and taught to appreciate the value of our West Indian possessions . . . and neither in the field nor the senate shall their just rights be infringed, while I have an arm to fight in their defense or a tongue to launch my voice against the damnable doctrine of Wilberforce and his hypocritical allies."

The cost to anyone taking a stand against the spirit of his age, and against "the great Goddess Interest," as Wesley had warned, was real indeed. In the civil rights battles in the United States in the last century, Jackie Robinson and the Reverend Martin Luther King Jr., to name just two, endured countless verbal attacks and many death threats. King, of course, was assassinated at the age of thirty-nine, and the stress on Robinson was so great that he seems to have aged prematurely, dying at fifty-two. Wilberforce's life and person too would be threatened many times during his campaign for abolition.

Wilberforce was a tiny, frail man; for him, being brave entailed being very brave indeed. Once he was challenged to a duel by an unhinged slave-ship captain named Rolleston. Wilberforce was passionately against dueling on moral grounds and a few years later took a public stand against his dearest friend Pitt when Pitt participated in one. But the palpable stress of such a challenge and having to parry it in the public sphere must have been very difficult for Wilberforce. He knew that many people would say he was a coward, that this tiny, frail man was conveniently hiding behind his Christianity to escape defending his manhood in such a contest.

In another such challenge, Wilberforce, during his testimony in the House of Commons in 1792, named a vicious Bristol slave-ship captain who had flogged to death a fifteen-year-old African girl. As a result of the evidence Wilberforce presented, this Captain Kimber was put on trial for murder. He was acquitted through what seemed an outrageous miscarriage of justice—another painful loss for the abolitionists. James Boswell sat in the gallery throughout Kimber's trial and gloated at the outcome, likely writing his denunciation around this time.

After the trial, Captain Kimber sent a letter to Wilberforce demanding £5,000, a public apology, and a government position such as "as would make me comfortable." Wilberforce, knowing the man to be guilt of this savage murder, ignored him. But Kimber took to waylaying Wilberforce in the street and grew increasingly threatening. Twice in one morning he showed up at Wilberforce's house. Wilberforce's servant described him as "very savage-looking," and his friends were concerned. On a trip to Yorkshire, one of them, carrying a pistol, insisted on "riding shotgun," as it were, alongside Wilberforce. Wilberforce said that any actual act of violence against him would be "beneficial rather than injurious to the cause," a staggering and telling statement that was not calculated to put his friends at ease, which it did not. Finally, a member of Parliament from Bristol was able to stop Kimber from continuing this threatening behavior.

The West Indian interests also had in their cabinet of torture implements every kind of lie imaginable, some blunt and some very pointed. All were deployed against Wilberforce and anyone who stood against them. Lies were used with special viciousness against the good doctor James Ramsay, whose essay on the horrors of West Indian slavery effectively launched the entire abolition campaign. He was personally despised by the slavers and had been singled out as their first target. So many savage untruths were said of him publicly that he was unable to refute them, especially given his ill health, and it is very likely that it was the stress of being subjected to such attacks that killed him. The leader in Parliament of the attack on Ramsay was Crisp Molyneux, who owned a slave plantation in St. Kitt's. Molyneux gloated to his son when he heard the news: "Ramsay is dead," he said. "I have killed him."

It is an extraordinary and happy fact that Wilberforce was never harmed very much by what was said of him—and much was indeed said and repeated and, in many cases, devoutly believed. On one of his endless travels, Clarkson met a man in a stagecoach who presented to him a dark and hitherto unknown aspect of Wilberforce's character. He "is no doubt a great philanthropist in public," the man allowed, "but I happen to know a little of his private history and can assure you that he is a cruel husband and beats his wife." Wilberforce was, of course, still a bachelor at the time—and how lucky for his wife.

Wilberforce seems eventually to have learned to laugh at what was said about him, or at least to ignore it. While he was still a bachelor, it was widely circulated that "his wife was a negress." There was also a story, oft repeated, that he had secretly married a "lady's maid." One of Wilberforce's constituents, a man who had indeed married his own cook, sent Wilberforce a note of heartiest congratulations for doing so, and for defying "the common prejudices of society" and pursuing his "own path to happiness."

In 1793 war came to England at last. Relations with France had become very troubling. That January, the mobs dragged their former king, Louis XVI, to the guillotine. For Pitt, this was enough. In February 1793, France declared war on Great Britain. And on the twenty-sixth of that month, doubtless influenced by the political situation with France, the House of Commons refused to confirm the previous year's vote for gradual abolition. Things were indeed now moving backward.

The more the Jacobins rioted and looted and killed, the more the British government became afraid of anything that smacked of human rights or liberty or equality. There was a very palpable fear that the trouble in France would leap across the Channel and light down upon their island with all the fury of a tornado, smashing and unraveling all that they knew and loved. To speak of human rights in 1793 and onward was suddenly beyond the pale. Anyone who did so was likely to be labeled a friend of the French Republic and an enemy of King George and England itself.

Wilberforce and abolition became victims of this new mind-set. When abolition came up in the House of Lords, sure enough, the Prince of Wales didn't mince words—he called Wilberforce "Republican at heart," referring to the French Republic. The debate on this issue also saw the maiden speech of the Duke of Clarence, the king's third profligate son. Clarence declared that "the promoters of the Abolition were either fanatics or hypocrites," and he boldly singled out Wilberforce by name. Clarence was a staunch enemy of abolition and would be so for many years. He had himself served in the Royal Navy in Jamaica, where he admitted having lived "a terrible debauched life."

Now, with this last defeat for abolition, rumors flew that Wilberforce, seeing the depressing handwriting on the wall, would step away from the fray. He would not. Two days after the House of Lords debate, on April 13, he wrote a letter that explains his thinking.

> In the case of every question of political expediency there appears to me room for consideration of times and seasons—at one period, under one set of circumstances it may be proper to push, at another, under another set of circumstances to withhold our efforts. But in the present instance where the actual commission of guilt is in question, a man who fears God is not at liberty. To you I will say a strong thing which the motive I have suggested will both explain and justify. If I thought that the immediate Abolition of the Slave Trade would cause an insurrection in our islands, I should not for an instant remit my most serious endeavours. Be persuaded then, I shall still even less make this grand cause the sport of caprice, or sacrifice it to motives of political convenience or personal feeling.

The issue of the slave trade was not merely a "political" issue for Wilberforce. The injustice of the trade was so clear to him that he would never relent, not even at this low point in the spring of 1793. In fact, one month after his defeat he was at it again, trying a new tactic. He put forward a bill that would stop British ships from carrying slaves to foreign countries. Half a loaf was always better than none. This so-called Foreign Slave Bill was politically brilliant and did something exceedingly clever and previously unthinkable: it set the slave merchants against the plantation owners. The plantation owners reasoned that if British slave ships couldn't sell slaves to other markets, the prices of slaves would drop and they would benefit, so they supported the bill.

This was Wilberforce's clever political mind at full stride; always looking for an angle, knowing when to move and how, and knowing when not to move. This bill came crushingly close to passing in its third reading, but lost by two votes. Still, he would never relent. One year later, in February 1794, he put the Foreign Slave Bill forward again. This time it actually was passed in Commons by eighteen votes. But then, in the House of Lords, it met yet another crushing defeat.

To be sure, all of these defeats, year after year, took their toll. Thomas Clarkson, having had more than enough discouragement and defeat for the time being, now stepped away from the cause; he would stay away for twelve years.

But the next year an energetic fresh recruit would arrive to take his place and buck up anyone weary from the battle. James Stephen that year left the West Indies for good and now arrived in London to stay. He'd brought with him his family, and would join the Clapham group as one of its most vital members, especially in the abolition cause. Stephen also brought with him to London three West Indian natives: turtles. And he gave the turtles to Wilberforce as a present. In just a few years, Wilberforce would be married with several children and many exotic animals running around his Clapham home. There would be pet hares and foxes and birds, but right now he was a bachelor and could hardly feed himself, much less care for three turtles from another hemisphere. So Wilberforce gave the three West Indian turtles to his friend the bishop of Durham, who in turn gave them to his cook, who in turn gave them to several waiters, who gave them to the bishop's guests at a banquet for fifty-five people, who all enjoyed them thoroughly, and who were all, the bishop informed Wilberforce in his thank-you note, supporters of abolition.

❧

As 1794 wound down, Wilberforce found himself beginning to diverge with his party—and with William Pitt—on the crucial issue of the war with France. Robespierre's fall and the abatement of the Terror made it look as though crushing France decisively was no longer necessary to ensure that Britain wouldn't itself be attacked. The threat was no longer so grave. Wilberforce felt that continuing the war at this point had mostly to do with the mercenary goal of snapping up France's sugar islands in the West Indies. Not only was continuing the war merely mercenary in purpose, he believed, but it would also surely increase the British slave trade there. So he felt that it was time to try for a negotiated peace. To move for that in the House of Commons, however, would be seen as practically treasonous, as giving comfort to the enemy and going over to the opposition, against Pitt. Wilberforce was politically independent, to be sure, but it was very rare that he found himself at cross-purposes with his dear friend and ally William Pitt, nor did he relish the idea. But now it seemed unavoidable.

In his diary of November 27 he writes: "I am making up my mind cautiously and maturely and therefore slowly as to the best conduct to be observed by Great Britain in the present critical emergency." In the last week of December, Wilberforce had several conversations with his friends and then finally decided upon his course: he would come out against the war. But it tore at him. Wilberforce knew that the opposition, Fox especially, whom he thought purely politically motivated and therefore fundamentally unprincipled, would seize upon his position and use it politically against Pitt. The thought that Pitt would be hurt was hard to bear. But Wilberforce felt that he had little choice. He couldn't be a mere party man; he was solemnly obliged to act in the best interests of the nation as he saw it. He would play to his audience of one.

Alas, Pitt didn't quite see it that way and took Wilberforce's opposition to continuing the war as a betrayal. Wilberforce often said that only twice in Pitt's career had Pitt lost sleep, first during the mutiny of the *Nore*—a long, drawn-out standoff that had the entire nation on tenterhooks—and now over this public breach with his old friend. The decision had real consequences, and this was not an easy time for Wilberforce. At the royal levee, the king, formally friendly to him and abolition, cut him dead, not even glancing at him. This was a world where being "cut" by the king was as close to not being a metaphor as we can imagine. And more painful to Wilberforce than literally being cut, the king from this point onward turned decidedly against abolition. Gone were the days when the king would ask Wilberforce, in a friendly and encouraging way: "How are your negroes?" It was a very real loss, but the times were harsh. Things were even said of Wilberforce now that painted him as a dyed-in-the-wool

Jacobin. "Your friend Mr. Wilberforce," said one Foxite MP to Lady Spencer, "will be very happy any morning to hand your Ladyship to the guillotine." Even when Wilberforce visited friends in York during this time, some refused to see him because of his public opposition to the war.

So for a brief moment now Wilberforce was the darling of Fox and the Whigs. But in a moment's time, they would vilify him for supporting Pitt's draconian suspension of habeas corpus. He would get it coming and going from both sides until the end of his career, and over a host of issues and votes.

Wilberforce had first come out against the war in January 1795, and the initial estrangement from Pitt was quite awkward. But already by the end of March, their mutual friend Bob Smith had brought them together over dinner. They saw each other twice again in April—once at Pitt's and over a weekend at Eliot's home in Clapham—and the breach was soon healed. To some degree it probably changed their friendship forever, but Wilberforce never regretted the stand he had taken.

In May, Wilberforce stood against the government once again, this time on the issue of giving the profligate Prince of Wales a staggering increase in his "allowance."

&

When 1796 dawned, Wilberforce yearned more than ever to pass a bill for abolition. This was, after all, the year when "gradual" abolition was to have taken effect. "Before this great cause," he wrote early that year, "all others dwindle in my eyes. . . . If it please God to honor me so far, may I be the instrument of stopping such a course of wickedness and cruelty as never before disgraced a Christian country."

There was no question that the prospects for abolition finally looked very promising again. How many years had he put a bill forward? Each year the defeat had been a surprise. Now, on February 18, Wilberforce again made his motion for abolition. And once again, the world-weary politicians yawned and prudently warned about the terrible dangers of being too hasty and recommended postponing all of this tiresome abolition business until the never-ending war had come to an end. The comments of one MP named Jenkinson about "suspending the question" until the end of the year seemed to set Wilberforce off, and he rose to say what was on his mind.

"There is something not a little provoking in the dry, calm way in which gentlemen are apt to speak of the sufferings of others," he said. "The question suspended! Is the desolation of wretched Africa suspended? Are all the complicated miseries of this atrocious trade—is the work of death suspended? No sir, I will not delay this motion, and I will call upon the House not to insult the forbearance of Heaven by delaying this tardy act of justice!"

Wilberforce was further incensed by the comments made by some in the West Indian contingent that the slaves were "decently" cared for, having food, clothing, and shelter. "What!" he exclaimed. "Are these the only claims of a rational being? Are the feelings of the heart nothing? Where are social intercourse and family endearment. . . . So far from thanking the honourable gentleman for the feeding, clothing, and lodging of which he boasts, I protest against the way in which he has mentioned them, as degrading men to the level of the brutes, and insulting all the qualities of our common nature."

One may see in these comments how Wilberforce years later came to be thought of as the "conscience" of the nation. A conscience reminds us of what we already know to be right. Wilberforce realized that Britain was a nation that had effectively lost its conscience or grown deaf to it, that claimed in every outward way to be a Christian nation, but that acted upon principles fundamentally at odds with the Christian view of human beings as immortal creatures, created in the image of God.

Of course, some of the members of Parliament made no pretense at all of harboring Christian beliefs. Among them was Banastre Tarleton of Liverpool, one of abolition's most ruthless and unprincipled opponents, quite a distinction indeed. Maimed and dashing, Tarleton had made a name for himself during the Revolutionary War as a depraved butcher who killed prisoners and civilians and did many sadistically cruel things, including compelling the widow of an American general to serve a meal to her husband's exhumed corpse. Tarleton presided over the infamous Waxhaw massacre of Virginia

Continentals, something so awful that many who had been previously neutral became zealous supporters of the Revolution. It was this pro-slavery charmer who now moved to adjourn the debate on abolition, but Tarleton's motion was defeated by twenty-six votes.

The bill's second reading came, prematurely, on March 3. One of its opponents made the motion to a mostly empty house, almost succeeding in his hope of catching the abolitionists unprepared. Wilberforce, however, got wind of the dastardly ruse and rushed over to the chamber from his home at 4 Palace Yard—practically next door—and bought time by speaking until enough of abolition's supporters could be rallied. And so the bill passed its second reading, 63–31. Success was so extremely close now that Wilberforce was optimistic, but he could hardly dare consider success just yet, not with all he'd been through. Still, little seemed to stand in the way of victory at this juncture; Wilberforce himself knew there were at long last enough supporters of abolition for the bill to pass.

But it didn't—and the blame for abolition's crushing defeat in 1796—yet again—could plausibly be laid on the implausibly hunched backs of a pair of Italians. For that very night in the city of London, the curtain had risen on the premiere of an Italian comic opera titled *I Dui Gobi* (The Two Hunchbacks), and to a full house too. The forgotten composer, Portugallo, and the lead singer, Vignoni, knew not what they did, but it was this otherwise forgotten performance that lured a handful of the pro-abolition votes away from their solemn duties and privileges in the chamber. Thus in such an exceedingly ignominious way did the anti-abolitionists win, by four votes, 74–70.

For Wilberforce, the defeat was unspeakably distressing. "Ten or twelve of those who had supported me absent in the country, or on pleasure," he writes in his diary. "Enough at the Opera to have carried it. Very much vexed, and incensed at our opponents." Wilberforce was, in truth, less vexed and incensed than heartbroken. He was heartbroken for the slaves and for their unfathomable sufferings, which would now continue for who could say how long, and he was heartbroken that the so-called friends whose votes could have so easily ended those sufferings had somehow reckoned an evening at the opera more important. Wilberforce was not given to self-pity or to depression. Everyone who knew him knew a perpetually sunny character, but there was something about this particular defeat that gave him pause. Perhaps he had at last come face-to-face with what John Wesley had warned of, with the evilness of evil. And perhaps he was seeing the banality of evil too, to borrow Hannah Arendt's phrase: the disturbing idea that the sufferings of men, women, and children should continue as a result of the laziness of a handful of politicians. But on just such things did the cancer of the slave trade grow.

That night in his diary he writes: "I am permanently hurt about the slave trade." Who can imagine what was going through his mind, knowing that he had so narrowly missed passing the bill after nine years of trying, knowing that it was growing not less but more difficult each year? As one might have expected, this particularly crushing defeat affected Wilberforce's health, and he now became quite ill and would remain so for a long time. His faithful friend Isaac Milner came down from Cambridge to attend to him.

CHAPTER 15

TWO LOVES

"Jacta est alea."

William Wilberforce's conversion to Christianity in 1785— what he called his "Great Change" —was without question for him the central and most important event of his life. Indeed, as far as Wilberforce was concerned, faith in Jesus Christ was the central and most important thing in life itself, so it can hardly surprise us that sharing this faith with others was central and important to Wilberforce too. And so, everywhere he went, and with everyone he met, he tried, as best he could, to bring the conversation around to the question of eternity. Wilberforce would prepare lists of his friends' names and next to the entries make notes on how he might best encourage them in their faith, if they had faith, and toward a faith if they still had none. He would list subjects he could bring up with each friend that might launch them into a conversation about spiritual issues. He even called these subjects and questions "launchers" and was always looking for opportunities to introduce them.

His efforts to draw his friends into conversation about "first things" sometimes failed, and the objects of his kindness may on occasion have felt more like his quarry. But in many cases Wilberforce's conversations bore great fruit, and some who hadn't known it was possible to be sincerely Christian and yet witty and charming found in Wilberforce an inspiration. If he, being so brilliant and sociable and wealthy—and a close friend of the prime minister's!—could be so serious about his faith, perhaps it might be acceptable after all. It was in his public person that Wilberforce may have done the most to "make goodness fashionable." An indisputably captivating figure who defied easy categorization (not that many didn't try), Wilberforce became something akin to an icon for serious Christian faith. But he was certainly no moralizing lummox. His brilliance and good cheer and wealth and charm and obvious earnestness made him too slippery to grasp easily. For a nation that knew serious Christianity principally through the black-robed figures of John Wesley, John Newton, and George Whitefield, Wilberforce was an undeniably fascinating and intriguing figure.

In 1793 Wilberforce began to write a tract on the rudiments of what he had to say on the subject of faith, but as often happened with Wilberforce's letters and speeches, it ballooned of its own accord into something far beyond the original idea. The tract, such as Wilberforce first planned it, was never written. Eventually, he began thinking that he should put his myriad thoughts into a book, and now and again he would jot things down on bits of paper.

An overactive mind like Wilberforce's was never easily channeled and did not lend itself well to organization. There was something inescapably wild and beautiful about his mind, and it's as if he spent his whole life trying to tame it without breaking it. One might say that this was the essence of his genius and charm—that he did not break the beautiful creature that was his own mind and did not set himself to become another stereotypically dour Methodist from whom his social peers would have recoiled, as they had with all the others. In its own way, remaining thus true to himself was an act of self-discipline for which we might give Wilberforce great credit, not to say gratitude.

Many years later his friend Maria Edgeworth described his conversational style:

His thoughts flow in such abundance, and from so many sources, that they often cross one another; and sometimes a reporter would be quite at a loss. As he literally seems to speak all his thoughts as they occur, he produces what strikes him on both sides of any question. This often puzzles his hearers, but to me it is a proof of candour and sincerity; and it is both amusing and instructive to see him thus balancing accounts out loud. He is very lively and full of odd contortions: no matter. His indulgent, benevolent temper strikes one particularly: he makes no pretension to superior sanctity or strictness.

For a man with such a mind, getting his thoughts on the Christian faith between the covers of a book was inescapably a task on the order of herding cats and shoveling smoke. Still, he knew that he must do it. What he had to say was really rather elementary: basic Christianity such as was professed in the Bible and in the doctrines of the Church of England, and to which almost everyone claimed to subscribe, was practically nonexistent in British society. Most people who went to church and thought themselves "decent Christian people" actually knew little or nothing about the faith they claimed to practice and did not practice the Christianity of the Bible or of the Church of England at all. Moreover, they were quite unaware that this was the case.

The principal problem was the Anglican clerics themselves, who mostly didn't believe the basic tenets of orthodox Christian faith but didn't want to declare themselves for fear of losing their salaries and positions. Wilberforce did not want to scold his readers or badger them into believing as he believed, but he did want to tell them what their ministers in the pulpits were keeping from them. He wanted to expose these ministers for what they were: dishonest members of a caste that refused to be thrown out because they had, as it were, a good thing going and seemed to think they knew better than the people in the pews anyway. Wilberforce wanted to speak directly to the people in those pews and tell them what many of them already suspected, that the emperor had no theological clothes, and was hiding behind silly fig leaves of mere propriety. Wilberforce wanted to point out the logical disconnect, to show the vast gulf separating "real Christianity," as he called it, from the ersatz "religious system" that prevailed in its place. The book's long title, *A Practical View of the Prevailing Religious System of Professed Christians, in the Higher and Middle Classes in This Country, Contrasted with Real Christianity,* made it difficult to miss the point.

The book's style, being similar to Wilberforce's style of speaking, was atypical of the time. Like his speeches in the House of Commons, the book was conversational and sometimes rambled every which way, as distinguished from the much more polished and organized oratory of Pitt and Burke and other masters of the form. Pollock calls it a "slippery eel of a book," but that, of course, was its charm—just as it was the author's charm. The book certainly isn't ponderous and, unlike most other religious tracts of the time, remains quite readable two centuries later. It simply describes what Christianity is and then shows what the reality of religious belief was in British society. Wilberforce's point was that this difference between theory and practice was vast and needed to be noted. And noted it was. The book's reception was remarkable. When Wilberforce approached the publisher, a Mr. Cadell, in February 1797, he was not at all interested. But when Cadell realized that Wilberforce would not publish the book anonymously, as so many did in those days, but planned to affix his somewhat famous name to it—well, that was another story. Even so, he agreed to print only 500 copies. Wilberforce assented and the book was published on April 12. Within just a few days, every copy had been sold. Within six months, it had been reprinted five times and had sold 7,500 copies.

Wilberforce explained that real Christianity had evaporated from England principally because it was woven into the social fabric and therefore was easier to ignore and take for granted. "Christianity especially," he wrote, "has always thrived under persecution. For then it has no lukewarm professors." Wilberforce was exactly right. Not only was there no persecution of Christianity in England at that time, but the entire nation was officially Christian—in name only. England's pulpits were filled with just such "lukewarm professors" lukewarmly professing a lukewarm faith that thrilled no one and challenged no one, lacking, as it did, the indispensable tang of otherness that is at the heart of Christian belief.

Wilberforce's main charge against the faux Christianity of his day was that it pretended to be the real thing but wasn't—yet few dared to rock the boat and say as much. Wilberforce couldn't stand this tepid version of the real thing and labored to show that this practice that everyone thought was Christianity was in fact not Christianity at all. It was an uphill battle.

Wilberforce knew that if Britain took its faith seriously, if it actually believed the doctrines it claimed to believe, it could never have countenanced the slave trade or the institution of slavery itself. He knew that if Britain began to see what real Christianity was, it would begin to take an interest in the sufferings of the poor and feel an obligation toward them, as well as toward prisoners and others who suffered. That sort of concern was always the mark of real Christianity, but it was utterly absent from Britain in the last years of the eighteenth century. Wilberforce knew that the upper classes were complacent and had easily substituted for real Christianity a philosophy more akin to the view of many Eastern religions, in which the sufferings of the poor were an important outworking of karmic justice and mustn't be meddled with.

In his book Wilberforce was essentially calling Britain to repent, to turn back to its true faith, the faith it had abandoned on the far side of the seventeenth century. Real Christianity, which they purported to believe, was wonderful and bracing and beautiful, but they had been getting the lukewarm version. It was a winsome and unprecedented appeal to a nation, specifically to its middle and upper classes, and ultimately it had a very great effect. Wilberforce knew that many people didn't know what real Christianity was; though they attended church, they'd never seen it and though they'd heard hundreds of sermons they had never heard it preached. Now, using the bully pulpit of his national celebrity, he would tell them that he believed it and had given his life to it. He was issuing, as it were, a warm invitation to join him.

Many would take Wilberforce at his word, both at the time the book was published and for decades afterward. It was a great comfort to many readers to learn that even if their own clergy did not understand what Christianity was—or perhaps they understood it and didn't much like it—at least this one man, this Wilberforce, understood it and recommended it. No less than Edmund Burke on his deathbed drew solace from the book. Henry Thornton wrote of it to Hannah More. "Have you been told," he asked her, "that Burke spent much of the two last days of his life reading Wilberforce's book, and said that he derived much comfort from it, and that if he lived he would thank Wilberforce for having sent such a book into the world?"

Wilberforce's book was published on April 12, 1797. He was at Bath at this time and in his diary laconically writes: "My book out today." Wilberforce knew that the publisher, Mr. Cadell, had hardly thought the book worth the trouble of publishing: "He evidently regarded me an amiable enthusiast."

As we already know, however, no sooner did the booksellers put a fresh copy of Wilberforce's book on their shelves than the unruly volume leapt off again, and flew directly into the open arms of a reader eager for spiritual sustenance. It was an extraordinary phenomenon, and the publisher was caught quite unawares. The author too was all that week observably beside himself, giddy and distracted to a degree that is difficult to fathom unless one has fallen in love. Wilberforce could hardly think or sleep all week long. But let us not mislead the reader any longer: it was not the five hundred books a-leaping that had robbed Mr. Wilberforce of sleep and peace. It was one maid a-flirting. Her name was Barbara Spooner. She was twenty years old, and it was love at first sight.

No one was more surprised than he was, but William Wilberforce was in love. He was now thirty-seven and certainly not what one would consider robust in his health. The "little fellow of the callico guts" was still suffering from terrible spells and still taking significant quantities of opium on a regular basis to ease things for himself. His eyesight, which had always been poor, had become poorer still, and he suffered from episodes during which it was very poor indeed. He was physically so slight as to appear ethereal. Romance had simply not been in the picture for many years. Seven years earlier, Dorothy Wordsworth, the sister of the poet William Wordsworth, had expressed to a mutual friend an interest in Wilberforce but had thought herself unworthy of him; Wilberforce had never expressed any particular affections toward her. Indeed, at the very time that Dorothy expressed interest in him, a letter tells us that Wilberforce was having strong romantic feelings toward another, a certain "Miss H." The secret letters compressed into the period after that tantalizing initial will probably never be released to reveal her mysterious identity. It seems that Wilberforce had had some irreconcilable differences with this Miss H. on matters of some importance—one assumes theological—and that he had elected, in the end, not to propose marriage, though he admitted that the temptation had been strong and the decision difficult. Soon she had married another.

Wilberforce had taken the whole experience as an indication that he was likely to stay as he was, as St. Paul had famously enjoined believers to do. "I doubt if I shall ever change my situation," he wrote to a friend in the winter of 1796. "The state of public affairs concurs with other causes in making me believe I must finish my journey alone." He was also convinced that he would finish his journey well ahead of the natural pace, because he seriously believed he was likely to die violently when some enemy of abolition made good on one of the several threats he had received since becoming the cause's chiefest champion. "I do assure you," he continued, "that in my own case I think it highly probable. Then consider how extremely I am occupied. What should I have done had I been a family man for the last three weeks, worried from morning to night. But I must not think of such matters now, it make me feel my solitary state too sensibly."

But in early 1796 the equation of his life had been altered. His dearest friend, Henry Thornton, got married—and to Marianne Sykes, who had been friends with Wilberforce since their childhood in Hull. This scrambled things unconscionably. For nearly five years, Wilberforce had lived with Thornton as a co-tenant at Battersea Rise in Clapham, and from their "chummery" the two friends had been busy bachelors engaged in many of the same things—abolition, of course, and the various projects related to the "reformation of manners." But suddenly his old friend Marianne, now styled as the new Mrs. Thornton, had supplanted him. It's very likely that this change in his situation and the loss of Henry to marriage started Wilberforce thinking again along matrimonial lines and wondering whether he was supposed to "finish his journey alone" after all.

This we know: by April 1797 Wilberforce had reversed course and was once again open to marrying. Indeed, he was more than open to the idea—he was positively interested in it. While at Bath that month, he confided his thoughts on the subject to another of his dearest friends, Thomas Babington. And that, it seems in retrospect, was about all it took: for didn't Babington that minute have just the girl in mind for his dearest Wilber? (Wilberforce's close friends unanimously called him Wilber.) Babington now told Wilberforce about a lovely young woman, twenty years of age, who had recently become deeply serious in her religious views and whose family were alarmed and bothered by her sudden conversion to what seemed like disturbingly Methodist views. Her name was Barbara Ann Spooner, and she was the third of ten children of Isaac Spooner, a wealthy banker from Birmingham.

The Spooners lived at Elmdon Hall and had a second home in Bath. But suddenly their Barbara no longer skittered along to each ball and assembly, as she must do. What was the blessed point of being in Bath at all if not to display to eligible bachelors one's marriageable daughters? And there was a giggling queue of Spooner girls just behind Barbara who needed marrying off once she'd been settled. But now she'd gone Methodist. Her parents surely feared she would end an old maid—their beautiful Barbara! It is no wonder Jane Austen set several of her novels in Bath during this time. One can almost hear Mrs. Spooner assaulting the ears of her dear husband with keening lamentations over their unprecedented tragedy: "O! Mr. Spooner! Our dear girl has gone Methodist—*Methodist!* And she the prettiest of the bunch! O! What shall we do now? O! Mr. Spooner. I tell you we are ruined—*ruined!* Call the apothecary! *O!*"

Not long afterward, whether prodded by Babington we don't know (but do guess), Barbara wrote a letter to Mr. William Wilberforce, asking his advice in "spiritual matters." It seemed that her new views on religion—to which she knew Mr. Wilberforce would be sensitive—were some cause of strife with the rest of her family. Wilberforce's curiosity was piqued by her letter, and on April 13, Holy Thursday, and the very day after his book came out,

Wilberforce writes: "Babington has strongly recommended Miss Spooner for wife for me. We talked about it."

April 14 was Good Friday, and Wilberforce's diary shows him to be in a rare state of spiritual satisfaction:

> I thank God that I now do feel in some degree as I ought this day. I trust that I feel true humiliation of soul from a sense of my own extreme unworthiness a humble hope in the favour of God in Christ; some emotion from the contemplation of him who at this very moment was hanging on the cross; some desire to devote myself to Him who has so dearly bought me; some degree of that universal love and good—which the sight of Christ crucified is calculated to inspire. Oh if the contemplation here can produce these effects on my hard heart, what will the vision of Christ in glory produce hereafter!

For those who believe in random coincidences, it was an extraordinary coincidence by any account that on the day after registering what for him was a very rare sense of peace with God that he should meet the woman for whom he had been waiting and praying so many years. For it was that next day, Holy Saturday, that Wilberforce met his future wife for the very first time. They dined in a party, and before all of the courses had been served Wilberforce had fallen headlong for her, and eight days later they were engaged, and a month after that married—and within ten years had six children, four boys and two girls. But we may be getting ahead of ourselves.

In his diary that night, after this inaugural meeting, Wilberforce writes the phrase "Pleased with Miss Spooner." And then, perhaps thinking that a bit of an understatement, he underlines it: *"Pleased with Miss Spooner."*

On Easter Sunday, Wilberforce writes that during services at church he had been "very much affected by my own meditations about Miss Spooner and mind sadly rambling at the dinner. . . . I in danger of falling in love with creature of my own imagination." It's hard not to be amused by his mind, so characteristically leaping wildly ahead and then instantly stopping on a dime to double back and repent of having leapt ahead, before leaping wildly ahead again, stopping dead, and doubling back again. At the end of the day he writes: "What a blessed Sunday have I been permitted to spend, how happy at dinner and in love."

He saw her practically every day that week and was kept awake most nights thinking of her. On Saturday he writes: "Morning. Miss Spooner to Pump Room. . . . Supped with Spooners—captivated with Miss Spooner. My heart gone, but that would forbear openly for a while, as advised by Henry [Thornton] and H[annah]. More, tho' they imperfect judges."

On Sunday the wave crests:

After sad night haunted with Miss Spooner rose to prayer. Miss Spooner to Pump Room, Randolph's. Much affected and at length I fear too hastily wrote, I fear rather too hastily declaring to Miss Spooner state of my mind and she dined with us. Afternoon. Babington rather advised me to put off for 2 or 3 days. I vexed, having got over the Struggle. But at length gave way. When going to Miss Babington found that my letter had actually gone. That night I had a formal favourable answer—kept awake all night.

That same day, in a separate journal, he writes:

This last week seems a month. Alas—I fear I have been too eager about earthly things. It seems as if I have been in a fever. I have constantly however prayed to God for his direction and read his word—yesterday had resolved to wait before I determined about Miss Spooner, but she quite captivated me last night by her behavior to her parents, the Lillingstones and myself and the Babingtons. Such frankness and native dignity, such cheerful waggish innocence from a good conscience, such mutual confidence and affection towards her parents . . . her modesty and propriety. . . . I could not sleep for thinking of her and being much agitated this morning at and after Church, wrote a long rambling letter to her which she has just returned with favourable answer. *Jacta est alea.* [The die is cast.] I believe indeed she is admirably suited to me, and there are many circumstances which seem to advise the step. I trust God will bless me; I go to pray to Him.

It was over. Wilberforce had proposed marriage and had been accepted, and now each friend must hear every detail. Pollock says Wilberforce's friends were "deafened with carillons of joy." All of Bath was atwitter with the news at the same time that it was abuzz with the phenomenon that was his book. It was as though one bold declaration of his affections had been instantly followed by a second, and it was an unprecedented and unexpected confluence of exceedingly happy events. Enthusiasts couldn't help seeing the Divine Hand at work—but "amiable enthusiasts" saw it at play too.

Wilberforce summoned Milner from Cambridge and Thornton from London to meet his Barbara, and dutifully they flew thither to inspect the gladsome situation firsthand and to clap their little friend on his back. In his letter, Wilberforce had also mentioned to Milner that Barbara was ill and needed his medical attentions. But when both friends arrived at Bath, after their hundred-mile journeys, they found Barbara beaming with health and Wilberforce leaving for London, summoned by Pitt on some important business regarding the Austrian loan. He had sent notes to intercept them and return them to their respective homes, but as sometimes happened in those days, the missives failed to hit their moving targets.

In any event, they were happy to be there, and so very happy for their friend. Also amused by the happy turn of events, Hannah More, whose life had been as single-mindedly literary as she was literally single, wrote to him: "I dare say if I were now to fill up my paper with any other subject but this fair Barbara you would think me a dull, prosing, pedantic unfeeling Old Maid who was prating of the book when she should be talking of the Wife."

❦

On May 30, in a typically quiet ceremony in the local parish church, William Wilberforce, age thirty-seven, was married to Barbara Ann, twenty, eldest daughter of Isaac Spooner, Esquire, of Elmdon Hall in the county of Warwick.

"Writings signed to Church about 11 o/c and married," he confides to his diary that day. "Miss Anne Chapman and Miss Lillingstone for Bridesmaids and my dearest Barbara, composed but inwardly agitated—suddenly moved to tears at service much affected. I but queer in my feelings all day. Dined Mr. Spooner's. In evening to Beacon Hill. My dearest B desired me to join in prayers with her." He concludes, "Oh that I might be worthy of her."

There can be little question from any quarter that their marriage was, from the start, filled with mutual love and affection. After four days, they traveled to Cowslip Green to visit Hannah More and her admiring quartet of sisters. Wilberforce had years before said that if ever he were to marry he would want to honeymoon with his wife there and take her on a tour of Hannah's Mendip Schools, which he had helped her start and which she and her sisters oversaw. He thought a tour of that place, in all of its poverty, combined with the great philanthropy of the More sisters, would be a fitting way of inaugurating their relationship, of further consecrating it to God. Every visit he had made to Cowslip Green was a tonic to any worldly mind-set and selfish ambitions, and he wanted to begin his married life on the right foot, with a visit to the poor.

On the day he and his new bride set off alone for Cowslip Green, he wrote to his friend Matthew Montagu: "She wishes to retire as much as possible from the giddy crowd, and to employ herself in 'keeping her own heart' and in promoting the happiness of her fellow creatures. I really did not think there had been such a woman. There seems to be entire coincidence in our intimacy and interests and pursuits." The next thirty-five years attest to the overwhelming truth of this early observation. To be sure, as in all marriages, hidden differences would weep out over time, but inasmuch as love covereth a multitude of sins, it covereth a smaller number too.

There were some who thought the match somewhat below Wilberforce, socially speaking. Henry Thornton tells us that her fortune, at only £5,000, was very modest compared to what others might have expected Wilberforce to achieve. But Wilberforce had, of course, introduced other variables into the equation, which his friends surely knew. "The match is not what the world would account to be a good match—" wrote Henry Thornton, "that is to say he has not insisted on some things which the world most esteems, because he has thought it indispensable that the lady should have certain other qualities." Henry Duncombe wrote: "You will perhaps judge my way of thinking old-fashioned and queer but I am greatly pleased that you have not chosen your partner from among the titled fair ones of the land. Do not however tell Lady C so."

CHAPTER 16

CLAPHAM'S GOLDEN AGE

". . . and that at Clapham."

After their honeymoon week with the five More sisters at
Cowslip Green, our newlyweds proceeded to London
and lived at 4 Palace Yard, for Parliament was still in session. Pitt
had offered them his Holwood Estate, but they decided instead to
lease Broomfield at Clapham, Edward Eliot's home. Eliot was in the
West Country, and very sick at the time. When Parliament rose, the
William Wilberforces—now comfortably pluralized—decided to
travel up to Hull to introduce Barbara to Wilberforce's mother and
publicly introduce her to the county that her husband represented.

But on the way there they received shocking news: Wilberforce's
brother-in-law, Dr. Clarke—his sister Sally's husband—had died
suddenly, at forty-five. Barbara's first visit to Hull thus took place
during a time of mourning. Wilberforce's mother was also quite
sickly and would die the next year. Dr. Clarke had been the rector
of the Hull church, and Wilberforce now used his influence to gain
the living for his dear old friend Joseph Milner. But Milner died a
few weeks later too. And that September, when Wilberforce and his
wife returned to Bath, the hardest death of them all came: one of

Wilberforce's oldest friends, Edward Eliot, died. Eliot had been one of the first whom Wilberforce had led to faith.

Wilberforce and Barbara now bought Eliot's Broomfield Lodge and would live there for ten years. Their moving into Broomfield Lodge would inaugurate a kind of Golden Age of Clapham, a ten-year period during which Wilberforce lived there with Barbara, and during which they would bring their six children into the world, and the culmination of which would be finally achieving abolition itself.

The unofficial community of Clapham had, of course, existed before then. Wilberforce had been living there with Henry Thornton, Edward Eliot, and Charles Grant, and many others lived nearby. But things now moved into a new phase.

But before we talk about any so-called Golden Age of Clapham, we must talk about Clapham more generally. We often hear about Wilberforce and the "Clapham Sect," or Wilberforce and the "Clapham Saints." Those terms have been used in books, but to be perfectly accurate, there was no such thing as the Clapham Sect, nor ever was. The erroneous term "Clapham Sect" was most likely coined after Wilberforce's death, and it is misleading because a sect is a group whose theology is somehow deviant from the norm, while the Clapham folks were about as theologically deviant as the Nicene Creed. The word sect also implies a group with an official membership, and the Clapham folks were utterly informal, just a group of friends with common interests. Several of them who were members of Parliament voted together on certain issues and shared a similar evangelical perspective; it was that link that was responsible for their sometimes being referred to as "the Saints."

This group of people who lived at Clapham at the end of the eighteenth century and the beginning of the nineteenth, most of whom we have already met, have been called the Clapham Community, the Clapham Group, and the Clapham Circle; the last term should suffice for our purposes. Whatever they are called, it's no exaggeration to say that over the course of a few decades, with William Wilberforce as their unofficial leader, they quite literally and only somewhat inadvertently changed the world forever.

Although he had no idea exactly what would come of it, the community was, truth be told, Henry Thornton's idea. Thornton thought that creating a kind of community—revolving principally around Wilberforce—would be beneficial in two ways. First, it would foster the faith of each of those who lived there, and second, it would create a place for them to plan together and dream together and console each other and encourage each other in their common efforts, most notably abolition. Such communities have often been at the core of movements. Thornton wisely saw that people of serious faith were not in the majority in the worlds in which they traveled. In the upper echelons of British society at the time, one needed a place to retire to where one was not thought odd or "Methodist." Clapham would be that place.

But he could never have foreseen exactly what might arise from his wonderful idea. "On the whole," Thornton wrote in 1793, "I am in hopes that some good may come of our Clapham system. Mr. Wilberforce is a candle that should not be hid under a bushel. The influence of his conversation is great and striking. . . . I am not surprised to find how much religion everybody seems to have when they get into our house."

The quaint village of Clapham was a suburb of London at the time, being just four miles from Westminster. When we talk about the Clapham Circle, or "Clapham," we are talking about something that transcends mere geography and is, more than anything else, a tangled skein of friendships and families, all bound up together with a cheerful and passionate evangelical impulse to serve God, most notably by ending the horror of the slave trade. To understand properly the full degree to which the members of the Clapham Circle were intermarried and intermingled would require a separate chapter, or another book.

We can say that the whole happy birds' nest started with Henry's father, John Thornton, who had become an evangelical early on, in 1754, through the ministry of George Whitefield. He had been living in Clapham when, in 1756, Henry Venn, a well-known evangelical at that time, began his ministry there. We remember that John Thornton's sister, Hannah, had married William Wilberforce's uncle—also named William Wilberforce—and that when the young Wilberforce lived with them, between the ages of nine and eleven or twelve, they had exposed him to the remarkable community of

evangelicals that included John Newton. Thornton had also been responsible for a few years later bringing Newton from rural Olney
to St. Mary Woolnoth's in London, which made him available to
Wilberforce at the beginning of his "Great Change." So you could say
that John Thornton established the beachhead at Clapham both geo-
graphically and spiritually. He was the first point that, with Henry
Venn, became a line; that connected to another line, and another,
until it became a nine-dimensional spider's web of lines that might
drive mad anyone attempting to untangle it—so let's don't.

John Thornton had three sons, all of whom became members
of Parliament and all of whom lived in Clapham. But it was his son
Henry who deliberately began to think that something like the
Clapham Circle might be possible. On his father's death, he bought
Battersea Rise and in 1792 invited Wilberforce to move in with him,
creating the chummery.

Battersea Rise was the magnificent Queen Anne house on the
west side of Clapham Common that would become the center of the
Clapham Community. Battersea Rise was quite grand, but Henry
Thornton was quite rich, and after he added two wings to the house,
each as big as the original house itself, it had thirty-four bedrooms
in total.

The central feature of Battersea Rise was the oval library. The
oval was a highly fashionable shape at the tail end of the eighteenth
century, the most popular example of which, of course, is the Oval
Office in the White House. The oval shape was used for very special
rooms because it enables a dignitary or honoree to be surrounded by
a circle of admirers without seeming to have a favorite.

The oval library at Battersea Rise had the distinction of having been designed by William Pitt, who, though not a member of
the Clapham Circle, was obviously well connected to many who
were, most notably Thornton, Eliot, and Wilberforce. Pitt had told
Thornton that he'd always wanted to design a library. From our modern point of view, this may seem like a surprising ambition for Pitt,
but at the end of the Enlightenment it was not so out of the ordinary
for bright, wealthy young men to want to do such things. The love of
reason and rationality that typified the Enlightenment lent itself rather
well to design, and eighteenth-century men were able to look back to

the Romans and the Greeks for their inspiration. Thomas Jefferson designed Monticello and the University of Virginia, of course, and George Washington oversaw all of the designs for the vast city that would posthumously bear his name. Before that, while in the field leading the Continental forces, he closely supervised the smallest details of Mount Vernon's renovation, down to moldings and paint colors, via letters. So Pitt was in good company. And naturally, as with practically everything else he put his mind to, he did a singular job.

Three walls of the capacious, high-ceilinged room were covered with books, and the fourth looked out through high glass doors onto venerable elms, firs, and giant tulip trees; beyond them to the lawns of the estate; and beyond the lawns to picturesque farmland. This library became the focal point and main meeting place for the Clapham Circle, the place where they held their "cabinet meetings," and it contained marble busts of both Fox and Pitt, presumably to underscore Thornton's political independence. The idea of marble busts of Pitt and Fox seems perfectly apt from the distance of two centuries, though it is hard for contemporary minds to imagine what it would have been like to have marble busts of living friends and acquaintances. But of course it was the fashion to do so, especially when one's friends were the nation's political leaders.

Thornton built two more impressive houses on the property: the first of these, Broomfield, was for Edward Eliot; the second, Glenelg, was for Charles Grant. After the 1787 death of Eliot's wife, Pitt's sister Harriot, Eliot continued to live there with their daughter, also named Harriot, until his death in 1798. Wilberforce and Barbara bought the house after his death. Charles Grant was a member of Parliament for Invernessshire [*sssic*] and a director of the East India Company. In 1793 Henry Venn's son, John Venn, became the resident clergyman at Clapham; he was a key figure in everything that transpired there, preaching sermons every Sunday that would spoil the group for anyone else and being their very capable spiritual head. Venn was such a good preacher that all who were at Clapham could trace to him a good deal of their spiritual growth and maturity. The historian Robin Furneaux tells us what happened when a visiting preacher came to Clapham: "Preaching to the Clapham Sect must have been the equivalent of singing at La Scala or playing on the centre court at

Wimbledon. But the miserable substitute failed to realise the quality of his audience. 'He chose to extemporise,' was the chilling verdict, 'and that at Clapham.'" Furneaux sees this as an example of spiritual pride, which it would be if it weren't meant to be humorous; but given the level of wit at Clapham, it almost certainly was. Furneaux chose a literal interpretation—and that of Clapham.

Granville Sharp lived in Clapham village, and James Stephen, the passionate lawyer who had lived in St. Kitt's, also came to live there, as did Zachary Macaulay, who had been a slave overseer in Barbados but who had become disgusted with the brutality of slavery and had returned to England to join the abolitionist cause. Another prominent figure, John Shore, or Lord Teignmouth, who had lately returned from India, also moved there. All of these men and their wives were evangelicals, all lived to abolish the slave trade and slavery, and all were instrumental in various aspects of "the reformation of manners."

But this is merely a list of those who actually lived there. A list of those who visited, and whom the Claphamites visited when venturing abroad, would be just as long, and when we speak of "Clapham" we are really speaking of all of them. The roll of these nonresidents is as distinguished as that of the residents. No one could have been more central to their various causes, or to what we mean by "Clapham," than Hannah More, who visited often. And then there was Charles Simeon of Cambridge. According to Ernest Marshal Howse, the "intellectual center of Clapham" was at Cambridge. Simeon, whom some called "St. Charles of Cambridge," was an especially important figure in the evangelical movement of this time and had close ties with the Clapham Group.

Sir James Stephen, the famous son of Clapham's James Stephen, in writing about Clapham would call Wilberforce "the Agamemnon of the host . . . the very sun of the Claphamic system." Physically, but certainly not intellectually, the "Telamonian Ajax" of the group might have been Isaac Milner, also of Cambridge. By this time he was the dean of Carlisle and was called Dean Milner. He was a frequent visitor to the Wilberforces' home at Broomfield, where he could often be heard calling for more food, which had partly to do with his size and appetite—and partly to do with Mrs. Wilberforce's evangelical abstemiousness.

Thomas Gisborne, Wilberforce's neighbor at St. John's College all those years before, had reconnected with Wilberforce and was now a key figure in their circle as well. Gisborne had come to be known as one of the finest preachers in England. His country home, Yoxall Lodge, was a kind of second Clapham. He had married the sister of Thomas Babington, another St. John's classmate, and Babington had married the sister of Zachary Macaulay.

To cross the reader's eyes we may now cinch the Georgian knot of Clapham interconnectivity beyond all human untangling by quoting from Howse's book, *Saints in Politics:*

> As we have seen, Henry Thornton was Wilberforce's cousin; Gisborne married Babington's sister; and Babington married Macaulay's sister. In addition Charles Eliot married John Venn's sister; [James] Stephen married Wilberforce's sister [Sally]; and, all the available sisters having been taken, Macaulay married a pupil of Hannah More. Soon, too, the next generation added its ties, and the son of James Stephen married the daughter of John Venn. . . .

Into this intellectually and spiritually verdant setting Barbara Wilberforce now came, from the decidedly less verdant environment of Elmdon Hall. It must have been a bit overwhelming for this twenty-year-old woman who couldn't have had a tenth of an idea of what she was getting into. And this so-called Golden Age of Clapham, as we have described it, began, quite literally, with a bang. The literal bang—we are sorry to say—came from the pistol of the prime minister of the nation, William Pitt. And the fired pistol was pointed in the direction of a member of Parliament. There was also a bang from another pistol, aimed at Pitt, and then two more bangs, one from each of the aforementioned pistols. The Wilberforces had moved their things into Broomfield only a few days before, and Barbara was already seven months pregnant with their first child, William. That Monday morning, the twenty-eighth of May, 1798, Wilberforce was dressing when his secretary, Ashley, entered with the shocking news that Mr. Pitt had been in a duel.

The revelation was extremely upsetting to Wilberforce, who hated dueling for several reasons. To begin with, he considered a duel a barbaric offense against God. As he saw it, dueling was the sanctioned, cold-blooded murder of a human being, and an act undertaken principally to avoid being seen as a coward, a motivation that, ironically, was a bit cowardly in and of itself. Wilberforce knew that dueling had everything to do with one's pride, in the negative sense of that word, and little or nothing to do with honor. Wilberforce himself had refused a challenge some years before from an opponent of abolition. That Pitt of all people—in the midst of an extremely serious war for the life of the nation—would risk his life in a duel was appalling. Pitt knew that Wilberforce would feel this way and took the trouble to conceal the affair from him until it was over. The duel had been with a Whig MP named Tierney, who opposed Pitt's policies and constantly attacked him over the war with France. Pitt finally blew up and accused Tierney, in effect, of aiding the enemy.

Furneaux's account is worth quoting:

On May 25 Pitt accused Tierney of deliberately sabotaging the country's defence, a remark that was ruled out of order by the Speaker. When Pitt refused to apologise Tierney issued a challenge, which he at once accepted. Pitt's thin, almost cadaverous figure was a joy to cartoonists, but Tierney was a fat little man. The wits in Parliament therefore suggested that, to make the contest more even, Pitt's figure should be chalked on to Tierney and no shots outside it should count.

The duelers fired at each other twice, from the curiously abbreviated distance of twelve paces. Pitt fired his second bullet into the air, deliberately. Nevertheless, the fact that they weren't both killed at such a distance makes one wonder how much for show such duels actually were. Still, Wilberforce was outraged. Not only was Pitt setting a horrid example for the rest of the nation and risking the life of the leader of the nation at a terribly crucial time, but he had done his awful deed on the Sabbath. It's impossible for us—who do everything imaginable on a Sunday—to understand how sacrosanct that day was to Wilberforce. For him the Sabbath had been set apart by

God, and to trespass on it as Pitt had done was to thumb one's nose at God himself. To Wilberforce, Pitt's deed was something grotesque, as though he had presided over a bull-baiting on the high altar at St. Paul's.

But Wilberforce had been disappointed with Pitt even before hearing about the duel. Pitt's ardor for abolition seemed to have cooled, and just that Friday, the twenty-fifth—the same day he had his confrontation in the House with Tierney—Pitt had angered Wilberforce by putting off a slave-carrying bill. Pitt might understandably have been feeling politically distracted and at cross-purposes as he tried to hold the country together during a war, with a Jacobite revolution threatening to leap the few miles across the Channel and a fierce enemy on the high seas. But there was more than that to Wilberforce's unease, as he himself knew. Pitt seemed to have become so distracted that he had forgotten about the suffering of the slaves. Wilberforce never lost the taste of the horrors of slavery, not even when abolition seemed politically impossible, such as now. He could never dismiss it and he lived and breathed to see it come to an end. He gave it no quarter and pushed against it whenever there was any opportunity. So Pitt's recent delaying of the slave-carrying bill had bothered him. And now this.

Wilberforce straightaway decided that he would put forth a bill in the House to outlaw dueling. It was about time, and he thought it was critical to send a message to the public that such behavior was neither laudable nor acceptable, whether their prime minister had engaged in it or not. Pitt, understandably, was rather vexed to hear of Wilberforce's intentions. He felt that under the current political circumstances such a bill would discredit him enough that he might well be turned out of office. In any case, he wrote Wilberforce a long letter saying so. Wilberforce hated to hurt his dear friend and so was persuaded to stand down. As usual, the two old friends made it up. But Wilberforce had gotten his point across.

Just a few weeks after this Wilberforce's mother died. Wilberforce had traveled to Hull to be with her. "My dear mother did not suffer in death," he wrote to Barbara, "and I trust she is happy. The change

gradually produced in her over the last eight years was highly grati-
fying to all who loved her. . . . It was a solemn and affecting scene to
me, yesterday evening, to be in my mother's room, and see the bed
where I was born, and where my father and my mother died, and
where she then lay in her coffin."

Alone in the room with his mother's body, he prayed. What
gratitude must have poured from his heart there, to know that the
very one who had once feared his incipient faith had come round
the bend herself to see its beauty. And what gratitude he must have
felt to know that he had been God's chiefest instrument in opening her eyes. Fourteen days after bidding his dear mother farewell,
Wilberforce was home to greet her grandchild, his first son.

All six of the Wilberforce children would be born at Broomfield
in the next nine years. Little William was born in 1798, Barbara in
1799, Elizabeth in 1801, Robert in 1802, Samuel in 1805, and Henry
in 1807. After the sixth child, Mrs. Wilberforce pronounced them
all good, and rested.

∽

The Clapham Circle was involved in a seemingly endless number of
ventures, but at the center, always, was the fight for abolition and
the slaves. One of the projects closest to the heart of the abolition
movement was the establishment, with great effort and difficulty,
of a free and self-governing colony of former slaves in Sierra Leone,
a venture whose beginnings predated Wilberforce's involvement in
the abolitionist cause. On May 10, 1787, two days before the famous
conversation under the oak at Holwood, a ship full of former slaves
had dropped anchor off the coast of Sierra Leone. But of course, this
experiment, for such it was, had originated long before that.

We will remember that back in 1772 Granville Sharp had first
appeared in Lord Mansfield's courtroom, causing that venerable
magistrate to seethe with anger and nearly flip his powdered wig.
Mansfield had been forced to rule in the Somerset case, and his ruling had effectively established the freedom of all slaves throughout
England. As Cowper wrote: "Slaves cannot breathe in England; if
their lungs/ Receive our air, that moment they are free." But quite

as Mansfield foresaw, these newly freed people would not mix into
the population and society without difficulty. It wasn't as though they
would simply inhale a lungful of British air, shed their shackles, and
take a flat on Easy Street. At the time of the Somerset ruling, there
were fourteen thousand blacks in England, and their integration into
society did indeed prove difficult. The "negro beggar," as Sir Reginald
Coupland tells us, became a common sight throughout England. From
1776 onward, the numerous American slaves who had broken their
shackles by joining the British forces during the war added to the
number.

So in 1786 a "Committee for Relieving the Black Poor" had been
formed. Among those involved was a Dr. Smeathman, who had lived
for some years in Sierra Leone on the west coast of Africa and who
suggested forming a colony for these Africans there. Most abolitionists felt that the continent of Africa itself had been injured by the
slave trade and was owed a great debt; they wanted not merely to
abolish the trade but also to restore some of what the British nation
and others had taken. The establishment of a successful colony of free
blacks in Africa was thought a capital beginning toward that end,
and in two ways. First, it would demonstrate that blacks were not
savages incapable of governing themselves, as the racist slave lobby
held, but human beings every bit as capable as the Europeans who
had enslaved them. And second, such a colony would help create a
thriving African economy trading in something other than enslaved
human beings. This colony would create a beachhead of freedom and
self-government on the Dark Continent, whose liberal light in time
might penetrate the furthest reaches of "Afric' gloom."

To modern ears, the idea of sending the blacks back to Africa
may sound racist, but the intentions of the abolitionists were as pure
as human intentions could be, and their high regard and hopes for the
blacks were nothing less than revolutionary at the time. The aim was
to bless these displaced men and women and make up to them and
their continent some measure of what had been wrongly taken.

On May 10, 1787, a few hundred blacks and some sixty whites
debarked on the shore of St. George's Bay in Sierra Leone and began
the noble experiment. Life was crushingly difficult for the infant
colony. Just as with another colony of pilgrims across the Atlantic

in the previous century, about half of those who arrived died within the year. In both cases diseases ran rampant, and poor timing exacerbated the adjustment to the strange climate. In Sierra Leone no Squanto appeared out of the woods to plant corn and solve most of the colonists' problems. And of course, in both places there were hostile locals. In Sierra Leone these included British and French slave traders, who recognized the powerful symbolism of this brave and fragile undertaking and would do all they could to murder it in its cradle. And in 1789 the fledgling town was burned to the ground by a neighboring African chief.

It was then that the cry of the embattled colonists was heard at Clapham, and now the Claphamite host and its Agamemnon, William Wilberforce, would be roused. Abolition stood to gain much from the success of this colony, and they would do whatever they could to make it succeed. Granville Sharp, always itching to vanquish troublemakers, girded his loins for the battle. In 1790 the St. George's Bay Association was formed, given a charter, and incorporated by an act of Parliament. The Sierra Leone Company, as it was called, would have Granville Sharp for president and Henry Thornton for chairman, and two of its first directors were Charles Grant and William Wilberforce. There was much to be done.

In 1792 one thousand fresh recruits arrived in Sierra Leone from Nova Scotia. The Sierra Leone Company raised £240,000 in capital, and a new town, called Freetown, was put on the map. Several schools were built and well run; both a hospital and a church were built. The Clapham Circle didn't know, as they say, the meaning of the word "discouragement"—which was a good thing, because there were towering heaps of reasons to be seriously discouraged. Fresh horrors arose constantly, including aggressive armies of ants who *literally* didn't know the meaning of the word "discouragement." Nor were the Nova Scotian reinforcements the cyclones of optimism and hard work they had promised to be. They seemed immune to the feverish enthusiasm for the colony that its directors at Clapham seemed to have. The Nova Scotians even dared to have grievances and sent a delegation home to air them. When they didn't get the response they were looking for, they staged a lackluster insurrection. So it went.

The Clapham Circle, however, would not yield to defeatism. They would now send to that distant shore one of their best, Zachary Macaulay, who was brilliant and capable and the most industrious and immune to despair of them all. And even he would be pushed to the brink. In 1794 French revolutionary forces, aided by an American slave-ship captain, attacked Freetown, pillaging and burning with a particular gratuitousness, slaughtering the livestock and killing every plant. In 1795 Macaulay's health and nerves collapsed. He returned to England, but in characteristic fashion he made the trip aboard a slave ship, so as to learn firsthand what the experience was like. In England, he fell in love with Selina Mills, a young teacher who worked with the More sisters in their Mendip Schools, another Claphamite project. They were engaged, but Macaulay returned to Sierra Leone in 1796 as governor and remained three more years before returning to England to be married.

The colony that Macaulay left in 1799 was substantially improved from the one he had found when he first arrived. The colony now had 1,200 inhabitants, and there was at least some stability. Sierra Leone was finally transferred to the Crown in 1807. Although it continued to struggle in various ways, it was a living, singular example of former slaves governing themselves and was therefore a powerful symbol and weapon for the abolitionist cause.

CHAPTER 17

DOMESTIC LIFE AT CLAPHAM

". . . that winged being and all his airy flight . . ."

Any picture of domestic life at Clapham as in any way pacific and ordered must be banished from the mind if ever such a false picture seeks to lodge there. The myriad activities, voluntary organizations, children, visitors, pets, and servants could never be described accurately, and at the center of it all, like a bumblebee or an electron, was William Wilberforce. Most of the descriptions we have of Clapham seem like a Georgian-era version of *You Can't Take It with You*. In place of Ann Miller pirouetting her way across the room and a few loud explosions from the basement, we substitute the grand entrances upon the scene of various inimitably colorful friends, such as Hannah More, Granville Sharp, and Isaac Milner.

Marianne Thornton, who lived at Battersea Rise, gives us a picture of Milner at the Wilberforce table: "He was a rough loud and rather coarse man," she writes,

> but he used to say all he thought and ask for all he wanted, in a way no one else ever ventured to do, in the many Wilberforce

homes he visited. The real bond of union between him and Mr. W. was that he was a deeply religious man, and how clever he was on the records of Cambridge honours shew. "Now W. listen, for no power on earth will make me repeat what I am going to say" used to be his rough exclamation when Mr. W. was flitting after a child, a cat or a flower or a new book, when they had met to discuss some important point. At the W. breakfast, when he chiefly received company, there was the most extraordinary mixture of guest, and an equally strange want of the common usages of life. To use a Yorkshire expression of his—Everyone was expected to fend for themselves. He was so short-sighted he could see nothing beyond his own plate, which Mrs. W. took care to supply with all he wanted till the Dean's stentorian voice was heard roaring "There [is] nothing on earth to eat," and desiring the servants to bring some bread and butter, he would add "and bring plenty without limit," while Mr. W. would join in with "thank you, thank you kindly Milner, for seeing to these things, Mrs. W. is not strong enough to meddle much in domestic matters."

By even charitable accounts, Barbara Wilberforce was not the best hostess, but she seems to have been a supremely devoted wife and mother, raising six children and assiduously attending to the needs of a husband who careered between having the energy of another six and then being bedridden and beset by his bevy of illnesses. We can only imagine what this reserved young woman thought of the giant Milner roaring for more food. Or of the endless parade of eccentric friends and visitors her husband attracted like a magnet from the four corners of the globe. The poet Robert Southey wrote: "His wife sits in the midst of it like Patience on a monument, and he frisks about as if every vein in his body were filled with quick-silver." But Barbara was thought by most to be a nervous woman, someone whose dark "gypsy" eyes in Russell's portrait betray an inner anxiety. Wilberforce seems to have been too distracted to allay her fears very effectively. Nor did either of them seem to be able to encourage the servants to bring some order to the situation.

Wilberforce had an old coachman, given to drink, who drove wildly, drunk or sober. Wilberforce several times nearly dismissed him but was simply too kind to let anyone go if he could possibly help it. But his feelings toward the coachman found egress in the witty comments for which he was privately so famous. One day, when visiting a friend, he found his host's housekeeper to be a woman of exceedingly bad temper. "You know the Indians have a way," Wilberforce said, "of getting oddly contrasted animals to fight each other. I really long to set our old coachman and this fine lady in single combat."

Few examples of the legendary Wilberforce wit and humor survive, but now and again there is a flash. After visiting the famous pavilion at Brighton that had been built by George IV, Wilberforce described it as "beautiful . . . though it looks very much as if St. Paul's had come down to the sea and left behind a litter of cupolas."

Wilberforce's humor must often have been crushed by the heavy concerns of abolition and the press of other parliamentary business, so that when he was at home, in his domestic element, he seems to have given his mind free rein and allowed himself to play with the children and the animals as though he were one of them.

It does seem, from all the accounts, that Wilberforce himself animated the chaos; when the children were wound up, it seems to have been their father who had turned the key to begin with, and who would turn it again when it had wound itself down. We get the idea that Wilberforce carried energy and chaos with him in his pockets along with his many books. The rest of the family, by comparison, was less wild and less interesting, certainly once they grew into adulthood. When, immediately after his death, Marianne Thornton learned that Robert and Samuel Wilberforce were collaborating on a book about their father—which eventually became the famous five-volume biography to which all subsequent biographers owe such a great debt—she expressed horror at the idea of these two rather straightforward figures trying their hand at capturing the ineffable sprite that was their father. She thought that asking them to capture "that winged being and all his airy flight" was like asking "a mole to talk about an eagle."

Wilberforce even brought the domestic chaos of his home life with him on the road. In 1818 he visited the Lake District and stayed at Keswick with Southey. "Wilberforce, also, has been here with all his household," wrote Southey, "and such a household. The principle of the family seems to be that, provided the servants have faith, good works are not to be expected from them, and the utter disorder which prevails in consequence is truly farcical. The old coachman would figure upon the stage."

It's impossible to get a snapshot of Wilberforce's life at any point, rather like trying to stick a pushpin in a cyclone. His mind and movements were so fast, his interests so varied, and his stream of visitors and correspondence so rapidly shuffled that the years he lived at Broomfield are a decade-long blur. But it's entertaining to freeze-frame the film now and again, just to see what turns up. For example, on the morning of July 30, 1804, Wilberforce's diary tells us that he had breakfast with one Mr. Norton, who was a Mohawk Indian chief, a Cherokee, and a Scottish Anglican, all rolled into one. Norton was visiting Clapham on the occasion of the inaugural effort of the British and Foreign Bible Society, another one of Wilberforce's innumerable projects. Wilberforce and company would pay for the translation of the Gospel into the Mohawk language and send Bibles with Mr. Norton to his compatriots across the Atlantic. The diary reads:

> Morning, breakfast—friends about sending the Gospel to the Indians. Mr. Norton's Mohawk's dance—Venn, Dealtry, Cookson, John Thornton—much discussion. We are all extremely struck with Mr. Norton, the Mohawk chief (Teyoninhokarawen); his blended modesty and self possession: his good sense and apparent simple propriety of demeanor. May it be a providential incident thrown in my way to send the gospel to those ill-used people. He again danced his war dance more moderately.

The scene of cultivated chaos was well and good in its way, but James Stephen, who married Wilberforce's sister Sally after she had been widowed by her first husband, was not shy about taking Wilberforce to task for being as scattered as he obviously was. Stephen, as we remember, was white-hot in his passion to end the slave trade, and it bothered him to see Wilberforce constantly spending energy in so many directions at once. He saw firsthand that his dear friend attended to every visitor and to every letter that came in the post when he might better have put them off for another time and attended to what was most important. The criticism seems at least half apt, especially with regard to the mountains of correspondence that Wilberforce was endlessly answering. "Millions will sigh in hopeless wretchedness," Stephen said, "that Wilberforce's correspondents may not think him unkind or uncivil. Why if you were my Lord Wellington and I Massena, I would undertake to draw off your whole attention from my grand movements, and ruin your army unperceived by teasing your piquets and burning a few cottages on your flanks."

At another time he spoke of Wilberforce's seat-of-the-pants way of living: "Your great defect has always been want of preparation . . . that you stand so high as you do, is because you could stand much higher if you would, i.e., if you could and would take time to analyze your material."

Wilberforce took all such criticism to heart, quite earnestly, and in some ways exerted terrific self-discipline, but in other ways he was quite hopeless. As Southey has already told us, Wilberforce even took the chaos with him when he and his family left Clapham. But Wilberforce did manage to find great tranquillity in his private times for prayer and meditation on the Scriptures—solitary activities he pursued with impressive assiduousness—and on the many long walks and hikes he took in the country, usually carrying books to read along the way. It was in solitude that he restored his soul to some equilibrium.

In September, the Wilberforces, with their four children, went to Lyme in Dorsetshire. This was one of those rare times when Wilberforce was able to truly get away from his many worthy involvements and, even more important, from the fatiguing fatuities of society. Everywhere else he went he was quickly found out. Wilberforce erred badly on the side of graciousness, and for fear of seeming ungracious the word "no" seems rarely to have escaped his mouth. But at Lyme, somehow, he found real rest.

"The place," he wrote to a friend,

> suits me mightily: a bold coast, a fine sea view—the clouds
> often shrouding the tops of the cliffs; a very varied surface
> of ground; a mild climate, and either fresh air or sheltered
> walks as you please. I allow myself two or three hours open
> air daily, and have enjoyed more than one solitary stroll with
> a Testament, a Cowper, or a Psalter, for my companion. We
> have not had one call since we came. . . . I never was at any
> place where I had so much the command of my own time,
> and the power of living as I please.

Wilberforce spent much time reading outdoors and "had many a delightful walk along the hoarse-resounding shore, meditating on better things than poor blind Homer knew or sung of."

Or than Pitt knew or sung of, now that he thought of it. Poor
Pitt! Wilberforce felt keenly his estrangement from his friend, sub-
tle and unspoken as it was. Wilberforce's love for his friend never
changed, but the tide of his own life had pulled him inexorably
away. He had, of course, become more and more surrounded by sincere Christians like himself. While a bachelor, he still had time for
friends like Pitt, but marriage changed that, as did the move out to
Clapham. And soon children were leaping into the picture with an
almost annual ferocity, filling all and any remaining moments. Pitt
had remained single and had naturally grown closer to others, such
as Dundas and Bishop Pretyman, both of whom took a powerfully
dim view of Methodists.

In 1805 a financial scandal involving Dundas erupted, and
Wilberforce's true value to the nation as someone who genuinely put
"principle above party" would show itself—as would, alas, the day-
light between him and his beloved friend and ally Pitt.

Dundas (now Lord Melville, having been made a peer in 1802)
was first lord of the Admiralty in Pitt's government. Five years earlier, while treasurer for the Navy, he looked the other way when
an underling misappropriated some funds. A February 1805 report
had now implicated him. Wilberforce happened to be in Pitt's office when the report arrived. "I shall never forget the way he seized

it," Wilberforce wrote, "and how eagerly he looked into the leaves without waiting even to cut them open." Pitt and Dundas had become close over the years, and while Wilberforce certainly wasn't the type to be jealous of Dundas, neither did he feel comfortable with the influence that Dundas had on his beloved friend. For one thing, Dundas had encouraged Pitt's drinking, with which Pitt had struggled over the years. And now this.

When Melville didn't resign quietly, the opposition sensed an opportunity to weaken Pitt politically, and they took it. On April 8, Samuel Whitbread moved a resolution to censure Melville. Wilberforce was caught in the middle of it all. He never wanted to be a party to anything that hurt his friend, but nothing outraged him more than corruption in high office. The evidence was at first inconclusive, but as Wilberforce listened to the debates all night long, he realized that there was never any solid defense of Melville's conduct. Wilberforce kept waiting for such a defense, and it never came. Melville was obviously guilty, and Pitt's demeanor indicated as much. He seemed to know that Melville was guilty, but also to have calculated that, unless it was bungled, the crisis would pass and all would be well.

By 4:00 a.m., when Wilberforce finally rose to speak, he had still heard nothing to exonerate Melville. Pitt had tried to catch Wilberforce's eye as he rose to speak, to deter him from saying what Pitt feared he would say, but Wilberforce knew that he could not in good conscience allow his friendship with Pitt turn him from his duty to the nation. And so Wilberforce avoided Pitt's gaze and said what he thought of the situation, eloquently and powerfully, and with enough moral authority to devastate Pitt. "I must confess that it is impossible for me to leave the House this night," Wilberforce said, "without giving my vote in support of the Resolutions [to censure]." Those who watched Pitt watching Wilberforce said that, atypically, he was visibly agitated. Wilberforce continued. "Here is a plain, broad fact which no subsequent elucidation can possibly explain away. . . . Here is my Lord Melville publicly declaring on his oath that he has tolerated his dependent in a gross breach of an Act of Parliament for the purposes of private emolument. I really cannot find language sufficiently strong to express my utter detestation of such conduct." Wilberforce saw no options at all. If Melville was not censured for what he had clearly done, it would set a terribly damaging precedent. It would, Wilberforce said, "open a door to every species of corruption, and there would be no security left for the faithful discharge of any public trust."

There was no question that Wilberforce's speech, surely the best of the night, administered a powerful shove to all the tortured fence-sitters. When the vote was called, the highly implausible happened: it was a dead tie, 216–216. Inasmuch as it was a tie, the speaker, Abbot, would have to decide. Abbot, suddenly realizing this and feeling the hard stares of the House's 864 eyes pinning him to his chair like a beetle, turned visibly white. He remained silent for the longest time. Then, at last, he cast his vote. It was against Melville, and it landed like a bomb into the midst of the deadlock, creating instant bedlam. Many now burst into cries of "Resign! Resign!" directed at Pitt. And Pitt could take no more. He wept. It was quite unlike him, and the only time anyone had ever seen him display his emotions while in office. He cocked his hat over his face to hide his tears, but his enemies exulted shamelessly in his defeat, wild Whigs a-whooping like blood-smeared savages in some Dionysiac orgy. One of them, more civil but not less cruel, cast the scene through a fox-hunting lens, shouting, "View Holloa"—the ejaculation upon flushing a fox from its cover—and then: "We have killed the fox!" A few friends formed a phalanx around Pitt to shield him from his enemies' unseemly leers of *schadenfreude*. But it was a rout.

Wilberforce was not happy with the outcome, but his conscience and the inevitable logic of the situation overrode his feelings toward his friend. Many felt that Wilberforce's betrayal and this devastating political defeat were what sent Pitt into the illness that soon killed him. Wilberforce was sure that was not the case. There can be little question that Pitt felt hurt and betrayed by Wilberforce. But knowing Wilberforce as he did, it's also certain that Pitt knew him to be entirely incapable of playing the part of Brutus. He knew that Wilberforce was a noble friend, and that knowledge likely made the whole episode hurt the more.

Melville now resigned, was impeached, and then was acquitted—found guilty of negligence but not fraud. Interestingly, his departure opened the way for the eighty-year-old Charles Middleton to take the post of first lord of the Admiralty. Few doubted that

Middleton's entire life had been a preparation for this hour. As good as Melville was, the fast-unfolding events on the high seas now required the surer hand that Middleton could bring, and the rapport that he had with Nelson was nothing small; indeed, it was likely decisive in the incalculably crucial Trafalgar campaign.

Middleton's taking this post now was simply an extraordinary turn of events. That this man whom Wilberforce revered and loved and knew as a friend and a brother in the faith—and who had been at the forefront of the abolitionist movement—should now at his advanced age command His Majesty's Navy, at this gravest of hours, when the future of the empire and the next century so depended on him, was something monumental.

Hard as it was for both of them, there was no irrevocable breach with Pitt over this incident. Wilberforce saw him many times that fall, and all was as it had been. In November the cheering news of Trafalgar came. Middleton—now Lord Barham—was awakened with the news: "My Lord, we have gained a great victory, but Lord Nelson is dead!" Wilberforce was overcome with emotion at the news. "So overcome," he writes, "that I could not go on reading for tears."

Every British schoolchild has heard the mythic heroics and details of that day over and over and can recite them chapter and verse: how Nelson, aboard the HMS *Victory,* sent word to his fleet before the battle—"England expects every man will do his duty"; how during the battle he was mortally wounded by the musket ball of a sniper standing in the rigging of the French ship *Redoubtable;* how his final words were, "Thank God, I have done my duty"; how the fallen hero's body was preserved for the long journey home in a cask of brandy; and how today it lies below St. Paul's in a coffin made from the wood of the mast of *L'Orient,* a French ship that had been, happily, blown up. If anyone is in danger of missing the significance of Nelson and Trafalgar to British life, Nelson's eighteen-foot-high statue has been helpfully placed atop the aptly named Nelson's Column, which granite pillar soars 169 feet into the air at the center of the aptly named Trafalgar Square—the central hub of all London—and is flanked by four massive bronze lions cast from the formerly French bronze of Napoleon's cannons.

For Pitt, however, the glorious news of Trafalgar was only a temporary buoy. On December 2 came the crushing defeat at Austerlitz as Napoleon's armies overcame Austria and Russia. The blow to Pitt was ultimately a fatal one. He had spent much of the previous two years in a fever of diplomatic activity to build the Third Coalition—an alliance with Austria, Russia, Sweden, and Naples—and had at last succeeded. And now, after all of that, the coalition's armies had been vanquished and destroyed. Pitt's already poor health now suffered a blow from Austerlitz from which he would never recover.

When Wilberforce returned to London on January 21, 1806, he received word that Pitt was very ill. On the twenty-second, he writes: "Quite unsettled and uneasy about Pitt, so to town. Heard bad account. Called on Rose, who quite overcome. He had been long at Putney talking to Bishop of Lincoln [Pretyman]. Physicians said all was hopeless."

Before Wilberforce could even visit his friend, it was over. At four in the morning on the twenty-third of January, William Pitt the Younger died. He was forty-six.

Bishop Pretyman was quite typical of the Church of England clergy of his day. He was deeply suspicious of evangelicals, and had kept a close circle around Pitt since Pitt's Cambridge years. Years later Wilberforce wrote to Henry Bankes that he could "never forgive [Pretyman's] never proposing prayer to our poor old friend Pitt . . . till within about six hours before his dissolution."

In a letter to Muncaster: "This late event saddens rather than softens my heart. There is something weighing down the spirits. . . . I own I have a thousand times (aye, times without number) wished and hoped that a quiet interval would be afforded him, perhaps in the evening of his life, in which he and I might confer freely on the most important of all subjects. But the scene is closed—for ever."

It broke Wilberforce's heart. His dear friend was gone—gone forever. And he knew not where.

CHAPTER 18

∞∞∞

VICTORY!

"God will bless this country."

Wilberforce was now forty-seven years old, but for someone who'd been part of a veritable youth movement—a
boys' club that had taken over Parliament—he was now practically
an old man. And he felt it too. His always frail body, which had been
wracked with pain and discomfort ever since he could remember,
was the body of someone much further along in years. The constant
doses of opium pushed on him by his doctors for his ulcerative colitis
had taken their toll on his eyes, and the curvature of his spine and
the telltale slump of his head that would mark him in later years were
already discernible. He'd entered Parliament as a boy of twenty-one,
fresh from the bright green lawns of Cambridge—but how the years
and battles had aged him! As if to underscore things, Pitt, his ally and
friend since those carefree days, was dead, and from complications
brought on by gout, an old man's disease.

Since 1787, year after year after year, Wilberforce had put forth
his bill, and year after year after year it had been defeated, one way
or another. In twenty long years, he had still not brought the boat
into the harbor, though he had tacked and retacked and circled back

and tacked in again and again and again. There had always been some difficulty, some heartbreaking last-minute barrier to success. Wilberforce was tired. The abolitionists had come so tantalizingly, horribly close to success in 1796, only to be handed their most devastating defeat yet. At that time, Wilberforce had all but decided to quit public service for good. But no less than the encouragements of the aged patriarchs John Wesley and John Newton prevented him from doing that, and thank goodness. Now, ten long years later, the waters were quite suddenly smooth, and the harbor for which he had longed for two decades seemed finally to open her arms to him.

After Pitt died, William Grenville became the new prime minister. Grenville had been the third man under that fabled oak tree twenty years before when Wilberforce had decided to lead the abolitionist battle. How extraordinary to think of it, and to think that now, just as Grenville came to lead the country, public sentiment again turned in favor of abolition. Grenville himself saw the opportunity to make history, but Wilberforce, the veteran of a score of such battles, was far less sanguine.

"It seemed clear he would have no easy triumph," wrote Wilberforce's son Samuel. "The Dukes of Clarence and of Sussex [the two sons of the king] declared openly against the Bill, speaking, as it was understood, the sentiments of all the reigning family. Yet the ice of prejudice was rapidly dissolving." And indeed it was. Grenville's strategy would be to reverse the usual pattern and this time bring the bill before the House of Lords first, where it had always encountered its greatest difficulties. And he, the prime minister, would read the motion himself.

On the second day of the new year 1807, a bill "for the Abolition of the Slave Trade" had its first reading. The Duke of Clarence, pro-slavery to the end, managed to delay the bill's second reading for a month. But the month passed, as they all seem to do, and on the evening of Thursday, the fifth of February, the second reading and the long-awaited debate began.

Wilberforce was there for it all, watching from the gallery, and doubtless on pins and needles throughout. The debate opened with Grenville making a speech of atypical eloquence—focusing not on the soundness of abolition as a fiscal policy but directly, and surprisingly, on the moral question of the slave trade itself. "Is it to be endured," he asked, "that this detestable traffic is to be continued, and such a mass of human misery produced?" He ended by eulogizing Wilberforce, calling the abolition bill "a measure which will diffuse happiness among millions now in existence, and for which his memory will be blessed by millions yet unborn." The debate did not end until 5:00 a.m., and when the vote was taken it could scarcely be believed. Abolition had won, and by an astonishing majority of 64 votes, 100–36.

In Wilberforce's recollection, "Lord Grenville's speech concluded with a most handsome compliment to me, and several peers now speak with quite new civility. How striking to observe Pitt and Fox both dead before Abolition effected, and now Lord Grenville, without any particular deference from Court, carries it so triumphantly! But let us not be too sure."

The bill's third reading in the House of Lords was set for the following Tuesday, February 10. Wilberforce was again only cautiously optimistic, knowing that at any moment a parliamentary monkey wrench might knock the bill another year or indeed many years into the future, as had happened so many times before. But the bill passed surprisingly fast, emerging from the House of Lords and going straight to Commons that very same evening, quick as a rabbit. "Our success," Wilberforce writes, "altogether greatly surpassed my expectations."

The bill's passage in Commons seemed probable, and by now everyone could see the historic handwriting on the wall. But Wilberforce still wouldn't allow himself that luxury. The following day he writes that he had received "congratulations from all, as if all done. Yet I cannot be sure. May it please God to give us success."

Still, even Wilberforce couldn't guard his heart completely now. Very slowly he began to believe—to allow himself to believe—that it might be possible, that it might be happening at long last. As he considered Grenville's assessment of how many votes they had in Commons, we see the first twinkle of Wilberforce's optimism: "Lord Grenville not confident on looking at Abolition list; yet I think we shall carry it too. Several West Indians with us. How popular Abolition is just now! God can turn the hearts of men."

The idea that two West Indian planters might vote for abolition! As a group, they had always formed the staunchest opposition to abolition. How giddy Wilberforce must have been to think of it—but how characteristically and quickly he checked his giddiness, as though afraid of it: two days later, during his usual Sabbath devotions, he writes, "The decision of the great question approaches. May it please God, who has the hearts of all in His hands, to turn them as in the House of Lords; and enable me to have a single eye, and a simple heart, desiring to please God, to do good to my fellow-creatures, and to testify my gratitude to my adorable Redeemer."

Writing on the day before the second reading, Wilberforce finally allows himself to see the victory that stands before him:

> Never surely had I more cause for gratitude than now, when carrying the great object of my life, to which a gracious Providence directed my thoughts twenty-six or twenty-seven years ago, and led my endeavours in 1787 or 1788. O Lord, let me praise Thee with my whole heart: for never surely was there any one so deeply indebted as myself; which way soever I look I am crowded with blessings. Oh may my gratitude be in some degree proportionate.

It is a measure of the man's heart that he knew himself unworthy of the veneration he would soon likely receive, and that he sincerely longed not to be swollen with pride, but instead to deflect all praise away from himself and upward, as it were, to the One who in the first place had led him to this long and noble battle and who had held up his tired arms as it raged for twenty long years on the plain below. He was fully determined to give God the glory when the glory at last would fall.

The bill's third and final reading in the House of Commons was set for February 23. What a flurry and contradiction of emotions he must have felt, a kind of ticklish torture of anticipation leading up to the day—the Day—when the hopes of two decades would be realized.

It is a rare thing to be able to appreciate something extraordinary while in the midst of it, to be inside it and outside it at the same time, watching ourselves. So how can we fathom the feelings of those in the House that day who knew the import of what was about to happen? It was as if they had been walking through a wood and had suddenly come upon a river, and had suddenly realized that this river before them, on whose banks they now stood, was the very river of History itself. What should they do? How had they been afforded this ineffable gift, to stand so close to it, to see it with their own eyes, the magnificent living thing itself that they had thought existed only in stories and old books? It would be like seeing the equator, bright red and gleaming, bisecting a field in Africa. They were giddy, beside themselves. And who would not want to wade in and touch it, to tell others he had been there, that he had brushed the hem of History's garment with his own hand!

And so, conscious of the unprecedented Moment in which they now lived and whose very air they breathed, nearly every man there, and the young ones especially, wanted to speak, to be a part of the glorious piling on. And how many did speak! They all rushed to enter the fray. Just as one member had finished his speech six or eight others leapt up to be next. It was highly unusual for this body, but one could feel the intensity mounting and mounting. In what was his maiden speech, young Lord Mahon hailed Wilberforce as one "whose name will descend to the latest posterity with never fading honour!" It became unbearable.

And now came Romilly, the solicitor-general. Romilly loved and admired Wilberforce not merely for his abolitionist efforts but also for his efforts toward penal reform and his sincere devotion to the poor. His speech, which contrasted the strutting egomaniac across the Channel with the humble figure seated only a few yards away, became legendary. Its sentences charged the air and brought the room to its final frenzy. "When I look to the man at the head of the French monarchy," he said,

> surrounded as he is with all the pomp of power and all the price of victory, distributing kingdoms to his family and principalities to his followers, seeming when he sits upon his throne to have reached the summit of human ambition and the pinnacle of earthly happiness—and when I follow that man into his closet or to his bed, and consider the pangs with which his solitude must be tortured and his repose banished,

by the recollection of the blood he has spilled and the op-
pressions he has committed—and when I compare with
those pangs of remorse the feelings which must accompany
my honourable friend from this house to his home, after the
vote of this night shall have confirmed the object of his humane and unceasing labours; when he retires to the bosom
of his happy and delighted family, when he lays himself down
on his bed, reflecting on the innumerable voices that will
be raised in every quarter of the world to bless him, how
much more pure and perfect felicity must he enjoy, in the
consciousness of having preserved so many millions of his
fellow-creatures.

But when Romilly spoke of Wilberforce's reception at home it
was too much for Wilberforce. Until then he had sat composed,
quite composed, but now he was overcome, and taking his head in
his hands, he wept.

Romilly's moving oration, now halted and combined with the
tears of its subject, proved too much for the room. It was as if somewhere, in the heart of creation, a dam had burst.

Everyone caught up in the increasingly charged atmosphere had
been waiting, as it were, for some unconscious cue, something to
ground the electricity—and Wilberforce's tears were it. Almost simultaneously, every man in the chamber lost his composure and was
carried off by the flood of emotion. Everyone rose, and three deafening cheers rang out for Mr. Wilberforce; they echoed off those
historic walls and hallowed them, and all was lost to the tumult.

It was an exquisite tragicomic chain of events, at once sublime
and absurd: Romilly's last words had overwhelmed Wilberforce,
who wept, and whose tears in turn overwhelmed the entire room,
which erupted into a surging spontaneity of cheers and applause—
and doubtless these cataracts of praise thundering down upon him
from every corner and surging down from the packed gallery served
in turn to further overwhelm Wilberforce, whose tears were re-
newed—which renewal in turn further overwhelmed the room into
further deafening rounds of cheering and applause! The tiny trickle
from Wilberforce's ducts had loosed a diluvian apocalypse never

before seen in the chamber. But it was an apocalypse not of judgment but of grace. It was as if the entire nation—as if the entire empire that circled the human globe—was in this flood of tears and huzzahs baptized and sanctified and marked forever for what they were now doing.

And here we leave him, weeping there in his accustomed seat as the overswollen thunderclouds of praise and celebration and joy burst over him and heaven rains a deluge of approbation upon his bowed head. In a little while the House would decide 283–16 in favor of abolition, and the battle would be officially won. But let's not run ahead just yet. Let's behold him here for a little while longer, here in this Moment of moments, a man allowed that highest and rarest privilege, to be awake inside his own dream. Seated there, head in his hands, humbled and exalted in his humility, we have the apotheosis of William Wilberforce.

❧

After this historic victory, Wilberforce repaired to 4 Palace Yard, where he was joined in his joyous delirium by many of his dearest friends. The Clapham gang were all there, including Henry and Marianne Thornton and Zachary Macaulay and the Grants. Granville Sharp was there too. The atmosphere must have been far beyond mere celebration. Most of them had been working toward this moment for twenty years, Granville Sharp for thirty-five. "Well, Henry," joked Wilberforce, "what shall we abolish next?" But Thornton missed the joke. "The Lottery, I think," he replied. And yet it is true that they would not long rest on these laurels, well deserved though they were. Wilberforce's second "great object" had spawned a hundred small battles over every social issue, and they would all spend the rest of their lives fighting those battles. And the main battle, for the slaves, was far from over. The long battles to enforce abolition and then to work toward emancipation loomed ahead and would be formidable. But for tonight they would rejoice in their victory. The size of the majority, 283–16, was especially inspiring. William Smith was nonetheless outraged that anyone at all had voted against abolition. "Let us make out the names of these sixteen miscreants," he said. "I have four of them." But Wilberforce said, "Never mind the miserable 16, let us think of the glorious 283!"

In another part of London that day, word of the victory was brought to John Newton. He was eighty-two and in the last year of his life. How his heart must have leapt to hear it! The news exploded across the globe. Sir James Mackintosh, hearing it in Bombay, remarked: "We are apt, perpetually to express our wonder that so much exertion should be necessary to suppress such a flagrant injustice. The more just reflections will be, that a short period of the short life of one man is, well and wisely directed, sufficient to remedy the miseries of millions for ages."

As for Wilberforce, he hardly knew what to make of the new situation. To labor so long and to be met with defeat after crushing defeat was all he had known for the better part of two decades. To a friend he wrote, "I really cannot account for the fervour which happily has taken the places of that fastidious well-bred lukewarmness which used to display itself on this subject, except by supposing it to be produced by that almighty power which can influence at will the judgements and affections of men."

Wilberforce was a brilliant thinker and astute politician, well aware of the many factors that came into play to make such a long-awaited victory possible. The 1801 Act of Union with Ireland was one of them, for it had brought many pro-abolitionist MPs into Parliament. The constant drumbeat of popular support for abolition, coupled with the increasing movement toward democratization, was crucial too. And sad as it was for Wilberforce to consider, the death of his beloved Pitt the previous year was an important factor. As much as Pitt had personally wished abolition's success, he had formed a government that did not share his ardor and was politically hamstrung on the issue. His cousin and successor as prime minister, William Grenville, was not only more personally passionate about abolition, but better situated politically to bring it about, being a member of the House of Lords, where it had met its chief opposition. And of course, by 1807 the formerly hair-raising phantasm of Jacobinism had been exorcised.

Wilberforce understood all of these factors and many more in endless detail. But for him this victory was more than anything a time to express humble gratitude for what might so easily again not have happened, despite all of these positive factors, and for what despite many positive factors had not happened before now. But it had happened at last, and he could hardly believe it. "God will bless this country," he said.

The Irish historian William Lecky gives us his own oft-quoted verdict: "The unweary, unostentatious, and inglorious crusade of England against slavery may probably be regarded as among the three or four perfectly virtuous pages comprised in the history of nations."

CHAPTER 19

BEYOND ABOLITION

"It is like closing my account . . ."

It is easy to treat the victory of 1807 as the joy and crown of all of Wilberforce's efforts and regard all that followed it as anticlimax. This would be understandable, though mistaken. Wilberforce did not forget that although they had won an epochal victory to end the slave trade, slavery itself remained alive and thriving as ever. The morning after abolition's victory, 500,000 human beings remained imprisoned as slaves on the brutal, dangerous sugar plantations of the British West Indies, unaware of and unable to take part in the victory celebration. Wilberforce and the others would never lose sight of these men, women, and children, and now and for the rest of his days he and his colleagues turned to the continuing war and the battles ahead—the battle to enforce abolition, the battle to spread abolition to the other great powers, and the battle to lessen the sufferings of those still in slavery. And finally they would turn toward the final battle in the war: the emancipation of all the slaves and the end of slavery.

One might say that in legally abolishing the trade the British nation had affirmatively and officially answered the poignant question

on the Wedgwood cameos. The slave's humanity had been established; now it must be honored. The immediate and main challenge
in 1807 would be enforcing abolition, and at the moment things
looked promising. The Americans had just abolished their slave trade
that same year (although, of course, it would still be more than half a
century before Lincoln's Emancipation Proclamation), and Denmark
had done so in 1803. Because of the ongoing war, Holland, France,
and Spain were not engaged in the trade either. Portugal stood alone
in conducting a large-scale trade.

And so, following the great victory of 1807, Clapham felt free to
shift its immediate attentions to the continent of Africa itself. Establishing the colony of former slaves in Sierra Leone had been a terrible
struggle for two decades, but now at last, in the same year that abolition was passed, it would be turned over to the British Crown. Those
who had labored to bring it to this moment now founded the African Institution to continue their work. Wilberforce was vice president and the usual Claphamite gang would be its directors: Stephen,
Smith, Grant, Babington, Macaulay, Sharp, and Clarkson. Henry
Thornton would be the treasurer, and the president would be the
thirty-one-year-old Duke of Gloucester, whose childhood head Isaac
Milner, cooing "pretty boy," had clumsily pawed all those years ago
at Nice. The Duke of Gloucester had been a young war hero, and
through his friendships with Wilberforce and Hannah More had become a devout Christian. He married one of the king's daughters
and stood in striking contrast to his anti-abolitionist cousins, the
king's sons, who jealously dismissed him as "Silly Billy." He proved
a very active president of the African Institution, whose purpose, in
Wilberforce's own description, was "promoting the Civilization and
Improvement of Africa."

But as this wider African venture gained traction, it became
painfully clear that the immediate problem would be enforcing abolition. Those who had been involved in the lucrative slave trade were
not about to give it up without a fight, and much smuggling was
going on. British slavers used every devious stratagem, the first of
which was flying the American flag as they sailed so that Royal Navy
patrols wouldn't bother them. Under the false colors of the Stars
and Stripes, thousands of Africans continued to suffer the Middle

Passage and were sold into West Indian slavery. On September 8, 1808, Wilberforce wrote to future U.S. president James Madison, who was a friend, enclosing another letter to then-president Thomas Jefferson and entreating Madison to help. In his letter to Jefferson, Wilberforce begged the cause of the men, women, and children who were being sold into bondage, "the unknown multitudes whose fate is involved in the decision you may form on this particular case." Wilberforce hoped for an Anglo-American agreement on the matter; this would not happen for many years, but an 1809 ruling in the case of a British ship seized by the Royal Navy's HMS *Derwent* effectively ended the use of the American flag as cover for the slavers' illegal operations. But there were other flags. The slavers soon began to use the Spanish flag for the same purpose, for Spain was a war ally and the ships of allies could not be searched. Wilberforce sent Lord Wellesley as an ambassador to the Spanish to plead the cause there, and on and on it went. In 1810 Parliament made slave trading a felony, with the stiff sentence of transportation to the British penal colony of Botany Bay in Australia for fourteen years. Still the smuggling continued.

The Royal Navy would become the policemen of the high seas for many decades into the future, and incredible as it may seem, British patrols were still functioning in this noble capacity into the 1920s. By then the large-scale trade had disappeared, but enterprising criminals will find niche markets. Each year into the 1920s ten or twelve boats, each carrying fifteen to twenty children, mostly for sale into the sex trade, would cross the Red Sea from Eritrea up into Saudi Arabia.

The great victory of 1807 marked ten years since Wilberforce and Barbara had been married and made a home together at Clapham. His activities had made Clapham a launching pad for much of the cultural reform that would shape the next century. But now, in 1808, Wilberforce would leave Clapham, though only formally. The concept of "Clapham" had long since overgrown the geographical reality, and wherever Wilberforce was found, there would Clapham be too.

Clapham was a movable feast, comprising an endlessly connected network of friends and co-laborers. And the Wilberforces were moving only three miles away. They took a twenty-five-year lease on a 1750s house in Kensington Gore. Gore House sat on the site of the future Albert Hall, one mile from Hyde Park Corner, and faced Hyde Park. Splitting his time between Clapham and Palace Yard had become an inconvenience and a financial extravagance. Wilberforce told Marianne Thornton the move "really will save 5 or 6 hundred pounds per annum." Moving to Kensington Gore seemed the perfect compromise: the area was still somewhat rural—for this was two centuries ago—but still near enough to Parliament that Wilberforce could walk home from work. If he was alone, he would sometimes recite the exceedingly long 119th Psalm to himself as he walked.

The happy informality of reciting Scriptures aloud among the birds and flowers and tall grasses of Hyde Park was typical Wilberforce. The sheer force of his innate innocence and cheer did much to change the public perception of religion in his day. William Blake had recently published his lines about "priests in black gowns, walking their rounds and binding with briars my joys and desires," aptly describing a faith that seemed to trundle along gravely, wrapped in black crepe with wheels muffled. But Wilberforce's grateful joy and his ebullient love for nature and her Creator was something else entirely, recalling the full-bodied spirituality of St. Francis of Assisi. Wilberforce loved memorizing poetry, Cowper and Milton especially, and he often recited it as he walked. But he especially enjoyed reciting Scripture and took seriously the injunction—from Psalm 119 itself—to "hide God's word in one's heart."

Although being one mile from Parliament was a great boon in some ways, it had its drawbacks. Now more than ever, people from every station in life, friends and strangers both, could stop in for a visit, and did. Lord Erskine would often stop by during his morning ride, and anyone else who felt the need for a meeting with the great man needed only to appear and take a seat with the others. Pollock tells us that "Kensington Gore became a sort of clearinghouse for British philanthropy and moral reformation, with Wilberforce ready to encourage or advise, or to rebuke, as when the Society for the Suppression of Vice toyed with the idea of using deceit to secure convictions." People would just gather, looking for something from the great man: his blessing on a venture or his signature or his willingness to lend his name to a committee.

After the assembled had waited for a bit, "an inner door opened," Pollock says,

> and out hurried Wilberforce, a strange little figure with hair still powdered, though the fashion had almost died out, and a sometimes dingy black suit without ornament except for a diamond pin. He would almost skip from group to group, bringing up his eye-glass as he greeted and listened and sympathized. Face and eyes would reflect pity or indignation at some tale of woe, or ardent approval for a new idea. Old friends could detect when the character or the suggestion before him touched his strong sense of the ludicrous, but his laughter never was unkind.

Spencer Perceval, the Tory who succeeded Grenville as prime minister in 1809, became a frequent visitor to Gore House. Perceval's religious views were quite close to Wilberforce's—indeed, closer than any prime minister's had ever been or would be again. On the question of introducing missionaries to India, Perceval saw eye to eye with Wilberforce, and Wilberforce would need all the help he could get, for Commons was strongly against the idea. "I am fully impressed," Perceval said, "with the necessity of setting the face of government against the offensive and abominable project of interdicting the circulation of religious knowledge in India." It must have been encouraging to have Perceval's support in something so close to Wilberforce's heart. The campaign to allow missionaries into India would be another epic and historic battle for Clapham. But as it turned out, Perceval himself, who had helped bring it to pass, would not be around to see it.

Perceval had become prime minister in 1809, when King George III was still ruling. In 1810 the king's seventeen-year-old daughter, Amelia, died. As much as the king's sons gave him worries and grief, his daughters seemed to give him comfort and joy, and Amelia was said to be his favorite. The death of his dear "Emily" aggravated the king's illness, rendering him again "mad" and unable to govern. The Prince of Wales, always the king's least favorite son and well ahead of the pack, was once again made regent, albeit with limited powers for one year. It was assumed that the king would soon recover, as he had done twice before, but he did not. And so the prince regent, aggressively dim on moral issues, was an especially stark foil for the upright and religious Prime Minister Perceval. But the strange political marriage would be short-lived. On May 11, 1812, Wilberforce and the Thorntons were at Babington's house in Downing Street for dinner. They were awaiting Babington, who was coming directly from Parliament, when he suddenly burst in and told them that Perceval had just been killed. A man named Bellingham had approached the prime minister in the lobby of Commons and shot him in the heart.

Bellingham was clearly half-mad and blamed his financial ruin on the government. But Wilberforce and many others, including Perceval's family, prayed for him. "Oh wonderful power of Christianity!" Wilberforce writes.

> Never can it have been seen, since our Saviour prayed for his murderers, in a more lovely form than on the occasion of poor dear Perceval's death. Stephen, who had at first been so much overcome by the stroke, had been this morning and found, praying for the wretched murderer, and thinking that his being known to be a friend of Perceval's might affect him, he went and devoted himself to trying to bring him to repentance. . . . The poor creature [Bellingham] was much affected, and very humble and thankful. . . . Poor Mrs. Perceval . . . with all her children knelt down by the body, and prayed . . . for the murderer's forgiveness.

After Perceval's assassination, another dissolution of Parliament seemed imminent, and another election. Wilberforce was forced to think about his position as MP for Yorkshire and the great responsibilities that it entailed. He was in his twenty-eighth year in his Yorkshire seat, having entered upon that role in 1784, the year before his "Great Change." He had been twenty-four then, and was now fifty-two, with six children. The exigencies of his political position forced Wilberforce to spend much time away from his family, far too much time, he thought. Once when Wilberforce picked up one of his little sons, the child had cried, and the boy's nursemaid had helpfully explained, "He always is afraid of strangers."

Leaving his Yorkshire seat would be a dramatically life-changing event, and it wasn't something Wilberforce could entertain lightly. So he now set himself to praying for God's will on the matter. Wilberforce's faith was not what one could call mystical—nor what we might today term "charismatic." The hours he logged praying and meditating on the Scriptures over the years were truly impressive. But Wilberforce never seems to have "heard" from God in any distinctly supernatural way, nor do we read of his ever having anything like a divinely inspired vision or dream. His faith was exceedingly sober—and careful and humble. He was filled with constant thanksgiving toward God and was keenly aware of his state before God as the beneficiary of unmerited grace. He partook of enough Anglican reserve and Calvinism to say on his deathbed that he hoped he "had his feet on the Rock," which implied that he didn't know, and which is misleading. From all the other evidence it seems obvious that he did know, but his humility toward an exceedingly gracious God—and his natural British reserve—would have made him feel it somewhat presumptuous to actually *say* so.

Wilberforce certainly believed that one had to have a "personal" relationship with God and that one had to be "born again." He believed that moral efforts were worth nothing without an experience of transforming grace, which he had experienced during his "Great Change." "[All] men must be regenerated by the grace of God before they are fit to be inhabitants of heaven," he wrote, "before they are possessed of that holiness without which no man shall see the Lord." He had a wonderfully firm and unfussy theological grasp of the balance between grace and works and refused to get bogged down in theological swamps. To Babington he put it succinctly: "The Blood of Jesus Christ cleanses from all sin and there is the comfort which combines the deepest Humiliation with the firmest Hope." And to his cousin Mary Bird he wrote: "Look to Jesus. Devote yourself body and soul to His service, I pray to God through Christ to enable you to do this more sincerely, more willingly, unreservedly." Wilberforce understood that Jesus was Savior, but as he wrote to his son Henry, "You may really have that Saviour for a Friend." And it was because of this that joy could enter the picture and lift him above the cliché of the dour Calvinist and sour moralist. The poet Southey once described Wilberforce as having "such a constant hilarity in every look and motion, such a sweetness in all his tones, such a benignity in all his thoughts, words, and actions that . . . you can feel nothing but love and admiration for a creature of so happy and blessed a nature."

So now, on the question of whether to leave his Yorkshire seat, Wilberforce prayed and expected to discover God's will. The fact was that Wilberforce's influence no longer depended on his occupying the powerful position of an MP from Yorkshire. After the passing of the abolition bill, he had in the public's eye been feted and cosseted and crowned with such laurels and heaped with such mantles of moral authority as anyone might have conceivably borne without stiffening to marble and gold. Wilberforce was now seen as the nation's conscience more than as a mere politically powerful member of Parliament. He might easily step down to serve as the member from a far less important "pocket borough" without losing anything substantive in the transition. His work and responsibilities would be considerably lightened, but he could still stay in the public swim as he felt called, and could still participate in such debates as he felt important.

Also, Wilberforce's eldest son, William, was now thirteen, and Wilberforce felt a strong responsibility toward his children. He wanted to be a significant part of their upbringing, and of their moral and religious education especially. Wilberforce's habit was to write down, at great length, the pros and cons of any serious question on a piece of paper as he was praying for God's guidance, and he did that now in making his decision about whether to stay as MP for Yorkshire. The paper upon which he wrote out the factors in that difficult decision— on his fifty-second birthday, August 24, 1811—survives, along with many other treasures, in Oxford's Bodleian Library. Among the factors he jotted down were: "2. The state of my body and mind, especially the latter, intimate to me the *solve senescentem*,—particularly my memory, of the failure of which I find decisive proofs continually."

James Stephen—with whom Wilberforce dilated on this subject at length, as he surely did with most of his closer friends—said that he thought Wilberforce's mind was quite as good as ever, apart from difficulties with memory, but he did write to Wilberforce that "of late I have at times seen or conceived I saw symptoms of deterioration in your bodily appearance, as if you were getting older faster than I could wish. Your spirits, too, I have thought not uniformly so high and so long on the wing as they used to be." On this basis, Stephen strongly urged him to switch to a less demanding seat.

In the end, Wilberforce did just that, deciding at last to forgo re-election to Yorkshire and accept a lesser borough, Bramber, so that he might stay involved in Parliament, but at a greatly reduced level of responsibilities. As usual, he reproached himself before making the decision, while making it, and after making it. "It is like closing my account," he wrote, "and I seem to have done so little, and there seem some things which it would be so desirable to try to do before I quit parliament, that I shrink from retiring as from extinction." Of course, for anyone, even the right decisions can be difficult. After twenty-eight years as a Knight of the Shire of Yorkshire, he couldn't be expected to hang up his lance and shield without some emotion and internal turmoil. He thought of all of the battles over the past three decades and all the elections. When the next general election came and for the first time in his adult life he did not participate in it, he was forgivably wistful. "I feel somewhat like an old retired hunter," he wrote, "who grazing in a park, and hearing the cry of the hounds pricks up his ears and can scarce keep quiet or refrain from breaking out to join them."

CHAPTER 20

INDIA

" . . . next to the Slave Trade, the foulest blot
on the moral character of our country."

After he had traded his powerful and prominent Yorkshire seat for the lesser seat of Bramber, Wilberforce went down to the House far less often. He had been serious about wanting to spend more time with his family. Far from being the political cliché it is today, the idea was quite unheard of in Wilberforce's time. In fact, his public avowal about wanting more time with his children sent a powerful countercultural message to the nation about the importance of family and fatherhood, one whose effects would be felt far into the next century and on both sides of the ocean. Both Wilberforce's habit of twice each day conducting family prayers—with everyone kneeling against chairs for the ten minutes or so that they took—and his regard for the Sabbath as a time to be spent with one's family went a long way toward establishing these practices as a model for many in nineteenth-century Britain.

But even with a lesser seat in Parliament, Wilberforce remained extremely busy with a host of nonparliamentary associations and initiatives, most of them having to do with the "reformation of manners." And there was another cause that would draw him back into the fray of Parliament in 1813. Next to abolition it was the single most important issue for him, and the way he and Clapham engaged in this fight bore many parallels to their fight for abolition. The political battle to which he was now drawn concerned a long-standing law that forbade missionaries from entering India. Wilberforce would lead Clapham in an all-out effort to repeal this law. The results would have an historic and monumental effect on the way the British saw themselves and their role in the world—an effect almost as vital as that of abolition in forging a fundamentally different national identity for generations to come.

For many years and with the blessing of the British Crown, the British East India Company had been essentially overseeing India and turning a handsome profit for itself and its shareholders in the process. Far from home, it did mostly as it pleased, and treated the native population with something that vacillated between contempt and indifference. The sole caveat of the company's singularly felicitous situation was that every twenty years its charter came under parliamentary review. When the charter had last been up for renewal, in 1793, the young Wilberforce had put forward a pair of reasonable resolutions proposing that the East India Company send schoolmasters and chaplains into different parts of the country. The resolutions survived two readings in the House, but the moment that the directors of the company awoke to the situation, they put every ounce of their considerable political weight into defeating them. They loudly complained that the resolutions proposed using violence to impose the Christian faith on the native population, a charge that, though groundless and almost absurd, worked quite effectively. The resolutions were defeated in the bill's third reading.

Just as with the slave interests in his early battles for abolition, Wilberforce was at first naive in dealing with the East India Company. He hardly realized what he was stirring up—what depths of darkness he had roiled with his well-meaning resolutions. The same ruthless mind-set he was up against in the fight for abolition was present here too, a kind of social Darwinism years before the term was coined, and one in which racism, again, was central. Powerful Europeans were legally and very profitably oppressing members of a darker race and felt entirely justified in doing so; indeed, they would use every possible means to protect their situation. Just as many Europeans had seen the continent of Africa as an endless resource of expendable human labor—to be looted and subdued while one had the power to do so—so the East India Company saw the vast subcontinent of India. Anything that reminded them of their subjects' humanity was a distinct threat, and to speak of missionaries and chaplains was like rattling a saber. Just as the West Indian slave owners despised La Trobe and the Moravians for their mission work among the African slaves, and James Ramsay for ministering to the slaves on St. Kitt's, so the East India Company despised Wilberforce and his pious and meddling co-religionists. In 1793 they defeated his efforts soundly and would not have to bother about such things again for twenty long years.

But during those years he had become a battle-hardened warrior against similar opponents, and now he was well prepared for what lay ahead. Wilberforce regarded the British abuse of the Indians as "next to the Slave Trade, the foulest blot on the moral character of our country." In a letter to Hannah More, he referred tenderly to the East Indians as "our fellow-subjects (nay, they even stand towards us in the closer relation of our tenants)," and he denounced the East India Company's reprehensible refusal to lift a finger "to enlighten and reform them" while they suffered "under the grossest, the darkest, and most depraving system of idolatrous superstition that almost ever existed upon earth."

Wilberforce was speaking less of Hindu theology than of the barbaric cruelties of East Indian culture at the time, including the common practices of female infanticide and suttee, in which a widow was bound and burned alive on her husband's funeral pyre. Moreover, the caste system that prevailed throughout India was institutionalized slavery without the name. He knew that the merest introduction of Christian ideas into this deeply racist and sexist culture would bring hope to these suffering people, especially to the poorest and least powerful among them, who, as is usually the case, suffered the most. Wilberforce felt that, as the stronger and wealthier nation, it was Britain's responsibility to help the people of India, especially since Britain had profited greatly from India over the decades. It was unconscionable to turn a blind eye to India's people, and he knew that legalizing the introduction of missionaries would expose them to Christian notions of human rights and objective standards of justice that would eventually have a powerfully ameliorating effect.

What was most troubling to the East India Company was that the slightest hint of Christianity would affect how the British could treat the Indians. One practice especially threatened by any whiff of Christianity was the keeping of a retinue of underage "mistresses" who were in fact legally permitted child sex slaves. In 1810 the East India Company published a *Vade Mecum*—its official manual for the instruction of servants, forty-eight pages of which were devoted to the subject of "mistresses." It helpfully quoted an elderly British gentleman who kept sixteen such "girls" and who, when asked how he managed them, cheerfully replied: "Oh, I give them a little rice and let them run about."

Wilberforce knew that the East India Company's claim that introducing missionaries would not show "respect" for India's ancient civilization was shameless pretense, designed to mask the company's selfishness and indifference to the natives' suffering. He would at dinner sometimes read aloud the names of women who had recently been consumed alive in the flames of their husband's funeral pyre. At that time, in the Bengal Province alone, ten thousand women—many teenage girls among them, and many even younger—were burned alive each year. Wilberforce was so disturbed at this practice that he added to the published edition of his speech in Parliament the following written account of one eyewitness to this spectacle, a Mr. Marshman:

> A person informing us that a woman was about to be burnt with the corpse of her husband, near our house, I, with several of our brethren hastened to the place: but before we could arrive, the pile was in flames. It was a horrible sight. The most shocking indifference and levity appeared among those who were present. I never saw any thing more brutal than their behavior. The dreadful scene had not the least appearance of a religious ceremony. It resembled an abandoned rabble of boys in England, collected for the purpose of worrying to death a cat or a dog. A bamboo, perhaps twenty feet

long, had been fastened at one end to a stake driven into the ground, and held down over the fire by men at the other. Such were the confusion, the levity, the burst of brutal laughter, while the poor woman was burning alive before their eyes, that it seemed as if every spark of humanity were extinguished by this accursed superstition. That which added to the cruelty was the smallness of the fire. It did not consist of so much wood as we consume in dressing a dinner: no, not this fire that was to consume the living and the dead! I saw the legs of the poor creature hanging out of the fire while her body was in flames. After a while, they took a bamboo ten or twelve feet long and stirred it, pushing and beating the half consumed corpses, as you would repair a fire of green wood, by throwing the unconsumed pieces into the middle. Perceiving the legs hanging out, they beat them with the bamboo for some time, in order to break the ligatures which fastened them at the knees, (for they would not have come near to touch them for the world). At length they succeeded in bending them upwards into the fire, the skin and muscles giving way, and discovering the knee sockets bare, with the balls of the leg bones: a sight this which, I need not say, made me thrill with horror, especially when I recollected that this hapless victim of superstition was alive but a few minutes before. To have seen savage wolves thus tearing a human body, limb from limb, would have been shocking; but to see relations and neighbours do this to one with whom they had familiarly conversed not an hour before, and to do it with an air of levity, was almost too much for me to bear. You expect, perhaps to hear that this unhappy victim was the wife of some brahmin of high cast. She was the wife of a barber who dwelt in Serampore, and had died that morning, leaving the son I have mentioned, and a daughter of about eleven years of age. Thus has this infernal superstition aggravated the common miseries of life, and left these children stripped of both their parents in one day. Nor is this an uncommon case. It often happens to children far more helpless than these; sometimes to children possessed of property, which is then left, as well

as themselves, to the mercy of those who have decoyed their
mother to their father's funeral pile.

❦

The callous indifference to such suffering disturbed Wilberforce
greatly; that the British government should sanction it was an out-
rage. Wilberforce had been spoiling for this fight for two decades.
Already two years before the 1813 parliamentary debate, Clapham
began to mobilize in earnest for the political battle ahead. Their efforts now on the India Bill were a picture of the Claphamic fleet
under full sail: Grant, Babington, Stephen, and Thornton were all
involved, at times gathering almost daily in the oval library at Battersea Rise for "Cabinet Councils," to devise strategies and delegate
tasks. They hoped to influence the indifferent members of Parliament through the same method they had used so effectively and indeed had invented in fighting the abolition battle: they would appeal
directly to the people of the nation, via petitions.

And just as with abolition, they took great pains to educate the
populace on the subject beforehand. Macaulay was charged with
drafting and disseminating circulars, letters were published on the
subject in newspapers, and endless personal letters were written—
literally hundreds by Wilberforce himself. Writing to Hannah More,
he said, "You will agree with me, now the Slave Trade is abolished,
this is the greatest of our national sins." He then specifically asked
her help in circulating a petition to the citizens of Bristol. Babington
was charged with the huge job of organizing the hundreds of petitions, and Wilberforce wrote or met with everyone and anyone who
might advance the cause. Evidence and testimonies were prepared
well in advance. Clapham's India expert, Lord Teignmouth, would
give evidence before the House of Lords. Wilberforce also arranged
a series of "political breakfasts" on the subject. All in all, it was an
historic and herculean effort. And the increasingly confident voice
of the British people was now a lionhearted roar: by June, the month
of the debate, 837 petitions had been gathered, covered with half
a million signatures, rolled and tied and ready to be presented to
Parliament.

On June 22, 1813, the great effort culminated in the House. Several of the "Saints" spoke, and then it was Wilberforce's turn. He held the chamber spellbound for three hours, and by all accounts it was one of the great speeches of his life. He spoke of female infanticide, and he spoke of suttee. He spoke of the practice of geronticide—murdering the "useless" old—and he spoke of murdering those who were sick; and he spoke of human sacrifices for "religious" reasons. Surely the British had a responsibility to do anything they could to help the powerless victims of these horrors. Taking a more explicitly religious tone than he had ever taken before or would after, he made the case that Christianity alone could open a way to help the people of India and that it could provide the philosophical underpinnings for doing so. In every way this debate, as with the debate over abolition, was a debate about worldviews that were antithetical in their understanding of everything—most centrally in their definitions of what constituted a human being.

The East India Company interests held—just as the slave interests had done—that some human beings, especially by dint of their race or sex, were naturally and self-evidently inferior and should be treated as such by those who were naturally and self-evidently superior, and that this should be done without any hint of guilt about it. This was the "natural" way of things, in their view, and it was "God's will." To behave as though the simpering "untouchables" of India were equal to white British gentlemen was as unthinkable as regarding "primitive" Africans as their equals. But for Wilberforce such a view was unavoidable. He and his allies declared that every human being was equal in God's sight and made in the image of God, and must therefore be treated with equal dignity. The contrast between the two views was striking, and the battle for how the British would treat the people of India, no less than the battle for how the British people would treat the peoples of Africa, was more than anything else, according to Wilberforce, a referendum on the Bible and Christianity itself.

During his speech, Wilberforce said, "The most able of our opponents has told us that some classes of natives are as much below others as the inferior animals are below the human species . . . and it is because I wish to do away this unjust inequality, to raise these poor brutes out of their present degraded state to the just level of their nature, that I am now bringing before you their real character, and explaining to you their true condition."

Wilberforce admitted openly that as a Christian he was concerned for the eternal souls of the Indian people, but speaking to those in the chamber who would not share this concern, he made it clear that even if one was concerned only with the conditions of the Indian people in this life, Christianity was the answer. Christianity, he said, "assumes her true character . . . when she takes under her protection those poor degraded beings on whom philosophy looks down with disdain or perhaps with contemptuous condescension. . . . It was declared by its great Author as 'Glad tidings to the poor,' and . . . still delights . . . to succour the needy, to comfort the sorrowful, to visit the forsaken."

He also answered the charge that the advent of missionaries betokened forced conversions, explaining that the words "compulsion" and "Christianity" were incompatible. "Christianity has been called the 'law of liberty,'" he said, ". . . and they, let me add, will most advance her cause who contend for it in her own spirit and character."

A writer in the press gallery said that Wilberforce "spoke three hours but nobody seemed fatigued: all indeed were pleased, some with the ingenious artifices of his manner, but most with the glowing language of his heart. Much as I differed from him in opinion, it was impossible not to be delighted with his eloquence. . . . He never speaks without exciting a wish that he would say more." Lord Erskine said the speech "deserves a place in the library of every man of letters, even if he were an atheist."

Christianity had long been banished from India, and Wilberforce now only asked that it be legally tolerated—that it be allowed a place at the table, as we might say today. Wilberforce knew this was all that was necessary. The East India interests seemed to know this too and fought with all their might and main, but this time they went down in defeat. When the vote was finally taken, the motion carried by a vote of 89–36. Though little recognized as such, Wilberforce had given an historic speech, followed by an historic vote not far in its importance from the vote on abolition six years earlier: it marked a major turning point in Britain's dealings with the world. Furneaux said that the passage of this bill "marked the change from looting to paternalism." But the bill did more than usher in paternalism, which today carries connotations of condescension and even racism; indeed, the bill countenanced neither looting nor paternalism but instead argued for the full humanity of all those in the Indian nation. Just as abolition had established that Christian principles, chief among them the Golden Rule, should be acknowledged not merely privately but also in the public and political sphere—and generally codified there as law—so too this bill had taken the next historic step: establishing for the first time in the history of the world that the Golden Rule was to be raised as the standard of behavior not only between individuals but between entire nations and peoples.

In this historic vote and in so many other smaller ways, the culture and people of Britain had begun to follow Wilberforce around the corner, as it were, into a new world; it was as if Britain herself had experienced a "Great Change," or was doing so in varying stages. The idea, so obvious to us today and so taken for granted, that the powerful have an obligation to help the powerless was indefatigably working its way through the whole of British society, like leaven through the proverbial lump. The Christian notions of loving one's neighbor and servant leadership would soon find themselves newly expressed in the concepts of noblesse oblige and, later on, social conscience. These notions were increasingly evident in every sphere and on every scale. In this vote on India, the change had been formally and publicly acknowledged, much as it had been in abolition's passage a few years earlier. The selfish prerogatives of power had been publicly and legally condemned and disavowed, and a new and bright precedent had been set in international relations.

Quite fittingly, but perhaps most surprisingly, the changes that had been effected largely by political means touched the world of politics itself. As long as anyone could remember, a seat in Parliament had been a place from which one might unashamedly seek one's own advancement, but now it began to be thought of as a position from which one might help the poor, or the nation as a whole. "Petty party and personal struggles" were beginning to be put aside for working in the public interest. Wilberforce had once said that Parliament ought to be the "moral mint of the nation in which moral and political

principles receive their stamp and currency." When Wilberforce entered Parliament, there were three MPs who would have identified
themselves as seriously Christian, but half a century later there were
closer to two hundred. Politics had come to be thought of as a noble
calling. There would always be self-seekers—and few individuals
could be entirely free of selfish motivation—but the idea that politicians should be free of that motivation and work for the good of society was something new, and Wilberforce's influence in introducing
it is hard to avoid.

CHAPTER 21

ENFORCING ABOLITION

" . . . the father of our great cause."

uring the battle for the India Bill and afterward, the battle to enforce abolition continued, with numerous twists and turns. James Stephen, again functioning as the creative innovator and political strategist of Clapham, hit upon a brilliant solution that could once and for all end the illegal trade in slaves. He proposed that each of the slaves in the British West Indies be registered, so that no smuggled slaves could be added to the number without detection. In January 1812, Prime Minister Perceval got behind the idea and issued an "Order in Council," which put the registry immediately into effect in Trinidad. But a slave registry beyond Trinidad, throughout all of the British West Indies, would require Parliament's approval. So the "Saints" of Clapham now began to draft the Slave Registry Bill, and the political battle for its approval began.

In 1814, however, the world changed. Napoleon surrendered, and the war was over. Twenty-two years of fighting had come to an end as 100,000 allied troops (63,000 of them Russian) marched into Paris, led by Czar Alexander himself, whose offer Napoleon had accepted, renouncing his throne and retiring to Elba. In a letter to

Hannah More, Wilberforce wrote, "So the dynasty of Buonaparte has ceased to reign. . . . This hath God done. How can I but wish that my old friend Pitt were still alive to witness this catastrophe of the twenty-five years' drama?"

The abolition leaders now decided to halt the push for the Slave Registry Bill in favor of the greater possibility that suddenly presented itself. It was hoped that the grand dream of universal abolition might now be attainable, via a general peace treaty among all of the European powers. The prospect of such a thing was dizzying. As long as the war with Napoleon had continued, the French had been unable to conduct any trade in slaves, but that was temporary. Now they might be made to give their official assent to total abolition. And if the French agreed to abolish their slave trade, this would likely push the other major powers to end their own slave trades too. Even Spain and Portugal would feel the pressure to go along. Wilberforce could hardly contain his excitement at the prospect: "O for the Abolition of the Slave Trade, generally," he writes. "Could I but talk French I'd go to Paris immediately. How nobly the Emperor Alexr has behaved, I'm delighted Paris spared." Wilberforce began a long letter to Czar Alexander, hoping to persuade him to chair an international gathering on abolition; he seemed to be the one who might lead the way. Lesser powers such as Venezuela and Argentina had given up their slave trades by 1811, but now in a single historic moment the greatest powers on the globe would walk together into a new age, and the end of a far greater war—of the centuries-old Atlantic slave trade—would soon be sounded.

With this in mind, the peace negotiations with the restored Bourbon government became the focus of Wilberforce's attentions, for they would determine whether the universal agreement was possible. France would not want to give up its slave trade but was in no position to insist on anything at the bargaining table. And it was certainly in Britain's economic self-interest to prevent its long-standing enemy from profiting from a trade it had recently given up itself. Still, Wilberforce would take no chances, and he appealed to Commons to officially weigh in with the prince regent, asking him to instruct his ministers to use all their political power to see that abolition was part of the final peace agreement with France. The motion to do so passed, to his obvious delight, "with zealous and triumphant unanimity."

"It would be too shocking," he wrote to his friend Gisborne,

> to restore to Europe the blessings of peace with professions of our reverence for the principles of justice and humanity, and at the same moment to be creating, for so it would really be doing wherever the Slave Trade is extinct, this traffic in the persons of our fellow-creatures. We are much occupied with the grand object of prevailing on all the great European powers to agree to a convention for the general Abolition of the Slave Trade. Oh may God turn the hearts of these men! What a great and blessed close would it be of the twenty-two years' drama!

Lord Castlereagh, the foreign secretary, was already in France; if the French began to back away from abolition, he was expected to make the return of France's West Indian colonies contingent upon it. That was the abolitionists' ace in the hole. Wilberforce thought of crossing the Channel himself, but all things taken together, including his inability to speak French, he decided to send Macaulay in his stead. But he would write Talleyrand a letter, detailing the case for French abolition. As happened with so many of Wilberforce's letters, it got away from him and, like a spooked horse, ran on and on wildly, to near book length. Wilberforce wrote his old friend the Marquis de Lafayette too, asking his support. Even Madame de Staël, who deeply admired Wilberforce and had pronounced him not only the most religious but also "the wittiest man in all of England," lent her support to the cause.

But on June 3, disaster. Wilberforce received terrible news of failure: the French had pushed back on abolition, and Castlereagh, to get the peace agreement, had caved in. France had agreed to abolish its slave trade, but *gradually* . . . in five years' time. The idea of five years more of the trade was monstrous enough, but what made it unbearable was that Wilberforce knew that the French were not likely to abolish it in five years either: "France to receive back her colonies," he wrote in his diary, ". . . and to abolish in 5 years!!! Alas! Alas!

How can we hope she will … with so many additional motives to cling to the Trade give it up in 5 years. My spirits are quite lowered by it, yet let us do what we can and trust to God's blessing on our labours." The chances for a universal abolition were dashed. Thousands more would endure the tortures of the Middle Passage and drink the poison of a life in slavery. The thought was hard to bear.

If ever in his life Wilberforce would gladly play the role of the skunk at the garden party—and show plainly where his deepest allegiances lay—this would be the time. That Monday, Castlereagh returned to Britain in glorious triumph, the peace treaty under his arm. He had been in France for years, and as he returned home and entered the House that evening everyone leapt and cheered—for him, and for the document he carried, the physical embodiment of the triumphant end of twenty-one years of war. Who could resist the unbridled patriotic joy of such a moment? The cheering went on, thunderously, and every man in Commons, Whig and Tory alike, was on his feet. Every man but one. When at last the hundreds were again seated, Wilberforce rose—and explained his dissent. He said that his feelings and position were no less patriotic than anyone else's, and then, speaking of Castlereagh and the peace treaty Castlereagh still held, he said, "I cannot but conceive that in my noble friend's hands I behold the death-warrant of a multitude of innocent victims, men, women, and children…. When I consider the miseries we are about to renew, is it possible to regard them without the deepest emotions of sorrow?… For my own part I frankly declare no considerations could have induced me to consent to it." But Wilberforce was not grandstanding for political effect, for when he sat back down he was seen to be on the verge of weeping.

The next day Wilberforce was at Henry Thornton's home, Battersea Rise, for dinner. Macaulay was there, just returned from Paris. After their meal, Macaulay read aloud Talleyrand's answer to Wilberforce's long letter, translating as he went. The letter was larded with flattery, but Wilberforce, whom James Stephen had dubbed "praise-proof," was unimpressed. He pronounced it "all flummery."

Wilberforce's only real hope now lay with Czar Alexander, who had come to London on June 7, along with most of the other Euro-

pean heads of state, all invited by the prince regent to celebrate the
"Glorious Peace," as it was called, as well as the centennial of Ha-
noverian rule, begun in 1714 with George I. It was a riot of endless celebrations, with fireworks and extravagant spectacles of every
kind, and everywhere one went one saw the international celebrities
of that day—kings and queens and princes and princesses and military heroes. The British people had followed their lives in newspapers
over the years, and had read with excitement of the great battles and
campaigns and court intrigues, and now here they were, of a sudden
sprung to life, fallen out of the newspaper illustrations and into the
streets of London itself. The emperor of Russia, Czar Alexander,
was staying at Pulteney's Hotel, two miles from Kensington Gore,
having declined the prince regent's invitation to stay at St. James's
Palace. He squired the Princess of Oldenburgh, his sister, from one
gala function to another, and the same crowds who hissed the fat and
hated prince regent when his carriage passed now gathered beneath
the czar's hotel balcony, cheering until he appeared, tall and handsome and resplendent in a red suit and bright blue sash.

That Saturday, June 11, while at a family dinner party at his
home, Wilberforce received an exalted honor for any commoner of
his day: an invitation to an audience with the czar. It was for the
following day, and so the next morning Wilberforce arose early—
at six-thirty—"that I might pray to God for a blessing on my in-
terview." He donned his court dress—a tiny velvet green costume
one may still see today at Hull, where it is displayed in his boyhood
home—and the sword that completed it, and thus properly accou-
tred, he proceeded to the Lock Chapel at Hyde Park Corner for Sunday service. He was obliged to sneak out before the sermon's end, in
order to be on time for his audience, walking the rest of the way. He
was not late, but the emperor of Russia, who that morning had attended the Orthodox church, was. Wilberforce waited with several
of the emperor's nobles, including Prince Czartoriski and the Prince
of Oldenburgh, until the czar, with his sister the princess, arrived.

Czar Alexander was in his mid-thirties and was an evangelical
Christian too, though with leanings toward mysticism and apoca-
lyptic thinking of which Wilberforce would have been dubious. The
czar believed himself to be divinely ordained to bring peace to all of

Europe, sometimes brooded over the Scriptures for "signs," and attended prayer meetings of some theological iffiness. But Wilberforce would see none of this today. When at last ushered into the czar's imperial presence, Wilberforce was about to follow the prescriptions of protocol by kneeling and kissing the emperor's hand, but Alexander prevented it, shaking Wilberforce's hand warmly instead. They spoke of abolition, and Wilberforce expressed his fundamental concern that the French would likely not abandon abolition in five years, as they had said they would. Wilberforce records that the czar, speaking English, "replied heartily, we must make 'em, and then corrected himself, we must keep 'em to it." The czar was friendly and sincere in his desire to help end abolition in Europe, but Wilberforce also realized that any really bold leadership on the issue would have to come from England.

The following day Wilberforce was summoned to see Castlereagh, but as will happen when all of the allied sovereigns are in town, "something suddenly came up," and Castlereagh could not keep the appointment. Wilberforce was passed to the prime minister, Lord Liverpool. Wilberforce records that, in explaining the recent negotiations, Liverpool said that the French had "resented our dictating to them, believing that all our pleas of having abolished ourselves or urging them to abolish on grounds of Religion, Justice, Humanity were all moonshine, mere hypocrisy."

Wilberforce now went to a meeting of the African Institution. Romilly spoke, and proposed calling a great public meeting of all the "friends of Abolition" for the purpose of resolving to petition Parliament or the prince regent to amend the peace treaty. Wilberforce groused that no one would attend, for everyone was buzzing and goggling in the frothy vicinity of the gathered European heads of state. But Wilberforce was wrong. Four days later the Freemasons' Tavern was filled to bursting with persons of every station in life, from gentry and clergy to MPs and peers. When Wilberforce arrived, he could hardly enter for the throng. He appeared quite weak, his head sunk down upon his breast, as it would increasingly be over the years and as one sees it in his later portraits. He was supported as he walked by his Bristol banker friend, John Harwood. Still only in his midfifties, Wilberforce already appeared quite old, although it almost suited him somehow, for he had already achieved that iconic status usually reserved for much older persons. When some in the swollen crowd saw that Wilberforce was among them and trying to pass, they quickly made a lane for him so that he could proceed toward the stage. As word spread of his arrival, the room erupted into applause and cheering that continued for several minutes— Wilberforce asked Harwood what all the cheering was for, what had he missed?—until the precociously venerable hero finally emerged upon the platform and took his seat.

When his turn came to address the crowd, Wilberforce stood and before their eyes the frail little man blossomed into the impassioned and vigorous orator they had always known—and he inspired the jostling assemblage to a resolution: they would petition Parliament to amend the peace treaty, to remove the clause allowing the French five more years of the trade. The MPs in the room were mostly Whigs, and in a grand gesture of political bipartisanship they determined that they would not present their own petition to Parliament, which might embarrass their Tory counterparts. Instead, Wilberforce should present it, and they now hailed him, movingly, as "the father of our great cause."

A great petitioning effort ensued. By mid-June, 806 petitions had been gathered from every village and town across the British Isles, with one million signatures recorded from a population of fourteen million. The people, not so very long ago voiceless, had again spoken—had fairly shouted—on behalf of those who were voiceless still. Parliament would have to heed their cry, and on June 27, when the House gathered, they would have to heed the voice of Wilberforce too.

When he spoke that day, urging Parliament to strike from the peace agreement the clause that gave the French five more years of their commerce in human beings, he sounded, especially toward the end of his wholly unprepared speech, like what one could well imagine the conscience of the nation might sound:

> When the heads of all those now living are laid low, and the facts which now excite such powerful feeling are related by the pen of the cold, impartial historian; when it is seen that

an opportunity like the present has been lost, that the first act of the restored King of France was the restoration of a trade in slavery and blood, what will be the estimate formed of the exertions which this country has employed, of the effect which they have produced upon a people under such weighty obligations? Surely no very high opinion will be indulged either of British influence or of French gratitude.

The amendment passed in the House of Commons, as expected, and in the House of Lords too. Now Castlereagh had no choice but to return to the table and lean on the French yet again, and harder than he had previously done, for the British people had leaned on the government, which now leaned on him. The battle shifted to Paris and Vienna, and the main players were Castlereagh and the Duke of Wellington, a staunch supporter of abolition who was now the British ambassador to Paris. Thomas Clarkson reentered the fray too now, and Stephen and Macaulay again gathered evidence of the horrors of the slave trade to present to the French. The old gang were back together, doing what they had always done, and Wilberforce, as ever, fussed at the whole thing from across the water, writing endless letters to all and sundry, with his faith and the nib of his pen moving mountains.

As ever, too, Stephen and Macaulay were thorough. When Wellington took in all of the powerful and moving and incontrovertible evidence they had amassed, he couldn't imagine the French not being convinced by it. But he wouldn't have to imagine anything, for he would soon have the privilege of seeing the French shrug and sneer at it with his very own eyes. Horrific as it must have been for all who had fought for abolition and were fighting for it still, the French were now irremediably biased against it. Like Parliament twenty years before, the Bourbon government associated abolition with the revolutionary French Republic, which they loathed. They associated it with the English too, whom they also loathed. In the end, there was little that could be done. So much effort had been expended, and all to end here, where they had started. The negotiations went on, but in vain. The French threw the abolitionists the tiniest of sops, such as a promise to engage in the trade only south of the Niger. It was all despicable. But more despicable yet was a report Wilberforce received that October of nine slave ships preparing to sail from Le Havre with the help of Englishmen. "How I would like to catch the Englishmen some day when on shore and send them to slave in New South Wales," he wrote in a rare burst of anger. "I know not that in all my long experience of Abolitionism, I ever felt a keener paroxysm of grief and indignation. Oh that it might please God to dash to the ground that bloody cup which they are preparing to quaff with so much avidity. They really appear to my mind's eye to be so many demons exulting over their savage orgies with grim, ferocious joy."

The international gathering at the Congress of Vienna was only somewhat more promising. Russia and Austria, along with Prussia, agreed to an international prohibition of the trade, but had been little engaged in it in the first place; meanwhile, the major slave trade powers of Spain and Portugal dragged their feet, asking for an eight-year "grace" period in which they might "restock" their colonies. In February 1815 a toothless declaration condemning the trade was accepted in Vienna. Wilberforce and his praying colleagues had expended themselves tirelessly, and to the last drop, but they had failed.

Then, in March, what surely seemed a miracle occurred. Napoleon slipped the bonds of his exile in Elba, landed at Cannes, and suddenly reclaimed power. He knew all of Europe would soon again be arrayed against him, and in a canny preemptive effort to placate his chief enemy, Britain, he quickly proclaimed the immediate abolition of the slave trade throughout the French empire. It was a glorious turn of events for abolition, unexpected as summer snow, but it was confusing too, for even the staunchest friend of abolition hardly wished to be at war again. For one hundred days, all of Europe was drawn back into turmoil once more. The allies had declared victory too soon. The Duke of Wellington now set aside his role as Britain's ambassador to the court of King Louis XVII and resumed his former martial identity, carving his name into history forever by leading a force of 68,000 British troops onto the rain-soaked fields of clover and rye near the village of Waterloo, just a few miles south of Brussels. The Prussian Marshal Blücher, having evaded Grouchy, led his troops northward to meet Wellington, and if the soaking rains had not delayed Napoleon's attack, Blücher would have been too late. But the rain did delay Napoleon, and

Blücher arrived in time. Wellington triumphed, and Napoleon, at long last, met his Waterloo.

Napoleon's final defeat marked the end of such a long era of strife that when the news reached London, it was very emotional for Wilberforce. The American inventor Samuel Morse, who gave us the telegraph and the Morse code, was a friend of Wilberforce's and was visiting him that very day for dinner at Kensington Gore. Zachary Macaulay was there, along with Charles Grant and his two sons. When Morse arrived, he had just walked through Hyde Park and had seen crowds gathering. The rumors were that Napoleon had been captured and the war was over. But Wilberforce, cautious as ever, couldn't believe it. "It is too good to be true," he said. "It cannot be true."

If it were true the cannons in Hyde Park would be fired to announce it officially. They discussed it feverishly all through dinner, and afterward, gathered in the drawing room, when they at last heard and saw the man-made thunder and lightning of the cannonade. Morse gives us his recollection of the moment. "I sat near a window which looked out in the direction of the distant park," he writes.

> Presently a flash and distant dull report of a gun attracted my attention, but was unnoticed by the rest of the company. Another flash and report assured me that the park guns were firing, and at once I called Mr. Wilberforce's attention to the fact. Running to the window he threw it up in time to see the next flash and hear the report. Clasping his hands in silence, with tears rolling down his cheeks, he stood for a few moments perfectly absorbed in thought, and before uttering a word, embraced his wife and daughters, and shook hands with every one in the room. The scene was not one to be forgotten.

As for abolition, there was even better news. The Bourbon government, once again restored, did not rescind Napoleon's decree abolishing the French trade. For his glorious victory on the muddy field at Waterloo, Wellington's stature had grown greatly in Europe's eyes. This, among other things, had turned the tide. Castlereagh had reapplied pressure for abolition with Talleyrand, and in the end the French king felt compelled to confirm abolition once and for all. On July 31, 1815, Castlereagh wrote to Wilberforce, "I have the gratification of acquainting you that the long desired object is accomplished and that the present messenger carries to Lord Liverpool the unqualified and total Abolition of the Slave Trade throughout the dominions of France."

This was one of those few sacred hours in Wilberforce's life when he could rest for a moment from the endless work and could rejoice in what had been accomplished, when he could take his eyes off the much that was yet to be done and behold what had been done, and could pronounce it good.

It was a triumphant moment for Wilberforce, and the whole world seemed to know it. As abolition had gained favor throughout the world, and now especially, Wilberforce's star had risen to an impossible height throughout European society. Everyone wished to meet him, for he seemed a living piece of history, and he came to be hailed and celebrated as the very embodiment of abolition, much as Franklin had been hailed as the spirit of the Enlightenment thirty years earlier. But unlike Franklin—who regarded his celebrity with a twinkling pride and had been observed to currycomb its glossy coat—Wilberforce was terribly abashed and humbled by it, holding it lightly and at arm's length, like a snake.

But its lavish attentions were paid him nonetheless. Madame de Staël used every stratagem conceivable to lure Wilberforce to attend one of her famous dinners, and every prince and princess in Europe wished to meet him and pay their respects. The king of Prussia presented Wilberforce with a set of Dresden china, and Prince Blücher of Prussia paid Wilberforce an extraordinary honor when he dispatched his aide-de-camp fresh from the victory at Waterloo to tell the story of the battle to the prince regent—and to Wilberforce. Though Wilberforce was indeed "praise-proof," as Stephen had said, he was certainly not unmoved by such attention, nor ungrateful.

CHAPTER 22

PEACE AND TROUBLES

. . . the moral conscience of the nation.

A nd so in 1815 lasting peace had finally come to smooth the troubled brow of the great continent. Napoleon was safely on St. Helena and would have no more chances to conquer the world, and the noble cause of abolition, if not quite home, had made undeniably great strides toward its goal. But for Wilberforce these great joys were offset by personal sadnesses. In January his dearest friend, Henry Thornton, succumbed to tuberculosis, leaving his wife and nine children. Though John Thornton had laid the foundations for what would become Clapham, his son had been its chief architect, and not merely in building the three great houses that formed its geographical center but in conceiving the very idea of the community itself, of seeing the possibilities it might hold, and in luring Wilberforce and Edward Eliot and Charles Grant and Henry Venn to live there, with the hope that others might be drawn in their train, as so many had indeed been. And Thornton had married Wilberforce's dearest childhood friend, Marianne Sykes. In many ways, he was the brother that Wilberforce had never had.

Wilberforce went to see his friend's body. "I stood for some time looking upon his poor emaciated frame," he writes. "I cannot say countenance for that was no more. . . . I said to myself what was said by the angel to one of our Saviour's faithful female attendants, He is not here, He is gone to Paradise." When the nurse who had attended Thornton began to weep, Wilberforce said, "This is not our friend. This is but the earthly garment which he has thrown off. The man himself, the vital spirit has already begun to be clothed with immortality." He genuinely rejoiced that his friend had gone to a better place. Nonetheless, the human loss was palpable. In a letter to Marianne, Hannah More wrote, "Poor Wilberforce, he has lost a great part of himself—his right hand in all great and useful measures. Heavily indeed will he go down to the House of Commons without his own familiar friend."

But soon Marianne became ill with tuberculosis too. Visiting that September, Wilberforce was shocked at her appearance. The woman he had known since their childhood in Hull was dying. "I fear I have been misled into too favourable an opinion of Mrs. Thornton's case," he said to Macaulay, "and I have touched in conversing with her as strongly as I could on the guardianship of her children in the event of her death." To Wilberforce she said, "God is gently leading me to that blessed place which he has provided for those that love him." On October 12, she died. Two more close friends, John Bowdler and Dr. Buchanan, died shortly thereafter. In a letter to Hannah More, he writes: "Oh may the warnings have their due effect in rendering us fit for the summons!"

That next year another great blow fell when his sister Sally suddenly died. James Stephen, who had lost his first wife to illness too, was inconsolable. He had adored Sally, and now his deeply passionate nature felt profoundest grief. Wilberforce consoled him during this time, and their friendship afterward was one of his closest. Wilberforce was genuinely free of despair amidst death, for he knew it was only a transition and that one's external state was what mattered. But to his great credit, his resolve to dwell on eternal things never became cold and mechanical, never closed him to the tenderer, human side of loss. After his sister's death, he writes: "How affecting it is to leave the person we have known all our lives, on whom we should have been afraid to let the wind blow too roughly, to leave her in the cold ground alone!"

Like many struggles, the battle for abolition was fought in people's minds as much as in the halls of Parliament. Wilberforce knew most people would not believe blacks could be free citizens entrusted to the formidable task of governing themselves, but if these skeptics saw it, they wouldn't have any choice. This was why Sierra Leone was a symbol of supreme importance, and worth all of the endless trouble it caused. But in 1811 the island state of Haiti—formerly Saint-Domingue—presented the cause of abolition with a second signal opportunity to show the world that African blacks could be their own masters, and in the slave owners' backyard too.

It was in that year that Henri Christophe, a former slave who had risen in the ranks of the revolutionary army, suddenly found himself at the head of the country. He had had himself crowned King Henri I and was by all accounts an exceedingly capable man, possessing great abilities, intelligence, and vision. Christophe was a great admirer of the English—especially for their leadership in the struggle to abolish the slave trade—and he even styled his dress and other aspects of himself on George III. He loathed the French too, for their foot-dragging on abolition, among other things. Christophe set about creating a model state run completely by former slaves; the whites, naturally, had been murdered or driven away during the turmoil of the previous years. But out of the bloodshed had sprung great promise: slavery had been abolished, and a black former slave was now king of Haiti. In 1815 Christophe appealed to Wilberforce, seeking help with education. He also hoped his fledgling country might be officially recognized by England, in part as a protection against the French who, if given the opportunity, would have swallowed Haiti whole, *comme ça.*

Wilberforce and all of Clapham well understood the symbolic importance of this fledgling state, and they were eager to do all they could to help it succeed. Haiti was off to a galloping start too: Christophe busily and capably set about building schools and hospitals, and engaging in agricultural experiments of ambitious scope. When he first wrote to Wilberforce, it was to ask for help in finding teachers. Macaulay was quickly dispatched north to Edinburgh to find professors in the classics, mathematics, and surgery—and then to persuade them to cross the ocean to teach former slaves on an island whose white inhabitants had recently all been murdered or, if they had been lucky, driven into exile. But Macauley was, as ever, indefatigable, and ere long the Scottish professors had been found, convinced, and put aboard ships bound for Haiti. The men and women of Clapham had never been the sort to waver in these holy missions. Having put their hands to the plow, they would not look back. They now offered Christophe every kind of help, and Wilberforce himself directed most of it, even attending to the smallest details, such as handpicking Christophe's personal staff. And as ever, he wrote letters and more letters, good-naturedly but persistently poking the four corners of the world for support in this, another of his great causes. Clapham sent Christophe everything from virus vaccines, with instructions on how to vaccinate, to special New Testaments they had prepared with side-by-side French and English translations. They sent a copy of the *British Encyclopedia,* and Wilberforce continued to send letters offering advice on everything that related to the great project— including a plea to Christophe to do something many might have found scandalous: he persuaded him to educate the women of Haiti too.

One day during this period, when a Mr. Prince Saunders, a black Bostonian, visited Wilberforce, wanting to go to Sierra Leone, Wilberforce had a better solution: he diverted him back across the Atlantic to Haiti. Six months later, Saunders returned to London with a message from Christophe: "Tell the friends of the colored men all you have seen and heard in Hayti." The excitement over what seemed to be happening there and the possibilities it held was intoxicating. Wilberforce said to Macaulay, "Oh how I wish I was not too old and you too busy to go." And Sir Joseph Banks, writing to Wilberforce, declared, "Were I five and twenty, as I was when I embarked with Captain Cook, I am very sure I should not lose a day in embarking for Haiti. To see a set of human beings emerging from slavery, and making most rapid strides toward the perfection of civilization, must I think be the most delightful food of all for contemplation."

But for Britain the years after the war were horribly trying. The peace in 1815 did not alleviate the financial hardships of the country, but because people thought it would—and had been waiting for years for a respite from their difficulties—there was great anger at the government and growing social unrest. The harvests of those years had been poor, exacerbating the situation, and radical agitators like the racist populist William Cobbett gleefully stirred the pot. The fear that mobs might finally erupt into the same violence and anarchy as they had in France was palpable, and the horrors of that revolution were still fresh in the minds of the ruling classes. So the government took a number of measures that we can see, in comfortable retrospect, as having been too harsh. Wilberforce was not innocent in this, siding with the government on the Corn Laws, which made it impossible to import cheaper corn, and on the rightly controversial vote to suspend habeas corpus. The price of corn had fallen so precipitously that many farmers lost everything. But after so many years of war, agricultural self-sufficiency was an important goal. In any case, the poor went hungry, and for these votes and others Wilberforce was accused of being a wealthy, out-of-touch enemy of the common laborer. Cobbett led the charge in vilifying Wilberforce, painting him as the most despicable of hypocrites, and obviously taking great pleasure in it. "You seem to have great affection for the fat and lazy and laughing and singing negroes," Cobbett famously wrote. "Never have you done one single act in favour of the labourers of this country."

To accuse Wilberforce of tending to the cause of the African blacks while ignoring the white laborers of Britain was outrageous and absurd. The historian Howse likens the accusation to reproaching Columbus for not also discovering Australia. But it's even worse because Wilberforce did so much for the British working class that it's as if he really had discovered Australia too. He is so well known for his work on abolition that all he did for the British people—much of it in the pursuit of fulfilling his second "great object," the "reformation of manners"—is overshadowed, and the results of much of his work would not be seen for decades. Wilberforce was deeply moved by suffering or injustice wherever he found it. His efforts, both in and out of Parliament, on behalf of British laborers and the poorer classes of England can hardly be tallied. Wilberforce labored to reduce the number of crimes punishable by hanging; he worked with the

Quaker Elizabeth Fry to bring about penal reform for women prisoners at Newgate; and with Romilly on many other efforts at penal
reform, including improvement of the harsh penal code of the time
and investigation of the abuses and cruelties in penal colonies such as
Botany Bay. Wilberforce referred to floggings in the army as an "object of my abomination," and cruelty of any kind—whether against
slaves or prisoners or sailors in the Royal Navy or animals—always
touched him and roused him to action. He worked with Romilly
to end the horror of "climbing boys"—little boys who were cruelly
forced to clean twisting, cramped chimneys under conditions almost
too terrible to describe; he sponsored legislation for improving child
labor laws and helped to found the Society for the Relief of the Manu-
facturing Poor. On and on it went.

Wilberforce often approached things from a moral or religious
perspective because he genuinely believed that this was the best way
to help those who suffered, but Cobbett simply saw it as hypocrisy, as
moral priggishness disguised as social outreach. For example, Cobbett
and other radicals of the day saw Wilberforce's efforts to end bear-
baiting and bull-baiting as killjoy measures motivated by fussy dis-
approval of the lusty joys of the poorer classes, who had so little to
entertain them. But Wilberforce saw these activities as grotesque displays of cruelty to defenseless animals and as practices that contributed
to the general coarsening of those who indulged in them, vulgarizing
and further callousing them to suffering and cruelty—which led to
further social problems. The mantle of moral authority Wilberforce
wore, and for which he had certainly neither asked nor angled, often
weighed heavily on him. Not only did it attract partisan lightning, but
it also gave Wilberforce a sense of obligation to weigh in on certain issues—such as the Corn Laws—when it might have been more politically savvy to say nothing. His reputation suffered, but he sincerely felt
that he had no choice but to speak up and honestly express what he felt
was right for the nation, even when doing so caused him to be lumped
in with some who had voted the same way out of simple selfish class
interest.

While Cobbett proudly and volubly set himself up as an heroic
champion of the lower classes, it must be noted that he was also a devoted champion of West Indian slavery and therefore the dedicated

enemy of the lowest of all classes of British persons. But having the happy advantage of being a confirmed and outspoken racist, Cobbett saw no inconsistency in his thinking.

The list of societies created by Wilberforce or Clapham to help those Cobbett accused him of ignoring is almost comically long. There is the Asylum for the Support and Encouragement of the Deaf and Dumb Children of the Poor; the Society for Bettering the Condition and Increasing the Comforts of the Poor; the Institution for the Relief of the Poor of the City of London and Parts Adjacent; the Society for the Relief of the Industrious Poor; the British National Endeavour for the Orphans of Soldiers and Sailors; the Naval Asylum for the Support of the Orphans and Children of British Sailors and Marines; the Asylum House of Refuge for the Reception of Orphaned Girls the Settlements of Whose Parents Cannot Be Found; the Institute for the Protection of Young Girls; and finally, the interestingly named Friendly Female Society for the Relief of Poor, Infirm, Aged Widows and Single Women, of Good Character, Who Have Seen Better Days.

☙

It was in 1818, after many failed attempts to pass the Slave Registry Bill, that Wilberforce and Clapham began at last to think of emancipation as the only solution to the sufferings of the West Indian slaves. In the course of gathering evidence to convince Parliament to pass the registry bill, new investigations were launched into the state of the West Indian slaves. The horrors that Wilberforce and his Clapham colleagues now discovered, eleven years after abolition of the trade, shocked them. All hopes that the slaves' situation might have been slowly improving were dashed. In his diary of January 7, Wilberforce mentions the account he had received "of the dreadful murder of a poor slave—buried without a coroner's inquest—but dug up, and found all mangled—yet brought in by the jury. . . . My mind becomes so much affected by the sad state of those poor injured wretches that it keeps me awake at night. Oh may God enable us to possess the nation with a due sense of their wrongs, and that we may be the instrument of redressing them!"

The larger aim of the abolitionists had always been emancipation, but as the battle for the abolition of the trade had worn on and on over twenty difficult years, the larger goal had somewhat receded as a political possibility. The idea of gradually improving the conditions of the slaves had gained ground, in the hope that this would lead to eventual emancipation. In a letter that February to John Joseph Gurney, Wilberforce explains that "it has ever been and still is, both the real and the declared object of all the friends of the African Race to see the W.[est] I.[ndian] Slaves gradually transmuted into a free peasantry; but this, the Ultimate Object, was to be produced progressively by the operation of multiplied, chiefly moral causes & to appear at last to have been the almost insensible result of the various Improvements, not to have been an Object all alone in View." But now, in 1818, it could be seen that this hope had been naive. So once again the course was clear: immediate emancipation by political means.

There were instantly objections and barriers. Britain's horrendous domestic situation in 1818 prompted Castlereagh to strongly advise Wilberforce against pushing for emancipation just then. But Wilberforce was unhappy about waiting. That April, feeling ill, he poured out his feelings in his diary: "I feel more and more convinced of the decay of my own faculties both bodily and mental and I must try to husband the little that remains. Alas Alas how grieved I am, that I have not brought forward the state of [the] W. Indian slaves." His guilt over the situation grew when the next day, again obviously sick and weak, he fumbled an opportunity to bring the subject up at a meeting of the African Institution. In his diary, he pours out his misery ungrammatically: "Never so much discredited myself in any public meeting to my recollection as to-day. Was it not my state of mind bad angry and irritated more than contrite and humble Lord mercy mercy I am wretched and miserable and poor and blind and naked. O supply all my wants and give me all needful supplies of Grace and Strength."

⚬⚬⚬

It's little wonder, considering the crushing pressures he was under, that Wilberforce escaped from London whenever possible. That summer he traveled with Barbara and the family to the Westmoreland area of

Scotland, where he took many long walks amidst the peace and beauty of the countryside. "The heat of the summer is checked," he writes, "and we are enjoying sun and showers, with just such a temperature as makes exercise pleasant and allows one to enjoy a little fire at night. I am as true to the hearth as a cricket or a favourite spaniel and reckon it a privation when the weather is too hot for enjoying this indulgence."

But Wilberforce was never far from his usual concerns. On July 20, a Sunday, he cringes at the sloppy ministrations of yet another "lukewarm professor" at Grasmere, who "read a common-place sermon at cantering or rather galloping pace; he preached last Sunday a sad trifling sermon. In the afternoon I walked to two or three cottages, and talked on religion to the people." Wilberforce did much of this wherever he went, evangelizing or trying to fan into fire whatever real faith might be found among the deprived population, who were typical of so many throughout Great Britain, poor lost sheep without a real shepherd. Southey concurred on the state of religion in that area, calling the half-hearted priests "marrying and christening machines."

During this time Wilberforce read books, wrote endless letters, and visited many old and new friends. He spent time with his friend Southey, who was grieving over the recent loss of his son, and with another poet, William Wordsworth. In his diary, Wilberforce records the visit of a novelist: "Walter Scott came to dinner to stay some time— Scott very entertaining, full of stories, which he tells excellently."

The Wilberforces' 1818 sojourn came to an end in early October. In his diary, he writes that on October 2 they "exchanged Muncaster for Keswick, reaching it after dark by Ennerdale-head and Lowes-water, and got to very comfortable lodgings. . . . 3rd. On the lake with poor Thomas Hutton who, seventy-five or six, but still active." Wilberforce was now fifty-nine himself, and ever attentive to the passage of time and its effects on himself and others. "I found afterwards that Mrs. I., our hostess, had been a pretty young woman, whom I remember forty-two years ago as Polly Keen of Hawkshead; now she is a toothless, nut-cracker-jawed old woman, but quite upright and active."

The year 1819 came and the climate for emancipation did not improve. That year brought the horror of the so-called Peterloo Massacre, in which a peaceful demonstration for government reform at St. Peter's Fields was threatened by a troop of cavalry. In the crush and subsequent confusion, eleven people died and hundreds were injured. The brutality of the government's response lent the radicals a new air of respectability and added fuel to their fire. It was clear that introducing legislation toward full emancipation would have to wait still longer. In the midst of the ongoing domestic strife, another radical, Francis Place, labeled Wilberforce "an ugly epitome of the devil." No one said being the "moral conscience of the nation" would be easy. And in 1820 Wilberforce—reprising that same thankless role—would be called upon to step into the center of an impossible national soap opera.

By turns wildly comic, heartbreakingly sad, and often simply disgusting, the Queen Caroline Affair, as it came to be called, would captivate the nation and shake it to its core. The strange circus of events began on January 29 when the old king died, deaf, blind, and insane. George III had risen to the throne sixty years before, in 1760.

When the king died, his eldest son, the Prince of Wales, who had been ruling for a decade as prince regent, would now at long last ascend the throne, and it was his impending elevation that set off this memorably sordid episode in British history. The phrase "the Queen Caroline Affair" does not refer to the extramarital affair that became the focus of the queen's subsequent trial, but to the episode in general. The queen likely had many affairs over the years, though nothing approaching the four-figure numbers put up by her husband, whose "relationships" with women—a hundred quotation marks could not adequately protect that word—could not have been more confused and complicated. For ten years before his marriage to Caroline, George IV had been secretly married to a Catholic woman named Mrs. FitzHerbert, but he had also conducted numerous well-publicized affairs before, during, and after that "marriage" and before, during, and after his twenty-five-year marriage to Caroline. And as we have mentioned, he had also over the years liberally distributed his primogenital favors and lifegiving milt throughout the wide world, capitalizing not a few brothels and disorderly houses with taxpayers' money.

George IV's cautionary anti-fairytale wedding to Caroline took place in 1795. At that time his gambling debts had scrambled to such heights that, with an eye toward wresting more money from the Royal Treasury, he consented to marry, almost sight unseen, the Princess

Caroline of Brunswick. If a legitimate heir ensued from their union, the prince's income would increase significantly. Though there are likely worse reasons to marry, few leap to mind. The prince arrived drunk at the royal wedding, and things tobogganed speedily downhill from there. He made no secret of finding his bride stout and tedious, not to say hygienically unschooled. Nor did Caroline think her lothario prince much in the way of a catch either. It seems miraculous that they produced a child, and given their mutual repulsion, parthenogenesis must not be ruled out. But a daughter was born the following year, at which point the unhappy couple bade each other adieu and accelerated in opposite directions. Caroline eventually settled in Italy, like seeds in an appendix, and the prince remained in England to return to the never-ending fox hunt, as it were.

Sadly, their daughter died at seventeen, and the prince and princess lived quite separate lives for twenty-five years. But now, when Caroline learned of the death of her father-in-law, the world would be new again. Faster than a speeding billet-doux, Caroline would return to England, there to claim her rightful place as queen at last. At least that was the plan, and George IV was ashen-faced to hear of it. He'd had a quarter-century of barnyard freedom, but now the funky chicken was coming home to roost. Ambassadors were quickly dispatched to buy her off, but Caroline was in no mood to be denied what she thought rightly hers, and goaded by her attorney-general, Brougham, who smelled political opportunity, she refused all offers to stop her progress.

George IV was so hated by the populace for a decade of what they perceived as repressive government measures that any enemy of his was their dearest heroine. And so Princess Caroline, rather rightfully thought of as a "wronged woman," instantly became the darling of the English mob. They drank her health at every opportunity and cheered her when she brazenly rode into London to claim what was coming to her. And they exulted in the fact that she had found shelter in the swarthy arms of an Italian playboy, for his swarthiness bespoke sexual vigor and was thus an openhanded slap to the fishbelly pallor of their detested king.

It was also bruited about that the king's spies had for a time been following Caroline about the Continent and had supposedly collected the details of her adulteries in a so-called green bag. If she refused to retract her claims on the throne, the king would put her on trial, produce the evidence of her adulteries, and publicly divorce her.

Wilberforce observed what was developing and knew that it would lead to real trouble. He knew that Brougham was using Princess Caroline as a political weapon—more cudgel than rapier—against the king and the Tory government. The controversy could divide the nation dangerously and cause terrible civil disorder. If the king felt cornered and decided to play his trump card—putting the queen on trial for her adulteries—the populace would be flooded with the offal of their mutual infidelities and bitter hatred. Wilberforce wished to spare the nation the bloodletting of such a public clash.

Wilberforce was very much seen as an elder statesman and an impartial political figure of the highest standing whose efforts in this episode were needed for the sake of his country. In his diary, Wilberforce writes: "I resolved if possible to prevent the inquiry; an object which could only be attained by such an amicable adjustment as should give neither party cause for triumph."

So Wilberforce stepped into the breach. He put forward a motion in the House, wrote another MP, "upon pure motives of charity to spare the public *the horrid and disgusting details* of the King's green bag and of the green bag which the Queen might bring against the King." A trial would open a Pandora's box of venereal furies. But the king and queen hardly seemed to give a fig for how their actions might harm the nation.

The king's final offer was a large sum of cash, in return for which he expected the queen to go away forever. She could use the title of "Queen" wherever she roamed and would have a royal yacht at her disposal, a frigate, etc. But there was one thing the king would not give her, one concession he would not make: he emphatically refused to allow her name to be read in the official prayers of the liturgy of the Church of England. Like many of the more refined hypocrites in history, George IV now became a liturgical stickler, who strained at a gnat but swallowed a camel. For a few words in a liturgy that meant nothing to him, he gambled with the fate of the British nation.

Wilberforce would have his work cut out for him, but he meant to persuade both sides, for the good of the country, to yield on this little point. He brought to bear all of the gravitas and moral authority and political independence he had amassed over the years. But neither side would budge. Finally, Brougham gave Wilberforce a private assurance that if he and a House delegation were to visit the queen, she would yield on the point of the liturgy. "She will accede to your request," Brougham wrote to Wilberforce. "I pledge myself."

And so Wilberforce dusted off his velvet green court frock coat, strapped on his ceremonial sword, and with a delegation proceeded to visit the queen. One of the many violent mobs that had been spawned by these unfolding events now swarmed in front of her residence, adding to the unpleasantness and danger. In a letter to Barbara, Wilberforce reported that the mob didn't throw any stones, a miracle that can hardly have had the reassuring effect he intended in recounting it. Nonetheless, up the stairs and into the queen's presence Wilberforce and the delegation went. Pollock describes the queen now as "slatternly odiferous," and it seems that in preparation for the solemn meeting she had been drinking. Wilberforce describes her as "extremely dignified, but very stern and haughty." However she appeared, and whatever had been personally promised by Brougham, the queen certainly did *not* yield. For all his troubles, Wilberforce ended up looking publicly foolish and was accused in the press of meddling. To his credit, he never mentioned Brougham's false promise.

Wilberforce greatly feared that the political partisanship stirred up by this affair could end in civil war. Mobs continued to threaten violence. One mob cornered Lord Anglesey, the celebrated and heavily decorated military hero who had led the cavalry charge at Waterloo and who had lost his leg there to a cannon blast. ("By God, sir," he reportedly shouted to the Duke of Wellington, "I've lost my leg!" "By God, sir," Wellington replied, "so you have!") The mob demanded that Anglesey declare his loyalty to the queen. "God save the queen!" he shouted. "May all your wives be like her!"

❦

"Whatever ensues," Wilberforce wrote, "it will always be a consolation to me to reflect that I have done my best to prevent all the evils that may happen." But what Wilberforce had feared would happen now happened: in addition to the civil violence, there would indeed be a public trial in which the king would attempt to discredit Caroline and get a divorce by unveiling the aforementioned "horrid and disgusting details" of the green bag. Italian servants would be summoned as witnesses, and the nation would be regaled with details of bedsprings and soiled linens.

Something like the media circuses we see today now began, issuing endless reports of the trial in foul detail. The picture we have of the queen during these proceedings is inescapably creepy. The Whig politician and diarist Thomas Creevy wrote a friend that "to describe to you her appearance and manner is far beyond my powers. . . . The nearest resemblance I can recollect to this much-injured Princess is a toy which you used to call Fanny Royds." The modern descendant of this now-antique Dutch toy is called a Weeble; like its ancestor, it combines a pear shape with a heavily weighted posterior to remain indefatigably upright. Creevy also remarked on the queen's baffling and incongruous black wig over her natural blond hair. What "few straggling ringlets" of hair he spied did not seem to be "Her Majesty's own property." The queen wore a veil during the proceedings, though her face appeared to glow red.

"I will frankly confess," Wilberforce said in a letter, "that the present inclination of my judgement is strongly against receiving the Bill [against her]. . . . Our Saviour's decision 5 Matthew 32. 'He that putteth away his wife except for fornication, causeth her to commit adultery,' appeared to me to bear very strongly on this question." He surely regarded her as "more sinned against than sinning" and felt it was indeed the king who had pushed her into her grotesque situation. During the trial, however, it came out that while living abroad with her Italianate paramour Bergami, the queen had been receiving £50,000 per year—something the public found displeasing—and suddenly Her Majesty's star was no longer in its zenith. Her Whig solicitor bobbled the tail end of an eight-hour closing argument by clumsily referring to the Gospel account of the "woman taken in adultery." It was an appalling blunder, for he had until then fastidiously maintained her innocence. A rhyme in the newspapers expressed the public's mood:

Most gracious queen, we thee implore
To go away and sin no more,
Or if that effort be too great
To go away at any rate.

"What a mess have Ministers and the Queen's advisers and the House of Lords altogether made of this sad business," wrote Wilberforce. It was as if two people had been wrestling in an open sewer. At what price victory? And the spectators had been thoroughly bespattered too.

In the end, the queen was acquitted, paid off to keep her title and go away, and she did. As part of the agreement, she was not to take part in the coronation the following July. But when the day came, she shocked everyone by arriving in her coach at Westminster Abbey and demanding entrance. It was a scene. The Abbey's door was quite literally shut in her face. Incredibly, the forward momentum of her obstinacy was not exhausted. She ran to another door—and then another. But she was refused entrance again and again. Thricely rebuffed she at last departed in her coach and died two weeks later, somewhat suspiciously. The king was obviously pleased, many thought indecorously so.

But before this heartbreaking denouement, when she had first been acquitted, Wilberforce was pleased that she had not borne the entire brunt of the ugliness and that the king had not been able to get away with the monstrous hypocrisy of casting stones at her for her adultery when he himself lived in a glass palace. Wilberforce was taken to task by the press, however, for his own failure to broker a deal. "What a lesson it is to a man not to set his heart on low popularity," he writes, "when after 40 years disinterested public service, I'm believed by the Bulk to be a Hypocritical Rascal."

Marianne Thornton gives us her account of him shortly after his failed mission to visit the "haughty and stern" queen. "He used to go into ecstacies especially about flowers," she wrote.

When staying with us at the time of wicked Queen Caroline's trial he was one of a deputation of three from the House of Commons to persuade her to give up being crowned, for a large annual allowance. She was half drunk

I believe when they got there and she all but kicked them downstairs. Mr. Wilberforce came back very low and disspirited, thinking indeed that she would upset the monarchy; when stepping out of the library window before dinner he caught sight of a gorgeous moss-rose that grew up the wall, and seeing how it transfixed him I gathered it. Oh the beauty of it, Oh the goodness of God in giving us such alleviations in this hard world. The bell rang for dinner but there was no getting him to go in while he stood worshipping his flower and when he had lavished all other endearments and admirations he ended with "And Oh how unlike the Queen's countenance."

Later that summer, Wilberforce came face-to-face with another happy "alleviation," much like the moss-rose, though he in no wise could have appreciated the larger significance of it at the time. Just before departing with his family for Weymouth, Wilberforce was invited to call on the Duchess of Kent. "She received me," he writes, "with her fine animated child on the floor by her with its playthings, of which I soon became one." How like Wilberforce to stoop to the floor at sixty and engage an infant, but had he known whom he entertained there on the floor, he might have sung the *Nunc Dimittis* and departed in peace for Weymouth. For the rosy-faced, German-speaking fourteen-month-old was none other than the future Queen Victoria, whose cherubic countenance was as unlike Queen Caroline's countenance as that glorious moss-rose. And so here, on the miniature plain of the carpet, in a prophetically fitting tableau of domestic happiness, the child who would lend the future era her name met the man who would lend it his character.

CHAPTER 23

THE LAST BATTLE

" . . . blessing and honour are upon his head."

I n December 1820, after Queen Caroline's trial, the Wilberforces
traveled again to Bath. Here they received word of the suicide
of Christophe, King Henri of Haiti. Wilberforce and the others at
Clapham had expended great energies on Haiti and had put their
hopes into it, but the situation there had always been terribly difficult. Wilberforce may sometimes have been a bit too hopeful in
such situations, but Christophe possessed such impressive leadership abilities that he may well have triumphed over the situation had
things been ever so slightly different. Surely it weighed heavily on
Wilberforce to think of it now.

Under Christophe, Haiti had indeed been off to a terrifically
promising start, but over time Christophe became increasingly au-
thoritarian and less popular—and then he suffered a stroke. The Duke
of Marmalade (in a letter Wilberforce confused him with the Comte
de Limonade, conflating their names into the Duke of Lemonade) led
a rebellion against Christophe, who eventually committed suicide.
The improvements of a decade were quickly undone. Those who had
opposed abolition and now opposed emancipation were thrilled.

The Scottish physician Duncan Stewart, who had overseen Christophe's hospitals, wrote to Wilberforce some months later: "Every day something transpires to show the importance of King Henry to the Haytians. His greatest enemies now acknowledge that they never have had a chief whose powers of mind and body were so fitted for command. Had he reigned over a people untutored in the scepticism of modern infidelity, and uncontaminated by the licentiousness of French libertinism, Hayti must centuries hence have regarded his memory with veneration."

The following summer greater heartbreak visited the Wilberforces when their eldest daughter, Barbara, grew ill with "consumption," what we now call tuberculosis. Charming and pretty, she was just twenty-two. They had nearly lost her when she was six, and now, after a few months' battle, they did. She died in London on December 30, 1821.

Even into his sixties, Wilberforce was still active in Parliament. In 1821 he made an important speech on Catholic emancipation. "Persecution for religious opinions," he said, "is not only one of the wickedest, but one of the most foolish things in the world." Wilberforce's views on Catholicism were complicated and changed as he grew older. Initially he had seen it as the very epitome of "dead religion," as bad or worse than what he said about the Church of England in his book. But toward the end of his life he realized that the problems with the Catholic Church, like the problems with the Anglican Church, had less to do with theology than with practice. If the clergy didn't believe what their church taught, they certainly wouldn't communicate it to their flocks or put it into practice. Though it would have surprised Wilberforce, two of his sons, Henry and Robert, would be involved in the Oxford Movement and later in life be received into the Catholic Church.

But it was the battle for emancipation for the slaves that loomed ahead of all the others. In 1823, at last, the domestic situation seemed to warrant beginning a final push toward that happy end. Wilberforce would first and foremost set pen to paper and write the book that he called his manifesto, *Appeal in Behalf of the Negro Slaves in the West Indies*. As ever, the book was seasoned with grace toward those he might so easily have demonized. Wilberforce knew that there were indeed slave owners who actually treated their slaves kindly, and many more who were genuinely ignorant of many of the horrors of which he wrote. Throughout his life Wilberforce resisted the cheap temptation to point the finger at others while posturing as their moral superior. He succeeded in defusing the anger of some and drew them in to hear what he was saying. Cobbett, however, was never one of them; he called the book "a great deal of canting trash; a great deal of lying; a great deal of that cool impudent falsehood for which the Quakers are famed [*sic*]. . . . There is no man who knows anything at all of the real situation of the Blacks, who will not declare you to be totally ignorant of the subject on which you are writing, or to be a most consummate hypocrite." But many less confirmed enemies were indeed converted to abolition over the years, and now this book had a similar effect. The owner of one West Indian sugar plantation wrote Wilberforce to say that the book "had so affected me, that should it cost me my whole property, I [would] surrender it willingly, that my poor negroes may be brought not only to the liberty of Europeans, but especially to the liberty of Christians."

◦◦◦◦◦

Wilberforce was tired, and he feared that the battle ahead would need younger champions. He was only sixty-two, but he now wore a back brace for the curvature of his spine, which had worsened, as such things do, and his eyesight was poorer than ever, in part as a result of decades of taking opium for ulcerative colitis, which also continued to plague him. He suffered terribly from a breathing difficulty now too, and periodically from what he called a protrusion *a posteriori,* a malady today dispatched with lasers and cryogenics. After a few more battles with his health and a few speeches that didn't rise to previous levels, Wilberforce knew he was not the man to lead the final parliamentary push toward emancipation. It would be wiser to appoint—and in his case, perhaps anoint—a successor. The oil would be drizzled upon the head of Thomas Fowell Buxton, a devout evangelical MP who was politically independent, like Wilberforce, but who, unlike him, was young, vigorous, and healthy, having been born in 1786.

Even so, by 1824 Wilberforce felt that it was likely time he left the House altogether. Some kindly suggested that he take a life peerage and sit in the House of Lords, but for various reasons he decided against it. A peerage wasn't his style. Far better, he thought, simply to retire.

In 1825, on February 22—Washington's birthday again—Wilberforce announced his retirement from politics. Just as when he had left his seat for Yorkshire to take the lesser seat for Bramber, Wilberforce felt regret. "When I consider that my public life is nearly expired . . . ," he wrote to a friend,

> I am filled with the deepest compunction from the consciousness of my having made so poor a use of the talents committed to my stewardship. The heart knows its own bitterness. We alone know ourselves the opportunities we have enjoyed, and the comparative use we have made of them. . . . To your friendly ear . . . I breathe out my secret sorrows. I might be supposed by others to be fishing for a compliment. Well, it is an unspeakable consolation that we serve a gracious Master, who giveth liberally and upbraideth not. . . . I always spoke and voted according to the dictates of my conscience, for the public and not for my own private interest. . . . Yet I am but too conscious of numerous and great sins of omission, many opportunities of doing good whether not at all or very inadequately improved.

As his letters and diaries prove, Wilberforce's tenderness and sensitivity to the sufferings of others was heartfelt. Nor did his concern for the well-being of others end with his own species. Wilberforce's home was a menagerie of animals that included rabbits, turtles, and even a fox. In 1824—along with his successor in the abolition struggle, Thomas Fowell Buxton—he was one of the founding members of the Society for the Prevention of Cruelty to Animals. His Clapham friend Lord Teignmouth gives us this account of Wilberforce in later life. "In one of his last visits to Bath," wrote Teignmouth,

the little dwarfish figure, twisted now into a strange confirma-
tion, was wending its way up one of the steep streets by which
loaded cars bring coals to the inhabitants of Bath from the
port on the Avon. Two rough carters were urging their feeble
horse up one of the steepest of these streets, when one of the
horses slipped and fell. The man to whom the cart belonged,
a burly specimen of a savage race, infuriated by the stoppage,
rained blows and kicks, mingled with hoarse curses on the
prostrate animal. Wilberforce who was near, and who forgot
everything in his sympathy, rushed forward when the giant
had raised his hand for a further blow, and interfered, pouring upon him at the same time a torrent of eloquent rebuke.
The fellow arrested in the very height of passion, and furious
at the language used, stood with his face like a thundercloud,
as if meditating to turn his stroke on the puny elf who appeared before him. At this moment his companion, who had
recognised Wilberforce, stepped up to him and whispered
his name. The word acted like a charm. In an instant the low-
ering face cleared, and from rage and sullen hatred the look
passed at once into wondering reverence as if, in the midst of
his brutal passions and abasement, there was suddenly presented to him an object that awakened the better feelings of
his nature, and drew forth his slumbering sympathies.

In 1826 the Wilberforces moved to a farm called Highwood Hill,
where his eldest son, William, along with wife and child, soon joined
them. The plan was for William to farm the land, and he persuaded
his father to lend him a significant amount of money so that he could
become the partner in a dairy business nearby. William had sometimes displayed a certain shiftlessness of character and had caused
Wilberforce no small heartache. A few years earlier Wilberforce
had been compelled to pull him out of Trinity College, Cambridge,
for his behavior there. But now William had married and seemed at
last settled into the life of a farmer. The other three boys, Robert,
Samuel, and Henry, were all at Oxford together in the early twenties

and distinguished themselves spectacularly, each receiving a first, and Robert a double first.

Wherever Wilberforce lived—and Highwood Hill was no exception—the domestic chaos continued, even without the proximity to Parliament and his many friends and acquaintances. Also invincibly unchanged was Wilberforce's tenderness to others, evinced all his life in his difficulty in saying no or in turning out servants who were far from their proper usefulness. "Things go on in the old way," wrote Marianne Thornton, who visited them that year.

> The house thronged with servants who are all lame or impotent or blind, or kept from charity, an ex-secretary kept because he is grateful, and his wife because she nursed poor Barbara, and an old butler who they wish would not stay but then he is so attached, and his wife who was a cook but now she is so infirm. All this is rather as it should be however for one rather likes to see him so completely in character and would willingly despair of getting one's place changed at dinner and hear a chorus of Bells all day which nobody answers for the sake of seeing Mr. Wilberforce in his element.

In 1827 Wilberforce left Highwood for a time to travel through Yorkshire and pay a visit to the haunts of his early years. He met a shopkeeper named Smart, whom he had known from Hull a half-century before. "Knew me when himself a boy," Wilberforce writes in his diary, "—remembered the ox roasted whole." Wilberforce was during this nostalgic journey often reminded of his mortality, for it seemed that everyone but Sharp the shopkeeper had departed this life ahead of him.

In 1830 the last decade of Wilberforce's life dawned. The few years he had left held a serious trial or two and some joys as well. He did not appear in public often. In fact, it was on May 15, 1830, that he appeared for the last time in public in London, having been persuaded to take the chair at a meeting of the Anti-Slavery Society. But a terrible financial blow fell that year, eclipsing much else. The dairy business in which he had helped his eldest son, William, now required more capital, and

Wilberforce, always eager to help William, now went to great lengths to obtain it. He sold a great deal of stock and, most dramatically, even sold his boyhood home in Hull. But after all of this, the business was a failure: they lost everything. Now in his seventies, Wilberforce—formerly a very wealthy man—found himself nearly destitute. It was a serious blow, but those around him were deeply impressed at his equanimity and even joy in the midst of the drama. He had given away vast sums of money throughout his life, and the innumerable people and projects that had benefited from his personal generosity could never be tallied in this world. But now he was even forced to sell Highwood, and would end his life without a home of his own. Foxes had holes and birds had nests, but Wilberforce and Barbara were forced in old age to cast themselves upon the mercies of their second and third sons, living for alternating periods with each of them.

"The loss incurred," Wilberforce writes,

> has been so heavy as to compel me to descend from my present level and greatly to diminish my establishment. But I am bound to recognise in this dispensation the gracious mitigation of the severity of the stroke. Mrs. Wilberforce and I are supplied with a delightful asylum under the roofs of two of our own children. And what better could we desire? A kind Providence has enabled me with truth to adopt the declaration of David, that goodness and mercy have followed me all my days. And now, when the cup presented to me has some bitter ingredients, yet surely no draught can be deemed distasteful which comes from such a hand, and contains such grateful infusions as those of social intercourse and the sweet endearments of filial gratitude and affection.

In 1832 he suffered another devastating blow: his dearest Lizzie died, at the age of thirty-one. The loss hit Wilberforce hard, but Lizzie's own daughter, just an infant, gave her grandfather some consolation and prompted this rumination on God and suffering:

"I was much impressed yesterday," he wrote,

> with the similarity in some respects of my own situation to that of [Lizzie's] dear little innocent, who was undergoing

the operation of vaccination. The infant gave up its little arm to the operator without suspicion or fear. But when it felt the puncture, which must have been sharp, no words can express the astonishment and grief that followed. I could not have thought the mouth could have been distended so widely as it continued, till the nurse's soothing restored her usual calmness. What an illustration is this of the impatient feelings we are often apt to experience, and sometimes even to express, when suffering from the dispensations of a Being, whose wisdom we profess to believe to be unerring, whose kindness we know to be unfailing, whose truth also is sure, and who has declared to us, that all things shall work together for good to them that love Him, and that the object of His inflictions is to make us partakers of His holiness.

Toward the end of his days, Wilberforce's marked habit of perpetual gratitude in all circumstances actually seemed to increase. He judged that living with his two sons, both ministers, was a blessing he would not have experienced if his finances had not been devastated. "It gives me no little pleasure, and calls for a large return of gratitude to the Giver of all good, to witness the delightful scene that is here exhibited of pastoral service and domestic happiness. You are able from experience to judge how a parent must feel in witnessing the pastoral labours of his own child."

Of his son Samuel, who would later become the bishop of Oxford, he writes: "His lady was not well endowed with pecuniary charms: but they will have enough, I trust, for comfort; and even if it were not a sin, as it certainly is, to marry for money, I should deem it one of the basest actions a gentleman could commit. This house is enlivened by a delightful infant, which twaddles about most captivatingly, and begins to lisp out papa and mamma with more than Cicero's eloquence."

His final home was with his son Robert, who lived in a vicarage at East Fairleigh. Even there, many visitors of all social stations, shapes, and sizes would come to pay their respects. The Russian Prince Czartoriski, with whom he had waited for the czar that Sunday morning in 1814, made a visit, bringing with him his four-year-old son and, as Wilberforce put it in his diary, "a dwarf about the same size."

That spring the antislavery movement surged forward one last time. It was on the minds of many that the grand goal toward which they had been working for so long might indeed be reached while Wilberforce was still living. The date in Parliament for the opening of the great and final battle for the emancipation of all the slaves in the British Empire had at last been set. It would be May 14, and the abolitionists now went one more time into the mode they had invented, and to which they were now quite accustomed. There were lectures and meetings; letters were written and articles placed in newspapers. Two hundred thousand copies of a pamphlet written by a young man recently in the West Indies were printed and distributed. He reported that the floggings of the slaves had increased dramatically since the rules against using the whip in the fields had taken effect; how, in short, there was no improvement in the misery, just a different kind of misery, meted out by different hands—and how the only solution was emancipation. And again petitions, hundreds of them, were circulated throughout the country. The people of the nation would speak once more, and before it was all over nearly one and a half million British subjects would add their name to the noble list.

One meeting from which one of these petitions would officially be sent to Parliament was to be held on April 12 at Maidstone, near East Fairleigh. That petition's signatures would include the shaky penmanship of William Wilberforce, now one of the voices in the great *vox populi* whose very existence he had in part midwifed and whose development he had husbanded over the years. But a recent visit from young Buxton and young Stephen to tell their exiled hero the exciting details of this final campaign seemed to have the inadvertent effect of blowing oxygen onto a banked fire: the embers, thought nearly dead, once more burst into roaring flame. There was suddenly no question that Wilberforce might be contented with merely signing this great document. Like those young men who had giddily leapt up to speak on that cold February night in 1807, who had wished to dip their fingers in the great river of History suddenly boiling before them, so now the aged pilgrim, four months from his long journey's end, was swept up in the moment and felt impelled to appear at the historic meeting—and not only to appear but to speak too. Wilberforce would accept the unsurpassed honor, pressed upon him now, of proposing the petition to the Houses of Parliament himself.

⟳

When he spoke that day in mid-April, Wilberforce's voice was an indistinguishable echo of the silver-toned trumpet of yore, which had blasted through the violent weather in the castle yard at York and gripped the attentions of the assembled four thousand. But his audience was no less attentive now. He first spoke in favor of the money that was being proposed as a recompense to the planters, whose slaves would be set free. The final figure would come to £20 million. There were some in the abolitionist movement whose sense of justice was understandably offended at the idea that the men who had enslaved their human brothers and sisters should be in any way rewarded or compensated by their country for this evil, but Wilberforce had long ago learned to temper whatever sense of justice he had with grace, and more grace. He also knew that to purchase the freedom of these men and women was better by far than leaving one's sense of justice uninjured and leaving them in their chains. "I say, and I say honestly and fearlessly," Wilberforce declared, "that the same Being who commands us to love mercy says also 'Do justice'; and therefore I have no objection to grant the colonists the relief that may be due to them for any real injuries they may prove themselves to have sustained."

Old as he now was, hunched and wizened and weak, yet he rose and spoke one more time in the great cause to which he had given his life and whose old father he had become. It was a short speech, and unremarkable compared with any of those for which he had become so famous. But if such things are possible, his words seemed to find the ear of God. For it was in the last moments of this last speech that something startling and remarkable happened. "I trust," the old man said, "that we now approach the end of our career." The phrase evoked the blazing sun's bright career through the daytime sky, and he was speaking of the soon end of his own days, of his disappearance from this world, as when the sun's arcing journey is ended and its light extinguished. But in the very moment that ended this sentence, as if by design, a beam of sunlight burst into the room, flooding it and the speaker with light. It was a startling echo of that astonishing moment forty-one years before when, at the tail end of Pitt's magnificent peroration for abolition, the golden light of dawn had filled the House chamber—a moment Pitt had instantly seized upon by appending a quote from Virgil in a fitting flourish. At that moment so long ago, when Wilberforce was young, victory had seemed assured. But that auroral sign of favor was in retrospect a false dawn, for there were still fifteen long years of darkness ahead before abolition would pass. But the light that broke into the room now, as the old man stood there marveling, was no false harbinger, and Wilberforce knew it. "The object is bright before us," the old man said, quick as Pitt had been to seize the moment. "The light of heaven beams on it and is an earnest of success."

In May, Wilberforce traveled to Bath and remained until July, when his old friend, the Quaker Joseph John Gurney, visited him. "I was introduced to an apartment upstairs," wrote Gurney,

> where I found the veteran Christian reclining on a sofa, and his countenance bespeaking increased age. . . . I freely spoke to him of the good and glorious things which, as I believed, assuredly awaited him in the kingdom of rest and peace. The illuminated expression of his furrowed countenance, with his clasped and uplifted hands, were indicative of profound devotion and holy joy. "With regard to myself," he said, "I have nothing whatsoever to urge, but the poor publican's plea, 'God be merciful to me a sinner.'"

Wilberforce, who might have crowed with pride over his accomplishments, was very obviously humble about anything he might have done, and genuinely and keenly aware of how much he had failed.

But others aren't obliged to be so modest about him. In the estimation of Sir Reginald Coupland, who was Beit Professor of Colonial History at Oxford, "more than any man, he had founded in the conscience of the British people a tradition of humanity and of responsibility towards the weak and backward . . . whose fate lay in their hands. And that tradition has never died." As well versed as we are today in the manifold failings of colonial rule, the comparison to things before Wilberforce gives us another picture. Before Wilberforce, a world power like Great Britain could do what it liked with the people of Asia and Africa, and for two centuries and more did, treating human beings as they treated dumb beasts or insensate resources like timber, hemp, and ore; but after Wilberforce, all that changed. What "Wilberforce and his friends achieved . . ." Coupland tells us, "was nothing less, indeed, than a moral revolution."

As Wilberforce's health declined, the family decided to travel to London to see his doctor, and on July 19 they arrived at 44 Cadogan Place, between the Brompton Road and Sloane Street. It was the home of his cousin, Lucy Smith. With Parliament still meeting, many friends were still in town, and they flocked around to visit with him. Wilberforce swelled with gratitude and affection for them, some of whom he hadn't seen in years. "What cause it is for thankfulness," he said, "that God has always disposed people to treat me so kindly."

On July 25, a Thursday morning, Wilberforce's youngest son, Henry, brought a young member of Parliament to breakfast. His name was William Gladstone. The twenty-three-year-old future prime minister had never met Wilberforce, though his parents, who were both evangelicals, had known him. Gladstone would remain in British politics until 1895 and become one of the fixtures of the century. "He is cheerful and serene," Gladstone wrote of the meeting, "a beautiful picture of old age in sight of immortality. Heard him pray with his family. Blessing and honour are upon his head."

"I am like a clock that is almost run down," Wilberforce said to one friend. But he would have one more glimpse on this side of the veil. On Friday evening, July 26, Wilberforce received word of the very thing for which he had dreamed his entire adult life: the House had just passed the bill abolishing slavery in the British Empire. The West Indian planters would be compensated for approximately half the market value of their slaves. "Thank God," Wilberforce rejoiced, "that I should have lived to witness a day in which England is willing to give twenty millions sterling for the Abolition of Slavery."

Tom Macaulay, who had been in and around this battle and these warriors his whole life, was now a part of the battle himself as a member of Parliament. He was the eldest son of Zachary Macaulay, and would later become famous for his wildly popular four-volume *History of England*. He raced to see Wilberforce the next day, Saturday, and to rejoice in the presence of the one who more than anyone living could know the meaning of such a victory. Macaulay wrote that Wilberforce "exulted in the success . . . as much as the youngest and most ardent partisan." That he had been allowed to live to witness it must have been almost unbearably wonderful, for him and for all those who knew him and were gathering around him in his final days.

Who can dream what went through the old man's mind that day? To know that the battle for emancipation was really and truly over, and won—to know that every slave in the vast reaches of the British Empire would soon have his legal freedom and could never again suffer under such a system. Such a Saturday of joy as Wilberforce lived that day can only come after a thousand Saturdays of battle. But it *had* come. It was a dream come true.

Wilberforce felt improved most of the day, basking with those he loved in the glow of this penultimate crowning victory. But that night he fell ill again, and on Sunday, the following day and his last, he had a succession of fainting fits. Barbara and his youngest, Henry, were with him that night when he stirred one last time. "I am in a very distressed state," he said. "Yes," Henry said, "but you have your feet on the Rock." The man whose voice and words had changed the world now spoke his last. "I do not venture to speak so positively," he said. "But I hope I have." He was humble and hopeful to the end, and at 3:00 a.m. on Monday morning, July 29, 1833, William Wilberforce departed this world.

Within a few hours, the following letter arrived addressed to his sons:

> We, the undersigned members of both Houses of Parliament, being anxious upon public grounds to show our respect for the memory of the late William Wilberforce, and being also satisfied that public honours can never be more fitly bestowed than upon such benefactors of mankind, earnestly request that he may be buried in Westminster Abbey; and that we, and others who may agree with us in these sentiments, may have permission to attend his funeral.

The letter had been organized by Henry Brougham, the lord chancellor, and bore his signature and that of Wilberforce's old friend the Duke of Gloucester, along with thirty-seven members of the Lords and nearly one hundred of the Commons. Brougham appended a personal note: "Nearly all the members of both Houses would have joined, had the time allowed."

That next Saturday, August 3, public business was suspended. A long train of mourners' carriages proceeded from the house on Cadogan Place to Westminster Abbey. All along the way huge crowds flanked the eastward procession, and when it reached the Abbey it was joined by all of the members of Parliament. The speaker, the lord chancellor, and the Duke of Gloucester, along with another royal duke and four peers, supported the pall, and behind the simple bier walked Wilberforce's four sons, along with other members of his family and close friends. The funeral was attended by the Duke of Wellington, royal princes, and the highest-ranking bishops of the church. Wilberforce's body was laid in the North Transept, near those of Pitt, Fox, and Canning. The words inscribed upon his tomb there, probably written by Thomas Macaulay, appear at the end of this chapter.

A letter from a West Indian clergyman informed his sons that a "great part of our coloured population, who form here an important body, went into mourning at the news of his death." In the biography of their father, his sons wrote that

> the same honour was paid him by this class of persons at New York, where also an eulogium (since printed) was pronounced upon him by a person publicly selected for the task, and their brethren throughout the United States were called upon to pay the marks of external respect to the memory of their benefactor. For departed kings there are appointed honours, and the wealthy have their gorgeous obsequies: it was his nobler portion to clothe a people with spontaneous mourning, and go down to the grave amid the benedictions of the poor.

One year later Wilberforce would have his greatest memorial, and the one for which, unashamedly, he had labored. Sir Reginald

Coupland describes it in the last words of his 1923 biography: "A year later, at midnight on July 31, 1834, eight hundred thousand slaves became free. It was more than a great event in African or in British history. It was one of the greatest events in the history of mankind."

The historian G. M. Trevelyan describes what took place on the actual dawning of that new era in the history of the world: "On the last night of slavery, the negroes in our West Indian islands went up on to the hill-tops to watch the sun rise, bringing them freedom as its first rays struck the waters."

The image of these men and women facing the sunrise, freed as they beheld its rising—as the light eclipsed the darkness—is a fitting coda for our story. Those beams of sunlight that morning literally illuminated a new world, an undiscovered country that no one had seen before but which some had been privileged to glimpse by faith and knew existed. On that historic morning, as the sun rose, that new world was revealed at last as real, as having existed all along on the far side of the mountains through which William Wilberforce had been our guide.

S. D. G.

TO THE MEMORY OF

WILLIAM WILBERFORCE

(BORN IN HULL AUGUST 24TH 1759,

DIED IN LONDON JULY 29TH 1833;)

FOR NEARLY HALF A CENTURY A MEMBER OF THE HOUSE OF COMMONS,

AND, FOR SIX PARLIAMENTS DURING THAT PERIOD,

ONE OF THE TWO REPRESENTATIVES FOR YORKSHIRE.

IN AN AGE AND COUNTRY FERTILE IN GREAT AND GOOD MEN,

HE WAS AMONG THE FOREMOST OF THOSE WHO FIXED THE CHARACTER OF THEIR TIMES

BECAUSE TO HIGH AND VARIOUS TALENTS

TO WARM BENEVOLENCE, AND TO UNIVERSAL CANDOUR,

HE ADDED THE ABIDING ELOQUENCE OF A CHRISTIAN LIFE.

EMINENT AS HE WAS IN EVERY DEPARTMENT OF PUBLIC LABOUR,

AND A LEADER IN EVERY WORK OF CHARITY,

WHETHER TO RELIEVE THE TEMPORAL OR THE SPIRITUAL WANTS OF HIS FELLOW MEN

HIS NAME WILL EVER BE SPECIALLY IDENTIFIED

WITH THOSE EXERTIONS

WHICH, BY THE BLESSING OF GOD, REMOVED FROM ENGLAND

THE GUILT OF THE AFRICAN SLAVE TRADE,

AND PREPARED THE WAY FOR THE ABOLITION OF SLAVERY

IN EVERY COLONY OF THE EMPIRE:

IN THE PROSECUTION OF THESE OBJECTS,

HE RELIED, NOT IN VAIN, ON GOD;

BUT IN THE PROGRESS, HE WAS CALLED TO ENDURE

GREAT OBLOQUY AND GREAT OPPOSITION:

HE OUTLIVED, HOWEVER, ALL ENMITY:

AND, IN THE EVENING OF HIS DAYS,

WITHDREW FROM PUBLIC LIFE AND PUBLIC OBSERVATION

TO THE BOSOM OF HIS FAMILY.

YET HE DIED NOT UNNOTICED OR FORGOTTEN BY HIS COUNTRY:

THE PEERS AND COMMONS OF ENGLAND,

WITH THE LORD CHANCELLOR, AND THE SPEAKER, AT THEIR HEAD,

CARRIED HIM TO HIS FITTING PLACE

AMONG THE MIGHTY DEAD AROUND,

HERE TO REPOSE:

TILL, THROUGH THE MERITS OF JESUS CHRIST,

HIS ONLY REDEEMER AND SAVIOUR,

(WHOM, IN HIS LIFE AND IN HIS WRITINGS HE HAD DESIRED TO GLORIFY,)

HE SHALL RISE IN THE RESURRECTION OF THE JUST.

EPILOGUE

All works of art possess something of the rascal about them: not in the sense of that unpardonably silly cliche about all art being "transgressive", but in the sense that all art—which by definition partakes of eternity and immortality—somehow gives the slip to doddering Father Time and to his humorless brother Death. So that, inevitably, even the stateliest works of a Titian or Michelangelo have something of the Katzenjammer kids about them.

Of course the biography of a figure from the past escapes time in a more overt sense, too, by seeming to resurrect the subject of the biography. Inside the small eternity of the book the subject is once again brought to life, and in a kind of flipbook illusion he again disports himself through the *trompe-l'oeil* decades—and then, of course, dies once more. But his death at the end of the book comes to us afresh, as if we had just read about it in that morning's newspaper. We mourn his passing, and wish that we might see him once more alive, might have him with us for a few more pages, our new friend. And so it is that we sometimes find ourselves stumbling through such things as are called epilogues, looking again for the one just lost.

I confess that while writing this book I sometimes had the happy sense that Wilberforce was present, or on the very verge of it, twinkling with delight at my elbow, wearing that rosebud smile of his, head quizzically cocked. Then the idea of the past and time itself seemed a flimsy construct, one through which I might have very easily reached, as through a wall of wet tissue paper, to touch him. After months of reading his diaries, journals, and letters I was even sure I knew his voice. Pressed hard enough, I might reveal to friends that it sounds remarkably like that of the British actor Leslie Howard, who played Professor Henry Higgins in the 1938 movie *Pygmalion*. And strangely, like Rex Harrison too, who also played Professor Higgins, in *My Fair Lady*. What Wilberforce and Henry Higgins have to do with each other is unclear, but the voices of those actors—the fast rhythms of their speech and their nasal British accents—strongly suggest Wilberforce as I've heard him in my head through his own words. He even looks like each of them in different ways, though his nose is larger, and seems to sniff the air for cant. Whether I should reveal such information remains to be seen; presently I shall remain mum, for fear of ridicule.

Who among us doesn't at some time long to reenter the past, to touch and hear again what is lost? No human impulse is more fundamental than our desire to transcend time, and none argues better that time is not the medium for which we are finally meant. And in the case of such as Wilberforce, we strain for some link, some palpable connection, whether to stand where he stood or touch what he touched, or perhaps even to speak to a living descendant, and stare at their faces. Whether via relic or relative, we seem to await that fairytale moment when the dead, gray facade of years between us at last cracks and crumbles and falls away, revealing the real thing hiding beneath: eternity, fresh and green.

There was a turtle born in the Galapagos islands in 1830, three years before Wilberforce's death. It was collected by Charles Darwin's *Beagle* expedition in 1835 and brought to England. In 1841 the *Beagle*'s Captain brought it to Australia, where it lived in a zoo for many years, that being an understatement. The turtle, later named Harriet, lived to the end of the nineteenth century, and into the twentieth. Incredibly, she made it all the way through the twentieth century, stepped over its far border, and walked into the twenty-first. Needless to say, Harriet outlived everyone on the *Beagle*—and two Beatles. She died of a heart condition during the writing of this book, on June 23, 2006. Reading of Harriet's superlative journey seemed a link to Wilberforce and his time, and this cheered me.

But there is yet a way we may reach across the years and touch Wilberforce. John Pollock, the great Wilberforce biographer, whose magnificent 1977 book brought Wilberforce so powerfully to life for me and so many has written more recently of an extraordinary meeting that he had sometime in the 1980s with Wilberforce's last surviving great-grandson. Pollock writes:

> [The great-grandson, who] was then over a hundred and blind, told me how his father as a small boy was walking with Wilberforce on a hill near Bath when they saw a poor cart-horse being cruelly whipped by the carter as he struggled to

pull a load of stone up the hill. The little liberator expostulated with the carter who began to swear at him and tell him to mind his own business, and so forth. Suddenly the carter stopped and said, "Are you Mr. Wilberforce? . . . Then I will never beat my horse again."

There it was. Someone alive today has spoken to someone whose own father had held Wilberforce's hand. I was greatly moved reading of Pollock's account, as though the intervening years had indeed at long last fallen away and Wilberforce had somehow come to life again. I soon found myself hoping I might speak with Mr. Pollock, if such a thing were possible. A dear friend thought it might, and generously proffered a number.

Only yesterday morning I phoned Mr. Pollock at his home in Devon, England. He is eighty-three now and spoke to me across the great ocean in a British accent that itself hails from another era, now gone. I asked him about his conversation with Wilberforce's great-grandson and he repeated it to me, explaining that he had first corresponded with the blind man via "an ammanuensis." Years later he arranged to meet the ancient figure in his home near Bath, where the story of his father and Wilberforce took place. Listening to Mr. Pollock himself tell me of meeting the man whose father had walked with Wilberforce seemed to complete the connection, and I felt that even with all these years between us—nearly two centuries—I could somehow really touch him.

And yet these are all but shadows of the things that once were. To all of us wandering together here now, looking for William Wilberforce, I repeat the words Wilberforce repeated to himself that day when standing near the lifeless body of his own departed friend, Henry Thornton: "Why seek ye the living among the dead? He is not here. He is risen."

Ἀληθῶς Ἀνέστη.

Eric Metaxas

New York City
November 15, 2006

BIBLIOGRAPHY

If anything or anyone can ever rightly be said to stand tall upon the shoulders of giants, both this book and its author certainly can. Our mandate in writing this book was to tell well the story of Wilberforce to an audience mostly unfamiliar with him, not to break new ground in the world of Wilberforce scholarship. While we humbly hope to have done the former, we are cockily confident of having accomplished the latter. Without the scholarship contained in the great Wilberforce books already written, the book you are holding simply could not exist, and it is as much indebted to them as a bicyclist may be indebted for his record time to the eighteen-wheelers behind which he has drafted.

It was our sincerest hope in writing this book to whet the readers' appetite for these other books, each of which will add happy depth, breadth, and height to the portrait in your hands, and for which purpose I heartily recommend each of them.

First and foremost I recommend Kevin Belmonte's excellent *Hero for Humanity,* which is filled with information, and which is especially accessible to American readers. I have had the great pleasure of meeting Kevin Belmonte, and rejoice that such a Wilberforce scholar exists in our era, and on my continent.

Shortest and probably most readable of all Wilberforce books is Garth Lean's 1980 biography *God's Politician.* John Pollock's much longer and entirely fabulous 1977 biography, *Wilberforce: God's Statesman,* was of inestimable value and particularly enjoyable.

Robin Furneaux's *William Wilberforce,* published in 1974, was also a tremendous boon, as was Sir Reginald Coupland's *Wilberforce,* published in 1923. The information and smiles afforded by these books cannot be overstated.

Ernest Marshall Howse's 1953 book, *Saints in Politics: The "Clapham Sect" and the Growth of Freedom,* deals with the Clapham group in general, and widens one's understanding of the enviable context of friendships in which William Wilberforce operated.

And Adam Hochschild's excellent 2005 book *Bury the Chains* tells in scintillating prose the story of the other men and women in the British abolitionist movement, doing them much of the justice they are denied by the tight focus of this volume.

Of course the five-volume 1838 *Life of Wilberforce,* written by his sons Samuel and Robert, is the ur-text to which everyone is indebted, and for lending me his copy of Samuel's 1868 single-volume condensation of same, the author is entirely indebted to Os Guinness, who should be receiving it back very soon indeed.

All these books and their authors have been my friends and companions on an otherwise solitary journey, and it is with profoundest gratefulness and sincerest affection that I speak of them.

ACKNOWLEDGMENTS

Life is a collaborative effort. That books are is a cliché, but not a fiction. I wish first and foremost to thank my typist, yours truly, for quite literally transcribing my thoughts as I thought them, a feat hardly to be explained, and yet quite literally true. More seriously and less tautologically, I must thank Walden Media and Harper San Francisco; and more specifically and less corporately, Micheal Flaherty, the producer of the movie *Amazing Grace,* and Mickey Maudlin, my editor, for allowing me the decidedly humbling privilege of telling the story of one of the greatest men who ever walked among us.

I am deeply indebted to my dear friend Os Guinness, for first introducing me to William Wilberforce and Clapham, and for faithfully keeping that flame alive long before bicentennials or feature films were on the horizon.

I am also exceedingly grateful to my friends, Richard and Pam Scurry, and Manos and Camille Kampouris, without whose selfless expression of the love of Christ in my life this book could not have been written.

For supporting, encouraging, and inspiring me in any number of ways bearing on the composition of this book, and for being to me something very like a Claphamic system, I am grateful to many friends, including but emphatically not limited to Jim Lane and the men of the New Canaan Society; the Rev. B. J. and Sheila Weber and the New York Fellowship; the Rev. Tom Pike and the people of Calvary/St. George's Episcopal Church in Manhattan; Stan and Ginger Oakes and the staff and students of the King's College of Manhattan; and the board, staff, and students of the Geneva School of Manhattan; not to mention such unattached superluminaries and artistic geniuses as Norman Stone, Tom Howard, David and Susie Young, Jerry Eiseley, Dick Staub, Tim Raglin, and, yes, Gordon Pennington. And who knows not Mark Berner?

For such shameless jackanapes as Richard Egan, John Hackney, and Bob Monteleone, I regrettably now have nothing more than stony-faced indifference. *Mene, mene, tekel, upharsin,* and so on. Chumps. You had your chance.

Lastly, I hereby happily express that cliché for which I have previously scorned other authors without number: I thank my dearest wife for having weathered the long electrical storm of this book's composition, and for—with my daughter—walking and sometimes dancing upon such eggshells as were profligately strewn everywhere, very likely by someone using the passive voice quite intentionally. May the eggshells now at last be swept away forever. And as God is our witness, may our lives never be crunchy again.